Donated by
Joseph and Diane Bast
to The Heartland Institute
2015

LIVING PHILOSOPHIES

LIVING PHILOSOPHERS

Albert Einstein

Living Philosophies

BY

ALBERT EINSTEIN	JOHN DEWEY
SIR JAMES JEANS	H. G. WELLS
THEODORE DREISER	H. L. MENCKEN
JAMES TRUSLOW ADAMS	JULIA PETERKIN
SIR ARTHUR KEITH	IRVING BABBITT
BEATRICE WEBB	JOSEPH WOOD KRUTCH
FRIDTJOF NANSEN	LEWIS MUMFORD
ROBERT ANDREWS MILLIKAN	HU SHIH
HILAIRE BELLOC	J. B. S. HALDANE
GEORGE JEAN NATHAN	IRWIN EDMAN
BERTRAND RUSSELL	WILLIAM RALPH INGE

19 31

SIMON AND SCHUSTER · NEW YORK

SECOND PRINTING

ALL RIGHTS RESERVED
Copyright, 1930, by Forum Publishing Company
Copyright, 1931, by Simon and Schuster, Inc.

Manufactured in the United States of America

NOTES

THE publishers wish to acknowledge their indebtedness to DR. HENRY GODDARD LEACH, Editor of The *Forum* Magazine, for his invaluable coöperation in the arranging and publication of this symposium.

THE contributions of Sir James Jeans, Hilaire Belloc, William Ralph Inge and J. B. S. Haldane are reprinted, with the kind permission of George Allen and Unwin, Ltd., from two symposiums entitled *Points of View* and *More Points of View*.

CONTENTS

		PAGE
I.	ALBERT EINSTEIN	3
II.	BERTRAND RUSSELL	9
III.	JOHN DEWEY	21
IV.	ROBERT ANDREWS MILLIKAN	37
V.	THEODORE DREISER	55
VI.	H. G. WELLS	79
VII.	FRIDTJOF NANSEN	93
VIII.	SIR JAMES JEANS	107
IX.	IRVING BABBITT	121
X.	SIR ARTHUR KEITH	139
XI.	JAMES TRUSLOW ADAMS	153
XII.	H. L. MENCKEN	179
XIII.	JULIA PETERKIN	195
XIV.	LEWIS MUMFORD	205
XV.	GEORGE JEAN NATHAN	221
XVI.	HU SHIH	235
XVII.	JOSEPH WOOD KRUTCH	265
XVIII.	IRWIN EDMAN	277
XIX.	HILAIRE BELLOC	287
XX.	BEATRICE WEBB	295
XXI.	WILLIAM RALPH INGE	307
XXII.	J. B. S. HALDANE	319
	biographical notes	331

ILLUSTRATIONS

	FACING PAGE
ALBERT EINSTEIN	*frontispiece*
BERTRAND RUSSELL —*Courtesy Horace Liveright*	9
JOHN DEWEY	21
ROBERT ANDREWS MILLIKAN	36
THEODORE DREISER —*Courtesy Horace Liveright*	69
H. G. WELLS —*Courtesy Doubleday, Doran and Company, Inc.*	84
FRIDTJOF NANSEN —*Courtesy W. W. Norton & Co., Inc.*	101
SIR JAMES JEANS —*Courtesy The Macmillan Company*	116
IRVING BABBITT —*Courtesy Houghton Mifflin Company*	133
SIR ARTHUR KEITH —*Courtesy W. W. Norton & Co., Inc., and Mr. S. J. Woolf*	148
JAMES TRUSLOW ADAMS —*Courtesy Little, Brown & Company*	165
H. L. MENCKEN —*Courtesy Alfred A. Knopf, Inc.*	180
JULIA PETERKIN —*Courtesy The Bobbs-Merrill Company*	197
LEWIS MUMFORD —*Courtesy Harcourt, Brace and Company, Inc.*	212
GEORGE JEAN NATHAN —*Courtesy Alfred A. Knopf, Inc.*	229
HU SHIH	244

	FACING PAGE
JOSEPH WOOD KRUTCH —*Courtesy Jonathan Cape & Harrison Smith, Inc.*	265
IRWIN EDMAN —*Courtesy Jonathan Cape & Harrison Smith, Inc.*	277
HILAIRE BELLOC —*Courtesy J. B. Lippincott Company*	292
BEATRICE WEBB —*Courtesy Longmans, Green & Co.*	295
WILLIAM RALPH INGE —*Courtesy Longmans, Green & Co.*	309
J. B. S. HALDANE —*Courtesy Harper & Brothers*	324

LIVING PHILOSOPHIES

I.
ALBERT EINSTEIN

Strange is our situation here upon earth. Each of us comes for a short visit, not knowing why, yet sometimes seeming to divine a purpose.

From the standpoint of daily life, however, there is one thing we do know: that man is here for the sake of other men—above all for those upon whose smile and well-being our own happiness depends, and also for the countless unknown souls with whose fate we are connected by a bond of sympathy. Many times a day I realize how much my own outer and inner life is built upon the labors of my fellow-men, both living and dead, and how earnestly I must exert myself in order to give in return as much as I have received. My peace of mind is often troubled by the depressing sense that I have borrowed too heavily from the work of other men.

I do not believe we can have any freedom at all in the philosophical sense, for we act not only under external compulsion but also by inner necessity. Schopenhauer's saying—"A man can surely do what he wills to do, but he cannot determine what he wills"—impressed itself upon me in youth and has always consoled me when I have witnessed or suffered life's hardships. This conviction is a perpetual breeder of tolerance, for it does not allow us to take ourselves or others too seriously; it makes rather for a sense of humor.

To ponder interminably over the reason for one's own existence or the meaning of life in general seems to me, from an objective point of view, to be sheer folly. And yet everyone holds certain ideals by which he guides his aspiration and his judgment. The ideals which have always shone before me and filled me with the joy of living are goodness, beauty, and truth. To make a goal of comfort or happiness has never appealed to me; a system of ethics built on this basis would be sufficient only for a herd of cattle.

Without the sense of collaborating with like-minded beings in the pursuit of the ever unattainable in art and scientific research, my life would have been empty. Ever since childhood I have scorned the commonplace limits so often set upon human ambition. Possessions, outward success, publicity, luxury—to me these have always been contemptible. I believe that a simple and unassuming manner of life is best for everyone, best both for the body and the mind.

My passionate interest in social justice and social responsibility has always stood in curious contrast to a marked lack of desire for direct association with men and women. I am a horse for single harness, not cut out for tandem or team work. I have never belonged wholeheartedly to country or state, to my circle of friends, or even to my own family. These ties have always been accompanied by a vague aloofness, and the wish to withdraw into myself increases with the years.

Such isolation is sometimes bitter, but I do not regret being cut off from the understanding and sympathy of other men. I lose something by it, to be sure, but I am compensated for it in being rendered independent of the customs, opinions, and prejudices of others, and am not tempted to rest my peace of mind upon such shifting foundations.

My political ideal is democracy. Everyone should be respected as an individual, but no one idolized. It is an irony of fate that I should have been showered with so much uncalled-for and unmerited admiration and esteem. Perhaps this adulation springs from the unfulfilled wish of the multitude to comprehend the few ideas which I, with my weak powers, have advanced.

Full well do I know that in order to attain any definite goal it is imperative that *one* person should do the thinking and commanding and carry most of the responsibility. But those who are led should not be driven, and they should be allowed to choose their leader. It seems to me that the distinctions separating the social classes are false; in the last analysis they rest on force. I am convinced that degeneracy follows every autocratic system of violence, for violence inevitably attracts moral inferiors. Time has proved that illustrious tyrants are succeeded by scoundrels.

For this reason I have always been passionately opposed to such régimes as exist in Russia and Italy to-day. The thing which has discredited the European forms of democracy is not the basic theory of democracy itself, which some say is at fault, but the instability of our political leadership, as well as the impersonal character of party alignments.

I believe that those in the United States have hit upon the right idea. A President is chosen for a reasonable length of time and enough power is given him to acquit himself properly of his responsibilities. In the German Government, on the other hand, I like the state's more extensive care of the individual when he is ill or unemployed. What is truly valuable in our bustle of life is not the nation, I should say, but the creative and impressionable individuality, the personality

—he who produces the noble and sublime while the common herd remains dull in thought and insensible in feeling.

This subject brings me to that vilest offspring of the herd mind—the odious militia. The man who enjoys marching in line and file to the strains of music falls below my contempt; he received his great brain by mistake—the spinal cord would have been amply sufficient. This heroism at command, this senseless violence, this accursed bombast of patriotism—how intensely I despise them! War is low and despicable, and I had rather be smitten to shreds than participate in such doings.

Such a stain on humanity should be erased without delay. I think well enough of human nature to believe that it would have been wiped out long ago had not the common sense of nations been systematically corrupted through school and press for business and political reasons.

The most beautiful thing we can experience is the mysterious. It is the source of all true art and science. He to whom this emotion is a stranger, who can no longer pause to wonder and stand rapt in awe, is as good as dead: his eyes are closed. This insight into the mystery of life, coupled though it be with fear, has also given rise to religion. To know that what is impenetrable to us really exists, manifesting itself as the highest wisdom and the most radiant beauty which our dull faculties can comprehend only in their most primitive forms—this knowledge, this feeling, is at the center of true religiousness. In this sense, and in this sense only, I belong in the ranks of devoutly religious men.

I cannot imagine a God who rewards and punishes the objects of his creation, whose purposes are modeled after our own—a God, in short, who is but a reflection of human frailty. Neither can I believe that the individual survives the death of his body, although feeble souls harbor such thoughts through fear or ridiculous egotism. It is enough for me to contemplate the mystery of conscious life perpetuating itself through all eternity, to reflect upon the marvelous structure of the universe which we can dimly perceive, and to try humbly to comprehend even an infinitesimal part of the intelligence manifested in nature.

BERTRAND RUSSELL

II.
BERTRAND RUSSELL

My outlook on the world is, like other people's, the product partly of circumstance and partly of temperament. In regard to religious belief, those who were concerned with my education did not, perhaps, adopt the best methods for producing an unquestioning acceptance of orthodoxy. My father and mother were freethinkers, but one of them died when I was two years old and the other when I was three, and I did not know their opinions until I grew up. After my father's death I lived with my grandmother, who was a Scotch Presbyterian but at the age of seventy became converted to Unitarianism. I was taken on alternate Sundays to the parish church (Episcopalian) and to the Presbyterian church, while at home I was instructed in the tenets of the Unitarian faith. I liked the parish church best because there was a comfortable family pew next to the bell rope, and the rope moved up and down all the time the bell was ringing; also because I liked the royal arms which hung on the wall, and the beadle who walked up the steps to the pulpit after the clergyman to close the door upon him at the beginning of the sermon. Moreover, during the service I could study the tables for finding Easter and speculate upon the meaning of Golden Numbers and Sunday Letters and enjoy the pleasure of dividing by ninety, neglecting fractions.

But I was not taught to suppose that everything in the Bible was true, or to believe in miracles and eternal perdition. Darwinism was accepted as a matter of course. I remember a Swiss Protestant tutor, whom I had when I was eleven, saying to me, "If you are a Darwinian I pity you, for it is impossible to be a Darwinian and a Christian at the same time." I did not at that age believe in the incompatibility, but I was already certain that if I had to choose, I should choose to be a Darwinian. I continued, however, to believe devoutly in the Unitarian faith until the age of fourteen, at which period I became exceedingly religious and consequently anxious to know whether there was any good ground for supposing religion to be true. For the next four years a great part of my time was spent in secret meditation upon this subject; I could not speak to anybody about it for fear of giving pain. I suffered acutely, both from the gradual loss of faith and from the necessity of silence.

The first dogma which I came to disbelieve was that of free will. It seemed to me that all motions of matter were determined by the laws of dynamics and could not therefore be influenced by the human will, even in the instance of matter forming part of a human body. I had never heard of Cartesianism, or, indeed, of any of the great philosophies, but my thoughts ran spontaneously on Cartesian lines. The next dogma which I began to doubt was that of immortality, but I cannot clearly remember what were at that time my reasons for disbelieving in it. I continued to believe in God until the age of eighteen, since the First Cause argument appeared to me irrefutable. At eighteen, however, the reading of Mill's autobiography showed me the fallacy in this argument. I therefore definitely abandoned all the dogmas of Christianity, and to my surprise I found myself much happier than while I had been struggling to retain some sort of theological belief.

Just after arriving at this stage I went to the University, where for the first time in my life I met people to whom I could speak of matters that interested me. I studied philosophy and under the influence of McTaggart became for a time a Hegelian. This phase lasted about three years and was brought to an end by discussions with G. E. Moore. After leaving Cambridge I spent some years in more or less desultory studies. Two winters in Berlin I devoted mainly to economics. In 1896 I lectured at Johns Hopkins University and Bryn Mawr on non-Euclidean geometry. I spent a good deal of time among art connoisseurs in Florence, while I read Pater and Flaubert and the other gods of the cultured nineties. In the end I settled down in the country with a view to writing a *magnum opus* on the principles of mathematics, which had been my chief ambition ever since the age of eleven.

Indeed, it was at that very early age that one of the decisive experiences of my life occurred. My brother, who was seven years older than I was, undertook to teach me Euclid, and I was overjoyed, for I had been told that Euclid proved things, and I hoped at last to acquire some solid knowledge. I shall never forget my disappointment when I found that Euclid started with axioms. When my brother read the first axiom to me, I said that I saw no reason to admit it; to which he replied that such being the situation we could not go on. Since I was anxious to go on, I admitted it provisionally, but my belief that somewhere in the world solid knowledge was obtainable had received a rude shock.

The desire to discover some really certain knowledge inspired all my work up to the age of thirty-eight. It seemed clear that mathematics had a better claim to be considered knowledge than anything else; therefore it was to the principles of mathematics that I addressed myself. At thirty-eight I felt that I had done all that it lay in my power to do in this field, although I was far from having arrived at any absolute certainty. Indeed, the net result of my work was to throw doubts upon arithmetic which had never been thrown before. I was and am persuaded that the method I pursued brings one nearer to knowledge than any other that is available, but the knowledge it brings is only probable, and not so precise as it appears to be at first sight.

At this point, therefore, my life was rather sharply cut in two. I did not feel inclined to devote myself any longer to abstractions, where I had done what I could without arriving at the desired goal. My mood was not unlike that of Faust at the moment when Mephistopheles first appears to him, but Mephistopheles appeared to me not in the form of a poodle but in the form of the Great War. After Dr. Whitehead and I had finished *Principia Mathematica,* I remained for about three years uncertain what to do. I was teaching at Cambridge, but I did not feel that I wished to go on doing so forever. From sheer inertia I was still occupied mainly with mathematical logic, but I felt—half unconsciously—the desire for some wholly different kind of work.

Then came the war, and I knew without the faintest shadow of doubt what I had to do. I have never been so whole-hearted or so little troubled with hesitation in any work as in the pacifist work that I did during the war. For the first time I found something to do which involved my whole nature. My previous abstract work had left my human interests unsatisfied, and I had allowed them an occasional outlet by political speaking and writing, more particularly on free trade and votes for women. The aristocratic political tradition of the eighteenth and early nineteenth centuries, which I had imbibed in childhood, had made me feel an instinctive responsibility in regard to public affairs. And a strong parental instinct, at that time not satisfied in a personal way, caused me to feel a great indignation at the spectacle of the young men of Europe being deceived and butchered in order to gratify the evil passions of their elders.

Intellectual integrity made it quite impossible for me to accept the war myths of any of the belligerent nations. Indeed, those intellectuals who accepted them were abdicating their functions for the joy of feeling themselves at one with the herd, or in some instances from mere funk. This appeared to me ignoble. If the intellectual has any function in society, it is to preserve a cool and unbiased judgment in the face of all solicitations to passion. I found, however, that most intellectuals have no belief in the utility of the intellect except in quiet times.

Again, popular feeling during the war, especially in the first months, afforded me a keen though very painful scientific interest. I observed that at first most of those who stayed at home enjoyed the war, which showed me how much hatred and how little human affection exist in human nature educated on our present lines. I saw also how the ordinary virtues, such as thrift, industry, and public spirit, were used to swell the magnitude of the disaster by producing a greater energy in the work of mutual extermination. I feared that European civilization would perish, as indeed it easily might have done if the war had lasted a year longer. The feeling of security that characterized the nineteenth century perished in the war, but I could not cease to believe in the desirability of the ideals that I previously cherished. Among many of the younger generation, despair has produced cynicism, but for my part I have never felt complete despair and have never ceased, therefore, to believe that the road to a better state of affairs is still open to mankind.

All my thinking on political, sociological, and ethical questions during the last fifteen years has sprung from the impulse which came to me during the first days of the war. I soon became convinced that the study of diplomatic origins, though useful, did not go to the bottom of the matter, since popular passions enthusiastically supported governments in all the steps leading up to the war. I have found myself also unable to accept the view that the origins of wars are always economic, for it was obvious that most of the people who were enthusiastically in favor of the war were going to lose money by it, and the fact that they themselves did not think so showed that their economic thinking was biased, and that the passion causing the bias was the real source of their warlike feeling. The supposed economic causes of war, except in the case of certain capitalistic enterprises, are in the nature of a rationalization: people wish to fight, and they therefore persuade themselves that it is to their interest to do so. The important question, then, is the psychological one—"Why do people wish to fight?" And this leads on from war to a host of other questions concerning impulses to cruelty and oppression in general. These questions in their turn involve a study of the origins of malevolent passions, and thence of psychoanalysis and the theory of education.

Gradually, through the investigation of these questions, I have come to a certain philosophy of life, guided always by the desire to discover some way in which men, with the congenital characteristics which nature has given them, can live together in societies without devoting themselves to making each other miserable. The keynote of my social philosophy, from a scientific point of view, is the emphasis upon psychology and the practice of judging social institutions by their effects upon human character. During the war all the recognized virtues of sober citizens were turned to a use which I considered bad. Men abstained from alcohol in order to make shells; they worked long hours in order to destroy the kind of society that makes work worth doing. Venereal disease was thought more regrettable than usual because it interfered with the killing of enemies. All this made me acutely aware of the fact that rules of conduct, whatever they may be, are not sufficient to produce good results unless the ends sought are good. Sobriety, thrift, industry, and continence, in so far as they existed during the war, merely increased the orgy of destruction. The money spent on drink, on the other hand, saved men's lives, since it was taken away from the making of high explosives.

Being a pacifist forced one into opposition to the whole purpose of the community and made it very difficult to avoid a completely antinomian attitude of hostility to all recognized moral rules. My attitude, however, is not really one of hostility to moral rules; it is essentially that expressed by Saint Paul in the famous passage on charity. I do not always find myself in agreement with that apostle, but on this point my feeling is exactly the same as his—namely, that no obedience to moral rules can take the place of love, and that where love is genuine, it will, if combined with intelligence, suffice to generate whatever moral rules are necessary. The word "love," however, has become somewhat worn with usage and no longer conveys quite the right shade of meaning. One might start at the other end, from a behaviorist analysis, dividing movements into those of approach and those of withdrawal. In some of the humblest regions of the animal kingdom creatures can be divided, for example, into the phototropic and photophobic—that is, those which approach light and those which fly from it.

The same kind of distinction applies throughout the animal kingdom. In the presence of a new stimulus there may be an impulse of approach or an impulse of retreat. Translated into psychological terms, this may be expressed by saying that there may be an emotion of attraction or an emotion of fear. Both, of course, are necessary to survival, but emotions of fear are very much less necessary for survival in civilized life than they were at earlier stages of human development or among our prehuman ancestors. Before men had adequate weapons, fierce wild beasts must have made life very dangerous, so that men had reason to be as timorous as rabbits are now, and there was an ever-present danger of death by starvation, which has grown enormously less with the creation of modern means of transport.

At the present time the fiercest and most dangerous animal with which human beings have to contend is man, and the dangers arising from purely physical causes have been very rapidly reduced. In the present day, therefore, fear finds little scope except in relation to other human beings, and fear itself is one of the main reasons why human beings are formidable to each other. It is a recognized maxim that the best defense is attack; consequently people are continually attacking each other because they expect to be attacked. Our instinctive emotions are those that we have inherited from a much more dangerous world, and contain, therefore, a larger proportion of fear than they should; this fear, since it finds little outlet elsewhere, directs itself against the social environment, producing distrust and hate, envy, malice, and all uncharitableness. If we are to profit fully by our new-won mastery over nature, we must acquire a more lordly psychology:

instead of the cringing and resentful terror of the slave, we must learn to feel the calm dignity of the master. Reverting to the impulses of approach and withdrawal, this means that impulses of approach need to be encouraged, and those of withdrawal need to be discouraged. Like everything else, this is a matter of degree. I am not suggesting that people should approach tigers and pythons with friendly feelings; I am only saying that since tradition grew up in a more dangerous world, the present-day occasions for fear and withdrawal are less numerous than tradition would lead us to suppose.

It is the conquest of nature which has made possible a more friendly and coöperative attitude between human beings, and if rational men coöperated and used their scientific knowledge to the full, they could now secure the economic welfare of all —which was not possible in any earlier period. Life and death competition for the possession of fertile lands was reasonable enough in the past, but it has now become a folly. International government, business organization, and birth control should make the world comfortable for everybody. I do not say that everybody could be as rich as Crœsus, but everybody could have as much of this world's goods as is necessary for the happiness of sensible people. With the problem of poverty and destitution eliminated, men could devote themselves to the constructive arts of civilization—to the progress of science, the diminution of disease, the postponement of death, and the liberation of the impulses that make for joy.

Why do such ideas appear Utopian? The reasons lie solely in human psychology—not in the unalterable parts of human nature, but in those which we acquire from tradition, education, and the example of our environment. Take, first, international government. The necessity for this is patent to every person capable of political thought, but nationalistic passions stand in the way. Each nation is proud of its independence;

each nation is willing to fight till the last gasp to preserve its freedom. This, of course, is mere anarchy, and it leads to conditions exactly analogous to those in the feudal ages before the bold, bad barons were forced in the end to submit to the authority of the king. The attitude we have toward foreign nations is one of withdrawal: the foreigner may be all right in his place, but we become filled with alarm at the thought that he may have any say in our affairs. Each state, therefore, insists upon the right of private war. Treaties of arbitration, Kellogg Peace Pacts, and the rest are all very well as gestures, but everybody knows that they will not stand any severe strain. So long as each nation has its own army and navy and air force, it will use them when it gets excited, whatever treaties its government may have signed.

There will be no safety in the world until men have applied to the rules between different states the great principle which has produced internal security—namely, that in any dispute, force must not be employed by either interested party but only by a neutral authority after due investigation according to recognized principles of law. When all the armed forces of the world are controlled by one world-wide authority, we shall have reached the stage in the relation of states which was reached centuries ago in the relations of individuals. Nothing less than this will suffice.

The basis of international anarchy is men's proneness to fear and hatred. This is also the basis of economic disputes; for the love of power, which is at their root, is generally an embodiment of fear. Men desire to be in control because they are afraid that the control of others will be used unjustly to their detriment. The same thing applies in the sphere of sexual morals: the power of husbands over wives and of wives over husbands, which is conferred by the law, is derived from fear of the loss of possession. This motive is the negative emotion of jealousy, not the positive emotion of love. In education the same kind of thing occurs. The positive emotion which should supply the motive in education is curiosity, but the curiosity of the young is severely repressed in many directions—sexual, theological, and political. Instead of being encouraged in the practice of free inquiry, children are instructed in some brand of orthodoxy, with the result that unfamiliar ideas inspire them with terror rather than with interest. All these bad results spring from a pursuit of security—a pursuit inspired by irrational fears; the fears have become irrational, since in the modern world fearlessness and intelligence, if embodied in social organization, would in themselves suffice to produce security.

The road to Utopia is clear; it lies partly through politics and partly through changes in the individual. As for politics, far the most important thing is the establishment of an international government—a measure which I expect to be brought about through the world government of the United States. As for the individual, the problem is to make him less prone to hatred and fear, and this is a matter partly physiological and partly psychological. Much of the hatred in the world springs from bad digestion and inadequate functioning of the glands, which is a result of oppression and thwarting in youth. In a world where the health of the young is adequately cared for and their vital impulses are given the utmost scope compatible with their own health and that of their companions, men and women will grow up more courageous and less malevolent than they are at present.

Given such human beings and an international government, the world might become stable and yet civilized, whereas, with our present psychology and political organization, every increase in scientific knowledge brings the destruction of civilization nearer.

John Dewey

III.

JOHN DEWEY

FAITH was once almost universally thought to be acceptance of a definite body of intellectual propositions, acceptance being based upon authority—preferably that of revelation from on high. It meant adherence to a creed consisting of set articles. Such creeds are recited daily in our churches. Of late there has developed another conception of faith. This is suggested by the words of an American thinker: "Faith is tendency toward action." According to such a view, faith is the matrix of formulated creeds and the inspiration of endeavor. Change from the one conception of faith to the other is indicative of a profound alteration. Adherence to any body of doctrines and dogmas based upon a specific authority signifies distrust in the power of experience to provide, in its own ongoing movement, the needed principles of belief and action. Faith in its newer sense signifies that experience itself is the sole ultimate authority.

Such a faith has in it all the elements of a philosophy. For it implies that the course and material of experience give support and stay to life, and that its possibilities provide all the ends and ideals that are to regulate conduct. When these implications are made explicit, there emerges a definite philosophy. I have no intention here of trying to unfold such a philosophy, but rather to indicate what a philosophy based on experience as the ultimate authority in knowledge and conduct means in the present state of civilization, what its reactions are upon what is thought and done. For such a faith is not at present either articulate or widely held. If it were, it would be not so much a philosophy as a part of common sense.

In fact, it goes contrary to the whole trend of the traditions by which mankind is educated. On the whole it has been denied that experience and life can regulate themselves and provide their own means of direction and inspiration. Except for an occasional protest, historic philosophies have been "transcendental." And this trait of philosophies is a reflex of the fact that dominant moral codes and religious beliefs have appealed for support to something above and beyond experience. Experience has been systematically disparaged in contrast with something taken to be more fundamental and superior in worth.

Life as it is actually lived has been treated as a preparation for something outside of it and after it. It has been thought lawless, without meaning and value, except as it was taken to testify to a reality beyond itself. The creeds that have prevailed have been founded upon the supposed necessity of escape from the confusion and uncertainties of experience. Life has been thought to be evil and hopeless unless it could be shown to bear within itself the assured promise of a higher reality. Philosophies of escape have also been philosophies of compensation for the ills and sufferings of the experienced world.

Mankind has hardly inquired what would happen if the possibilities of experience were seriously explored and exploited. There has been much systematic exploration in science and much frantic exploitation in politics, business, and amusement. But this attention has been, so to say, incidental and in contravention to the professedly ruling scheme of belief. It has not been the product of belief in the power of experience to furnish organizing principles and directive ends. Religions have been saturated with the supernatural—and the supernatural signifies precisely that which lies beyond experience. Moral codes have been allied to this religious supernaturalism and have sought their foundation and sanction in it. Contrast with such ideas, deeply embedded in all Western culture, gives the philosophy of faith in experience a definite and profound meaning.

Why have men in the past resorted to philosophies of that which is above and beyond experience? And why should it be now thought possible to desist from such recourse? The answer to the first question is, undoubtedly, that the experience which men had, as well as any which they could reasonably anticipate, gave no signs of ability to furnish the means of its own regulation. It offered promises it refused to fulfill; it awakened desires only to frustrate them; it created hopes and blasted them; it evoked ideals and was indifferent and hostile to their realization. Men who were incompetent to cope with the troubles and evils that experience brought with it, naturally distrusted the capacity of experience to give authoritative guidance. Since experience did not contain the arts by which its own course could be directed, philosophies and religions of escape and consolatory compensation naturally ensued.

What are the grounds for supposing that this state of affairs has changed and that it is now possible to put trust in the possibilities of experience itself? The answer to this question supplies the content of a philosophy of experience. There are traits of present experience which were unknown and unpossessed when the ruling beliefs of the past were developed. Experience now owns as a part of itself scientific methods of discovery and test; it is marked by ability to create techniques and technologies—that is, arts which arrange and utilize all sorts of conditions and energies, physical and human. These new possessions give experience and its potentialities a radically new meaning. It is a commonplace that since the seventeenth century science has revolutionized our beliefs about outer nature, and it is also beginning to revolutionize those about man.

When our minds dwell on this extraordinary change, they are likely to think of the transformation that has taken place in the subject matter of astronomy, physics, chemistry, biology, psychology, anthropology, and so on. But great as is this change, it shrinks in comparison with the change that has occurred in method. The latter is the author of the revolution in the content of beliefs. The new methods have, moreover, brought with them a radical change in our intellectual attitude and its attendant morale. The method we term "scientific" forms for the modern man (and a man is not modern merely because he lives in 1931) the sole dependable means of disclosing the realities of existence. It is the sole authentic mode of revelation. This possession of a new method, to the use of which no limits can be put, signifies a new idea of the nature and possibilities of experience. It imports a new morale of confidence, control, and security.

The change in knowledge has its overt and practical counterpart in what we term the Industrial Revolution, with its creation of arts for directing and using the energies of nature. Technology includes, of course, the engineering arts that have produced the railway, steamship, automobile, and airplane, the telegraph, telephone, and radio, and the printing press. But it also includes new procedures in medicine and hygiene, the function of insurance in all its branches, and, in its potentiality if not actualization, radically new methods in education and other modes of human relationship. "Technology" signifies all the intelligent techniques by which the energies of nature and man are directed and used in satisfaction of human needs; it cannot be limited to a few outer and comparatively mechanical forms. In the face of its possibilities, the traditional conception of experience is obsolete.

Different theories have expressed with more or less success this and that phase of the newer movements. But there is no integration of them into the standing habits and the controlling outlook of men and women. There are two great signs and tests of this fact. In science and in industry the fact of constant change is generally accepted. Moral, religious, and articulate philosophic creeds are based upon the idea of fixity. In the history of the race, change has been feared. It has been looked upon as the source of decay and degeneration. It has been opposed as the cause of disorder, chaos, and anarchy. One chief reason for the appeal to something beyond experience was the fact that experience is always in such flux that men had to seek stability and peace outside of it. Until the seventeenth century, the natural sciences shared in the belief in the superiority of the immutable to the moving, and took for their ideal the discovery of the permanent and changeless. Ruling philosophies, whether materialistic or spiritual, accepted the same notion as their foundation.

In this attachment to the fixed and immutable, both science and philosophy reflected the universal and pervasive conviction of religion and morals. Impermanence meant insecurity; the permanent was the sole ground of assurance and support amid the vicissitudes of existence. Christianity proffered a fixed revelation of absolute, unchanging Being and truth; and the revelation was elaborated into a system of definite rules and ends for the direction of life. Hence "morals" were conceived as a code of laws, the same everywhere and at all times. The good life was one lived in fixed adherence to fixed principles.

In contrast with all such beliefs, the outstanding fact in all branches of natural science is that to exist is to be in process, in change. Nevertheless, although the idea of movement and change has made itself at home in the physical sciences, it has had comparatively little influence on the popular mind as the latter looks at religion, morals, economics, and politics. In these fields it is still supposed that our choice is between confusion, anarchy, and something fixed and immutable. It is assumed that Christianity is the final religion; Jesus the complete and unchanging embodiment of the divine and the human. It is assumed that our present economic régime, at least in principle, expresses something final, something to endure—with, it is incidentally hoped, some improvements in detail. It is assumed, in spite of evident flux in the actual situation, that the institutions of marriage and family that developed in medieval Europe are the last and unchanging word.

These examples hint at the extent to which ideals of fixity persist in a moving world. A philosophy of experience will accept at its full value the fact that social and moral existences are, like physical existences, in a state of continuous if obscure change. It will not try to cover up the fact of inevitable modification, and will make no attempt to set fixed limits to the extent of changes that are to occur. For the futile effort to achieve security and anchorage in something fixed, it will substitute the effort to determine the character of changes that are going on and to give them in the affairs that concern us most some measure of intelligent direction. It is not called upon to cherish Utopian notions about the imminence of such intelligent direction of social changes. But it is committed to faith in the possibility of its slow effectuation in the degree in which men realize the full import of the revolution that has already been effected in physical and technical regions.

Wherever the thought of fixity rules, that of all-inclusive unity rules also. The popular philosophy of life is filled with desire to attain such an all-embracing unity, and formal philosophies have been devoted to an intellectual fulfillment of the desire. Consider the place occupied in popular thought by search for *the* meaning of life and *the* purpose of the universe. Men who look for a single purport and a single end either frame an idea of them according to their private desires and tradition, or else, not finding any such single unity, give up in despair and conclude that there is no genuine meaning and value in any of life's episodes.

The alternatives are not exhaustive, however. There is no need of deciding between no meaning at all and one single, all-embracing meaning. There are many meanings and many purposes in the situations with which we are confronted—one, so to say, for each situation. Each offers its own challenge to thought and endeavor, and presents its own potential value.

It is impossible, I think, even to begin to imagine the changes that would come into life—personal and collective—if the idea of a plurality of interconnected meanings and purposes replaced that of *the* meaning and purpose. Search for a single, inclusive good is doomed to failure. Such happiness as life is capable of comes from the full participation of all our powers in the endeavor to wrest from each changing situation of experience its own full and unique meaning. Faith in the varied possibilities of diversified experience is attended with the joy of constant discovery and of constant growing. Such a joy is possible even in the midst of trouble and defeat, whenever life-experiences are treated as potential disclosures of meanings and values that are to be used as means to a fuller and more significant future experience. Belief in a single purpose distracts thought and wastes energy that would help make the world better if it were directed to attainable ends.

I have stated a general principle, because philosophy, I take it, is more than an enumeration of items of belief with respect to this and that question. But the principle can acquire definiteness only in application to actual issues. How about religion? Does renunciation of the extra-empirical compel also an abandonment of all religion? It certainly exacts a surrender of that supernaturalism and fixed dogma and rigid institutionalism with which Christianity has been historically associated. But as I read human nature and history, the intellectual content of religions has always finally adapted itself to scientific and social conditions after they have become clear. In a sense, it has been parasitic upon the latter.

For this reason I do not think that those who are concerned about the future of a religious attitude should trouble themselves about the conflict of science with traditional doctrines—though I can understand the perplexity of fundamentalists and liberals alike who have identified religion with a special set of beliefs. Concern about the future of religion should take, I think, a different direction. It is difficult to see how religion, after it has accommodated itself to the disintegrating effect of knowledge upon the dogmas of the church, can accommodate itself to traditional social institutions and remain vital.

It seems to me that the chief danger to religion lies in the fact that it has become so respectable. It has become largely a sanction of what socially exists—a kind of gloss upon institutions and conventions. Primitive Christianity was devastating in its claims. It was a religion of renunciation and denunciation of the "world"; it demanded a change of heart that entailed a revolutionary change in human relationships. Since the Western world is now alleged to be Christianized, a world of outworn institutions is accepted and blessed. A religion that began as a demand for a revolutionary change and that has become a sanction to established economic, political, and international institutions should perhaps lead its sincere devotees to reflect upon the sayings of the one worshiped as its founder: "Woe unto you when all men shall speak well of you," and, "Blessed are ye when men shall revile you and persecute you."

I do not mean by this that the future of religion is bound up with a return to the apocalyptic vision of the speedy coming of a heavenly kingdom. I do not mean that I think early Christianity has within itself even the germs of a ready-made remedy for present ills and a ready-made solution for present problems. Rather I would suggest that the future of religion is connected with the possibility of developing a faith in the possibilities of human experience and human relationships that will create a vital sense of the solidarity of human interests and inspire action to make that sense a reality. If our nominally religious institutions learn how to use their symbols and rites to express and enhance such a faith, they may become useful allies of a conception of life that is in harmony with knowledge and social needs.

Since existing Western civilization is what it is so largely because of the forces of industry and commerce, a genuinely religious attitude will be concerned with all that deeply affects human work and the leisure that is dependent upon the conditions and results of work. That is, it will acknowledge the significance of economic factors in life instead of evading the issue. The greatest obstacle that exists to the apprehension and actualization of the possibilities of experience is found in our economic régime. One does not have to accept the doctrine of economic determination of history and institutions to be aware that the opportunities of men in general to engage in an experience that is artistically and intellectually rich and rewarding in the daily modes of human intercourse is dependent upon economic conditions. As long as the supreme effort of those who influence thought and set the conditions under which men act is directed toward maintenance of the existing money economy and private profit, faith in the possibilities of an abundant and significant experience, participated in by all, will remain merely philosophic. While this matter was led up to by a consideration of religion, its significance extends far beyond the matter of religion. It affects every range and aspect of life.

Many persons have become acutely conscious of economic evils as far as they bear upon the life of wage earners, who form the great mass of mankind. It requires somewhat more imagination to see how the experience of those who are, as we say, well-to-do or are "comfortably off" is restricted and distorted. They seem to enjoy the advantages of the present situation. But they suffer as deeply from its defects. The artist and scientific inquirer are pushed outside the main currents of life and become appendages to its fringe or caterers to its injustices. All æsthetic and intellectual interests suffer in consequence. Useless display and luxury, the futile attempt to secure happiness through the possession of things, social position, and economic power over others, are manifestations of the restriction of experience that exists among those who seemingly profit by the present order. Mutual fear, suspicion, and jealousy are also its products. All of these things deflect and impoverish human experience beyond any calculation.

There may have been a time when such things had to be endured because mankind had neither the knowledge nor the arts by which to attain an abundant life shared by all. As it becomes increasingly evident that science and technology have given us the resources for dealing effectively with the workings of economic forces, the philosophy of the possibilities of experience takes on concrete meaning.

Our international system (since, with all its disorder, it *is* a system) presents another example, writ large, of the restriction of experience created by exclusiveness and isolation. In the arts and technical sciences, there already exist contacts and exchanges undreamed of even a century ago. Barring our execrable tariff walls, the same is true of commerce in physical commodities. But at the same time, race and color prejudice have never had such opportunity as they have now to poison the mind, while nationalism is elevated into a religion called patriotism. Peoples and nations exist in a state of latent antagonism when not engaged in overt conflict. This state of affairs narrows and impoverishes the experience of every individual in countless ways. An outward symbol of this restriction is found in the oft cited fact that eighty per cent of our national expenditure goes to pay for the results of past wars and preparing for future wars. The conditions of a vitally valuable experience for the individual are so bound up with complex, collective, social relationships that the individualism of the past has lost its meaning. Individuals will always be the center and the consummation of experience, but what an individual actually *is* in his life-experience depends upon the nature and movement of associated life. This is the lesson enforced by both our economic and our international systems.

Morals is not a theme by itself because it is not an episode nor department by itself. It marks the issue of all the converging forces of life. Codes that set up fixed and unchanging ends and rules have necessarily relaxed in the face of changing science and society. A new and effective morale can emerge only from an exploration of the realities of human association. Psychology and the social disciplines are beginning to furnish the instrumentalities of this inquiry. In no field has disrespect for experience had more disastrous consequences, for in no other has there been such waste. The experience of the past is largely thrown away. There has been no deliberate, cumulative process, no systematic transmission of what is learned in the contacts and intercourse of individuals with one another. It has been thought enough to hand on fixed rules and fixed ends. Controlled moral progress can begin only where there is the sifting and communication of the results of all relevant experiences of human association, such as now exists as a matter of course in the experiences of science with the natural world.

In popular speech, morals usually signifies matters of sex relationship. Phenomena of a period of acute transition like those of the present are poor material upon which to base prediction and foresight. But it is clear that the codes which still nominally prevail are the result of one-sided and restricted conditions. Present ideas of love, marriage, and the family are almost exclusively masculine constructions. Like all idealizations of human interests that express a dominantly one-sided experience, they are romantic in theory and prosaic in operation. Sentimental idealization on one side has its obverse in a literally conceived legal system. The realities of the relationships of men, women, and children to one another have been submerged in this fusion of sentimentalism and legalism. The growing freedom of women can hardly have any other outcome than the production of more realistic and more human morals. It will be marked by a new freedom, but also by a new severity. For it will be enforced by the realities of associated life as they are disclosed to careful and systematic inquiry, and not by a combination of convention and an exhausted legal system with sentimentality.

The chief intellectual characteristic of the present age is its despair of any constructive philosophy—not just in its technical meaning, but in the sense of any integrated outlook and attitude. The developments of the last century have gone so far that we are now aware of the shock and overturn in older beliefs. But the formation of a new, coherent view of nature and man based upon facts consonant with science and actual social conditions is still to be had. What we call the Victorian Age seemed to have such a philosophy. It was a philosophy of hope, of progress, of all that is called liberalism. The growing sense of unsolved social problems, accentuated by the war, has shaken that faith. It is impossible to recover its mood.

The result is disillusionment about all comprehensive and positive ideas. The possession of constructive ideals is taken to be an admission that one is living in a realm of fantasy. We have lost confidence in reason because we have learned that man is chiefly a creature of habit and emotion. The notion that habit and impulse can themselves be rendered intelligent on any large and social scale is felt to be only another illusion. Because the hopes and expectations of the past have been discredited, there is cynicism as to all far-reaching plans and policies. That the very knowledge which enables us to detect the illusory character of past hopes and aspirations—a knowledge denied those who held them—may enable us to form purposes and expectations that are better grounded, is overlooked.

In fact, the contrast with the optimism of the Victorian Age is significant of the need and possibility of a radically different type of philosophy. For that era did not question the essential validity of older ideas. It recognized that the new science demanded a certain purification of traditional beliefs —such, for example, as the elimination of the supernatural. But in the main, Victorian thought conceived of new conditions as if they merely put in our hands effective instruments for realizing old ideals. The shock and uncertainty so characteristic of the present marks the discovery that the older ideals themselves are undermined. Instead of science and technology giving us better means for bringing them to pass, they are shaking our confidence in all large and comprehensive beliefs and purposes.

Such a phenomenon is, however, transitory. The impact of the new forces is for the time being negative. Faith in the divine author and authority in which Western civilization confided, inherited ideas of the soul and its destiny, of fixed revelation, of completely stable institutions, of automatic progress, have been made impossible for the cultivated mind of the Western world. It is psychologically natural that the outcome should be a collapse of faith in all fundamental organizing and directive ideas. Skepticism becomes the mark and even the pose of the educated mind. It is the more influential because it is no longer directed against this and that article of the older creeds but is rather a bias against any kind of far-reaching ideas, and a denial of systematic participation on the part of such ideas in the intelligent direction of affairs.

It is in such a context that a thoroughgoing philosophy of experience, framed in the light of science and technique, has its significance. For it, the breakdown of traditional ideas is an opportunity. The possibility of producing the kind of experience in which science and the arts are brought unitedly to bear upon industry, politics, religion, domestic life, and human relations in general, is itself something novel. We are not accustomed to it even as an idea. But faith in it is neither a dream nor a demonstrated failure. It is a faith. Realization of the faith, so that we may work in larger measure by sight of things achieved, is in the future. But the conception of it as a possibility when it is worked out in a coherent body of ideas, critical and constructive, forms a philosophy, an organized attitude of outlook, interpretation, and construction. A philosophic faith, being a tendency to action, can be tried and tested only in action. I know of no viable alternative in the present day to such a philosophy as has been indicated.

Robert Andrews Millikan

IV.
ROBERT ANDREWS MILLIKAN

THERE are three ideas which seem to me to stand out above all others in the influence they have exerted and are destined to exert upon the development of the human race. They have appeared at widely separated epochs because they correspond to different stages in the growth of man's knowledge of himself and of his world. Each of these ideas can undoubtedly be traced back until its origins become lost in the dim mists of prehistoric times: for the sage and the prophet, the thinker and the dreamer, have probably existed since the days of the cave man, and the first has always seen, the second felt, truth to which his times were wholly unresponsive. But it is only *when the times are ripe* that an idea, which may have been adumbrated in individual minds miiienniums earlier, begins to work its way into the consciousness of the race as a whole, and from that time on to exert a powerful influence upon the springs of human progress. In this sense these three ideas may be called discoveries, and times may be set at which they began to appear. The first of these, and the most important of the three, was the gift of religion to the race; the other two sprang from the womb of science. They are the following:

1. The idea of the Golden Rule;
2. The idea of natural law;
3. The idea of age-long growth, or evolution.

The first idea—namely, that one's own happiness, one's own most permanent satisfactions are to be found through trying to forget oneself and seeking, instead, the common good—is an altruistic ideal so contrary to the immediate promptings of the animal within us that it is not strange that it found little place in the thinking or acting of the ancient world, or, for that matter, in the acting of the modern world either, in spite of the professions of Christianity. There will be common consent, however, that the greatest, most consistent, most influential proponent of this idea who has ever lived was Jesus of Nazareth. Buddha, Confucius, Socrates, all had now and then given voice to it, but Jesus made it the sum and substance of his whole philosophy of life. When he said, "All things whatsoever ye would that men should do to you, do ye even so to them: for this is the law and the prophets," I take it that he meant by that last phrase that this precept epitomized in his mind all that had been commanded and foretold—that it embodied the summation of duty and of aspiration.

Now, when the life and teachings of Jesus became the basis of the religion of the whole Western World, an event of stupendous importance for the destinies of mankind had certainly taken place, for a new set of ideals had been definitely and officially adopted by a very considerable fraction of the human race—a fraction which will be universally recognized to have held within it no small portion of the world's human energies and progressive capacities, and which has actually determined to no small degree the direction of human progress.

The significance of this event is completely independent even of the historicity of Jesus. The service of the Christian religion and my own faith in essential Christianity would not be diminished one iota if it should in some way be discovered that no such individual as Jesus ever existed. If the ideas and ideals for which he stood sprang up spontaneously in the minds of men without the stimulus of a single great character, the result would be even more wonderful and more inspiring than it is now, for it would mean that the spirit of Jesus is actually more widely spread throughout the world than we realize. In making this statement, I am endeavoring to say just as positively and emphatically as I can that the credentials of Jesus are found wholly in his teachings and in his character as recorded by his teachings, and not at all in any real or alleged historical events.

And in making that affirmation, let me also emphasize the fact that I am only paraphrasing Jesus' own words when he refused to let his disciples rest his credentials upon a sign.

My conception, then, of the essentials of religion, at least of the Christian religion, is that they consist in just two things: first, in inspiring mankind with the Christlike ideal—that is, the altruistic ideal which means, specifically, concern for the common good as contrasted with one's own individual impulses and interests, wherever in one's own judgment the two come into conflict; and second, inspiring mankind to do, rather than merely to think about, its duty, the definition of duty for each individual being what he himself conceives to be for the common good. In three words, I conceive the essential task of religion to be "to develop the *consciences,* the *ideals,* and the *aspirations* of mankind."

It is very important to notice that in the definitions I have given, duty has nothing to do with what somebody else conceives to be for the common good—that is, with morality in the derivative sense of the *mores* of a people. Endless confusion and no end of futility gets into popular discussion merely because of a failure to differentiate between these two conceptions. As I shall use the words, then—moral and immoral, or moral right and wrong, are purely subjective terms. The question of what actually is for the common good is the whole stupendous problem of science or of knowledge in the broad sense of that term; it has nothing to do with religion or with morals as I am using these words. There are only two kinds of immoral conduct. The first is due to indifference, thoughtlessness, failure to reflect upon what is for the common good; in other words, careless, impulsive, unreflective living on the part of people who know that they ought at least to try to think things through. I suspect that ninety-nine per cent of all immorality is of this type. This furnishes the chief reason for religious effort and the chief field for religious activity, for both example and precept unquestionably have the power to increase the relatively small fraction of the population that attempts to be reflectively moral. The second type of immorality is represented by "the unpardonable sin" of which Jesus spoke—deliberate refusal, after reflection, to follow the light when seen.

Thus far I have been dealing only with what seem to me to be obvious facts—mere platitudes, if you will—for the sake of not being misunderstood when I speak about the essentials of religion. I am not at this moment concerned with how far the *practice* of religion has at times fallen short of the ideals stated in the foregoing essentials. I am now merely reaffirming the belief with which I began: that the discovery of the foregoing ideals and their official adoption as the basis of the religion of the Western World has within the past two thousand years exercised a stupendous influence upon the destinies of the race.

But I shall go further and express some convictions about the relation of those ideals, not only to the past, but also to the present and future. I am going to affirm that those ideals are the most potent and significant element in the religion of the Western World to-day. It is true that many individual Western religions contain some elements in addition to these—some of them good, some harmless, some bad—and that the good and the bad are so mixed in some of them that it is not always easy, even from my own point of view, to determine whether a given branch of religion is worth while or not. Nevertheless, looking at Western religion as a whole, the following facts seem to me obvious and very significant.

First, that if the basis of Western religion is to be found in the element that is common to all its branches, then the one indispensable element in it now is just that element which formed the center of Jesus' teaching, and which I have called above the essence of religion. Second, that no man who believes in the fundamental value for the modern world of the essentials of religion as defined above, and in the necessity for the definite organization of religion for the sake of making it socially effective, needs to withdraw himself from the religious groups, and thereby to exert his personal influence against the spread of the essential religious ideals. In America, at least, he will have no difficulty in finding religious groups who demand nothing of their adherents more than belief in the foregoing ideals, coupled with an honest effort to live in conformity with them. Third, that a very large fraction of the altruistic, humanitarian, and forward-looking work of the world, in all its forms, has to-day its mainsprings in the Christian churches. My own judgment is that about ninety-five per cent of it has come and is coming, directly or indirectly, from the influence of organized religion in the United States. If the influence of American churches in the furtherance of socially wholesome and forward-looking movements, in the spread of conscientious and unselfish living of all sorts, were to be eliminated, it is my belief that our democracy would in a few years become so corrupt that it could not endure. These last two are, however, merely individual judgments, the correctness of which I cannot prove. Some will no doubt differ with them.

Now, looking to the influence of religion in the future, I have in the preceding paragraphs found the essence of the gospel of Jesus in the Golden Rule, which, broadly interpreted, means the development of a sense of social responsibility in the individual. In the last analysis, civilization itself is primarily dependent upon just this thing.

The change from the individual life of the animal to the group life of civilized man, which becomes a life of ever-expanding complexity as our scientific civilization advances, would obviously be impossible unless the individual learned in ever-increasing measure to subordinate his impulses and interests to the furtherance of the group life. The reason that the Western World adopted Christianity as its religion is to be found, I suspect, in the fact that Western civilization discovered that it could not possibly develop its highly organized group life without Christianity. If this is so, the future is certainly going to need the essentials of Christianity even more than the past has needed them. In other words, the principal job which the churches have been trying to do in the past, and which I think, on the whole, they have succeeded fairly well in doing in spite of their weaknesses and follies—namely, the job of developing the consciences, the ideals, and the aspirations of mankind—must be done by some agency in the future even more effectively than it has been done in the past.

There are just two ways in which this can be done. The first is by destroying organized religion as Russia has recently been attempting to do, and building upon its ruins some other organization which will carry on the work of the church— some other organization which will embody the essentials of religion but be free from its faults. The second way is to assist organized religion as it now exists, helping it to eliminate its faults and to be more effective in emphasizing and spreading its essentials with ever-increasing vigor. The second method may perhaps be impossible in some countries. I should need to know those countries better than I do now before I could express an opinion. But, for our own country I feel altogether sure of my ground, and I suspect that most thinking men will agree with me that the second way is the only feasible way.

In the United States, organized religion has already undergone an amazing evolution, which shows its capacity to adapt itself to new conditions. It first sloughed off, or had cut away from it, the terrible incubus of political power when the complete separation of church and state was decreed by the far-visioned men who made our Constitution. Second, to a considerable degree it has freed itself from the shackles that are imposed by central authority and vested rights, and has thus left itself free to evolve. Third, within recent years it has been rapidly freeing itself, despite some sporadic indications to the contrary, from the curse of superstition, and getting nearer and nearer to the essentials of religion. Finally, if the growth of modern science has taught anything to religion and to the modern world, it is that the method of progress is the method of evolution, not the method of revolution. Let every man reflect well on these things before he assists in stabbing to death, or in allowing to starve to death, organized religion in the United States.

Thus far I have presented the most conspicuous contribution of religion to the development of the race. I now turn to the two major contributions of science to human progress. The ancient world, in all the main body of its thinking, believed that God, or Nature, or the Universe, whichever term you prefer, was a being of caprice and whim. To-day, however, we think of a God who rules through law, or a Nature capable of being depended upon, or a Universe of consistency, of orderliness, and of the beauty that goes with order. This idea has *made* modern science, and it is unquestionably the foundation of modern civilization. Because of this discovery, or because of the introduction of this idea into human thinking, and because of the *faith* of the scientist in it, he has been able to harness the forces of nature and to make them do the work that enslaved human beings were forced to do in all preceding civilizations.

Yes, and much more than this; for it is not merely the material side of life that this idea has changed. It has also revolutionized the whole mode of thought of the race. It has changed the philosophical and religious conceptions of mankind. It has laid the foundations for a new and stupendous advance in man's conception of God, for a sublimer view of the world, and of man's place and destiny in it. The anthropomorphic God of the ancient world—the God of human passions, frailties, caprices, and whims—is gone, and with him the old duty to propitiate him, so that he might be induced to treat you better than your neighbor. Can anyone question the advance that has been made in diminishing the prevalence of these medieval, essentially childish, and essentially selfish ideas? The new God is the God of law and order; the new duty, to know that order and to get into harmony with it, to learn how to make the world a better place for mankind to live in, not merely how to save your individual soul.* However, once destroy our confidence in the principle of uniformity, our belief in the rule of law, and our effectiveness immediately disappears, our method ceases to be dependable, and our laboratories become deserted.

I am not worrying here over the recent introduction of the so-called "principle of uncertainty" in microscopic processes— an event that is causing so much excitement among physicists just now. This may indeed be consoling, or, at least, illuminating to those non-physicists who have been worrying their heads over their inability to reconcile the principle of law with the facts of free will and of responsibility. We physicists have had much worse contradictions than that to put up with in the subject of physics alone, as, for example, the reconciliation of the wave theory of light with the essentially corpuscular light-quant theory. Experiment has told us that both theories are right, and we have had the limitations of our knowledge jolted into us enough times lately in physics to believe it, in spite of

---

* "Concerning what ultimately becomes of *the individual* in the (evolutionary) process, science has added nothing and it has subtracted nothing. So far as science is concerned, religion can treat that problem precisely as it has in the past, or it can treat it in some entirely new way if it wishes. For that problem is entirely outside the field of science now, though it need not necessarily always remain so. Science has undoubtedly been responsible for a certain change in religious thinking as to the relative values of individual and race salvation. For obviously, by definitely introducing the most stimulating and inspiring motive for altruistic effort which has ever been introduced, namely, the motive arising from the conviction that we ourselves may be vital agents in the march of things, science has provided a reason for altruistic effort which is quite independent of the ultimate destination of the individual and is also much more alluring to some sorts of minds than that of singing hosannas forever around the throne. To that extent science is undoubtedly influencing and changing religion quite profoundly now. The emphasis upon making this world better is certainly the dominant and characteristic element in the religion of to-day."
—Robert A. Millikan, *Evolution in Science and Religion* (pp. 83 and 84), Yale University Press, 1927. The reader is referred to this volume for further elaboration of the author's point of view.

our inability to see as yet just how the reconciliation is to be made.

This fact worries Mr. Mencken, as it does all essentially assertive (that is, dogmatic) minds, so that in a recent review of Eddington's extraordinarily profound book, *The Nature of the Physical Universe,* he calls for another Huxley to tell us just exactly what is what in physics. But physicists have never been strong on dogmatism, not even in Huxley's day, and they are much less so now than then. We admit, to the complete bewilderment of minds like Mr. Mencken's, that we do not know everything yet. In this book, Eddington points out for the edification of those who worry about free will and determinism that the behavior of a very large number of human beings—such, for example, as the percentage of them who will get married each year—is accurately predictable on the basis of modern statistics, though the behavior of a particular individual in the group is completely unpredictable and his choice unhampered. Here is certainly a specific illustration of the coexistence of the reign of law with the practical freedom of choice which each individual knows he has.

But I don't think this particular problem ever worried the physicist, for he has always known that his ignorance was as yet quite ample enough to cover the links in the reconciliation that must exist. Eighteenth and nineteenth century materialism never had any lure for him, for it always represented quite as pure dogmatism—assertiveness without knowledge—as did medieval theology, and modern developments have pushed it completely out of sight. For *matter* is no longer a mere game of marbles played by blind men. An atom is now an amazingly complicated *organism,* possessing many interrelated parts and exhibiting many functions and properties—energy properties, radiating properties, wave properties, and other properties quite as mysterious as any that used to masquerade under the name of "mind." Hence the phrases—"All is matter," and "All is mind"—have now become mere shibboleths completely devoid of meaning.

It is not important here, however, to inquire whether the principle of determinism applies to infinitely minute and practically unattainable processes. For it is the existence of the *idea* of natural law or orderliness with which we are concerned, rather than with the proof of its universality; and no one who has any conception of what science has done since about A.D. 1600—the date at which this idea first began to spread throughout the consciousness of mankind—will be likely to question my initial statement that it is one of the three ideas which, whether true or false as a *universal* generalization, has at least exerted, and is undoubtedly still destined to exert, a stupendous influence upon the destinies of mankind.

The third, or evolutionary idea, is the youngest of the two great ideas born of modern science. It is not yet one hundred years old. Introduced by Darwin solely in its application to biological evolution, the evolutionary theory has come to dominate in a very broad way almost every aspect of human thought as discovery after discovery in modern science has pushed back farther and farther the age of the stars, the age of the solar system, the age of the earth, the age of the rocks, of fossil life, of prehistoric man, of recorded history, of social institutions. Thus we have discovered that our social institutions have evolved through a process identical with that which governed the evolution of biological forms. We have come to realize that if the family, the state, religion, or even war have survived, it is because, after ages of trial in which many other institutions have competed with them and disappeared, they have had survival value. Hence we have come to *study* institutions to see *why* they have survived.

And finally, if we wish to eliminate an old institution like war, for example, we have come to realize that we are not likely to succeed simply by wishing it gone, nor, indeed, simply by pacifistic propaganda of any sort. We are likely to succeed only if the conditions which gave it its survival value have been or can be eliminated. Hence the establishment of a League of Nations and of a World Court, aimed precisely at eliminating some, at least, of these conditions. In my judgment, however, war is now in process of being abolished chiefly through the relentless advance of modern science—the principal diverter of man's energies and interests from the warlike to the peaceful arts. War will disappear, like the dinosaur, when changes in world conditions have destroyed its survival value. Such changes are now being brought about primarily by the growth of modern science and its applications—changes due to the advent of world-wide and nearly instantaneous communication, to the enormous modern stimulation of international trade and commerce, bringing with it a sense of interdependence and of the necessity of international understandings.

Again, because of the growth of this evolutionary idea in human thinking, we have come to see that an institution like religion, in so far as it deals with conceptions of God—the integrating factor in this universe not merely of atoms but of ether and of mind, ideas, duties, and intelligence—has not been and cannot be a fixed thing; that it has been continually changing with the growth of human knowledge; and that it will continue to expand as knowledge continues to grow.

I have thus presented the most outstanding contribution of religion to human progress, and the two most representative and significant contributions of science. We are now ready to ask how they are interrelated. The answer is quite obvious. The world of science, dominated by the reign of law, has necessitated the increasing association of men into coöperating groups; but the effectiveness of those groups—indeed, the whole group life—becomes at once impossible unless the altruistic ideal of religion, the sense of social responsibility, permeates the whole; while the evolutionary concept is absolutely essential to an understanding of the development both of religion and of science. In a word, these three ideas and ideals interlock everywhere in a mutually helpful way. Not one of them can have a normal and effective existence without each of the other two.

Whence, then, arises this strange idea, so often heard in popular discussions, of an incompatibility between science and religion? Here again I think the answer is clear. There is obviously no incompatibility between science and *the essentials of religion* as I have defined them. But individual religions, or branches of a religion, often contain more than these essentials. Every movement which becomes popular and gains large numbers of adherents inevitably draws into itself men who are not actuated solely, or even at all, by its ideals, but who use it to further their own ends. Those ends may be very worthy ones, arising from the best of motives in minds of restricted understanding or limited intelligence, or they may be very unworthy ones, such as the desire for personal aggrandizement or political power. Everyone knows that the history of Christianity is not at all free even from influences of the latter sort. The so-called War of the Reformation is usually described as a religious war, and the horrors of it are sometimes attributed to the influence of Christianity; but I think that most historians will agree that it was not primarily a religious war at all, although both sides undoubtedly worked overtime, as they always do, to try to prove that God was on their side. In other words, religion was its shibboleth, not its cause. It represented simply the terrific struggle of a group of northern princes to free themselves from the yoke of a southern power which had used the machinery of a religious organization for cementing and perpetuating its control.

Again, the anticlerical parties in many countries to-day represent, in part, the efforts of real reformers to break the *political* power of groups that have seized it and hold it in the *name* of religion, when the real issues obviously have nothing whatever to do with religion. Still again, Voltaire in his attack on the church was not attacking religious ideals in the least. He did not even call himself an atheist. He was far too intelligent for that. Fullness of knowledge always and necessarily means some understanding of the depths of our ignorance, and that is always conducive to both humility and reverence. If you and I lived in some countries to-day, I have no doubt that we should be in the anticlerical groups; but it would not be because we had lost confidence in the essentials of religion, but rather because we thought that these essentials had become so buried under excrescences of the kind I have been describing that the net result was harmful rather than socially helpful.

I have here been talking, not about religion and science, but rather about organized religion and politics—a pair that all of us will agree ought never to have been mated. Where they have been so mated, they ought to be divorced with the same celerity that characterizes proceedings at Reno. Fortunately this problem does not exist for us in the United States. I have introduced the subject merely to show how the essentials of religion may, and sometimes do, become lost in the *organization* of religion. Present-day Buddhism is, I suppose, a more striking illustration of this than is anything that can be found among the many ramifications of Christianity.

But by the very same method described above in the discussion of politics and religion, there has grown up, as I think, another excrescence upon the essentials of religion which introduces us at once into the very heart of the alleged conflict between science and religion. This has come about not so much because of the selfishness and ambition of men (real motives, though often masked even in the minds of their possessors under softer names), as through the ignorance of men. The amazing insight of Jesus is revealed in his having kept himself free from creedal statements, particularly statements that reflected the state of man's knowledge or ignorance of the universe that was characteristic of his times. In spite of our enormously increased knowledge of the universe, a large part of his sayings seem to us to be just as true now as they seemed to be then. The things that a man does not say often reveal the understanding and penetration of his mind even more than the things he says. The fact that Jesus confined himself so largely to the statement of truths that still seem to us to have eternal value is what has made him a leader and teacher of such supreme influence throughout the centuries.

But throughout the past two thousand years, his followers, unlike him, have in many instances *loaded* their various branches of his religion with creedal statements which are full of their own woefully human frailties. The difference is so enormous as to justify calling his statements Godlike in comparison. For what are these man-made creeds? Admittedly they have been written by men, or groups of men, called together for the purpose—men so uninspired that very few of them have ever left any lasting memory of themselves. How many people now know of any name that was ever associated with any of them? In their creeds these men have often reflected in detail the state of knowledge, or the state of ignorance, of the universe, or of God—whichever term you prefer—characteristic of their times. If someone wishes me to change this implied definition of Deity so as to make it read, "the unifying principle in the universe," I shall not object; for there *is* a unity, an interrelatedness, a wholeness to it all, we ourselves being but parts of that whole, and this is attested by all experience, including the amazing new scientific developments in the fields of ether physics, relativity, and wave-mechanics. That is only my prosaic paraphrase of the lines of Tennyson, the poet of science, when he says:

> The sun, the moon, the stars, the hills and the plains,
> Are not these, O Soul, the vision of Him who reigns?
> The ear of man cannot hear, and the eye of man cannot see;
> But if we could see and hear this vision—were it not He?
> Speak to Him, thou, for He hears, and spirit with spirit shall meet.
> Closer is He than breathing, and nearer than hands and feet.

Now with the conception of God changing continuously as man has grown in knowledge, from the time when he pictured his God in the form of a calf, or a crocodile, or a monstrous man, to the time when the poet described God as the Soul of the Universe—what must be the relation between science, or the ever-expanding knowledge of man, and the long since vanished conceptions of the universe, or of God, frozen in ancient man-made creeds? Obviously one of inescapable conflict. And in so far as these creedal excrescences have covered up, or displaced, the essentials of religion, there are obviously no alternatives except (1) to remove that sort of a deadening growth from the heart of religion, or, failing that, either (2) to desert a hopeless religion or (3) to give up science.

A choice between the last two alternatives might be a necessity in some countries. Fortunately, no such choice is necessary in the United States. Since this nation is the widest flung democracy in the world, it needs—indeed, it must have—the essentials of religion more than any other country if it is to endure; and with us religion has been able to develop wholly untrammeled by political interference, and in many of its branches it has been absolutely free to evolve without the restraining influence of central authority. I have myself belonged to two churches, one a Union church and one a Congregational church, both of which were unhampered by a creed of any sort. Other churches are continually revising or modifying their creeds with our growing knowledge.

Within the United States, then, there is not the slightest reason why religion cannot keep completely in step with the demands of our continuously growing understanding of the world. Here religious groups are to be found which correspond to practically every stage in the development of our knowledge and understanding. Personally, I believe that essential religion is one of the world's supremest needs, and I believe that one of the greatest contributions that the United States ever can, or ever will, make to world progress— greater by far than any contribution which we ever have made, or can make, to the science of government—will consist in *furnishing an example to the world of how the religious life of a nation can evolve intelligently, inspiringly, reverently, completely divorced from all unreason, all superstition, and all unwholesome emotionalism.*

V.

THEODORE DREISER

THE original inquiry which is responsible for the ensuing fanfare requested information concerning my beliefs as to the nature of the world and of man—a spiritual (if only I or anybody knew what that word meant!) as opposed to a material (whatever that is!) last will and testament.

And because all my life I have speculated concerning the mystery of my being here and the (to me) lamentable finish to all the serious moods, sentiments, struggles, beliefs, and what not else to which from time to time I have lent myself, I do not now hesitate to undertake this serious, if ultimately unilluminating, labor. For, Messieurs and Mesdames, to be quite frank, I have thought of but little else. The mystery of life—its inexplicability, beauty, cruelty, tenderness, folly, etc., etc.—has occupied the greater part of my waking thoughts; and in reverence or rage or irony, as the moment or situation might dictate, I have pondered and even demanded of cosmic energy to know *Why*. But now I am told by the physicist as well as the biologist that there can be no *Why* but only a *How*, since to know *How* disposes finally of any possible *Why*.

Yet, just the same and notwithstanding, here I sit at this

NOTE: Mr. Dreiser's article is included in *Living Philosophies* by permission of Horace Liveright.

particular moment, pen in hand and scribbling briskly concerning something about which finally I know nothing at all, and worse yet, about which no one can tell me anything, and yet wishing to know *Why*. To be sure, I can turn to almost any religion and hear that God lives and reigns, that He is all-wise and all-good, and that, assuming ourselves to be sufficiently humble and worshipful, He may "save" us to a more agreeable hereafter—though why He should have chosen to invent such irritable and even ridiculous creatures as ourselves or the several chemical and physical processes of which we are compounded in order to ultimately "save" us is beyond me. He need never have troubled to create, and so might well have saved Himself the trouble of "saving" us.

But not only that. For I am not only puzzled, but even startled and all but struck dumb by the number and variety of the *creations* of this Creator of the religionists, or if there chances to be no such Creative Being, then by the will-less mechanism of the physicist and the chemist which just is and does, but without any traceable intention of doing so—a blind and yet deathless energy possessed of most amazing powers and attributes, but not that of intelligible intention. Sitting in a modern home or automobile, walking through a modern street or building, seeing for oneself what appears to be intention, direction, order, intelligence, and what not else in the way of forms and implements wherewith to protect and preserve as well as entertain and even educate—I will not say *all* of the inventions of this alleged Creator or this blind mechanism, but rather one only—Man; seeing this, one might almost be inclined to exclaim and even insist that here was order and intelligence at work. One might say that here was the obvious handiwork of an amazingly wise, although not necessarily a kindly, intelligence; for some of the adventurings and compulsions of Man in connection with himself and his fellows—

those of his own species as well as others—would soon make clear that kindness, although a fractional part, possibly, of the nature or at least the relationship of one individual of this species to another, was by no means the whole of it.

For here among men you soon find vitally and—strangest of all, perhaps—constructively operative: cruelty, greed, vanity, lust, gluttony, false witness, envy, and hatred; with their evoked and hence attendant wars, murders, injuries, and deaths; together with the possibly more admirable qualities of friendship, affection, admiration, charity, generosity, etc.—if, indeed, these qualities often be not mere figments or illusions of the human mind, or *élan vital,* or blood stream, or whatever it is that keeps us functioning in the very peculiar and not necessarily (except to ourselves) admirable forms or shapes in which we find ourselves. For, friends,—and much to my own astonishment it is that I am compelled to conclude this—I find life to be not only a complete illusion or mirage which changes and so escapes or eludes one at every point, but the most amazing fanfare of purely temporary and always changing and ever vanishing and, in the main, clownish and ever ridiculous interests that it has ever been my lot to witness—interests which concern at best the maintenance here of innumerable selfish, self-centered, and cruel organisms whose single and especial business it is to exist each at the expense of the other—no more and no less. If only it were by cutting each other's hair—and no more.

For what other incentive has Man than to feed, clothe, and entertain himself at the expense of others—whether little or much? And when you pass into the realms of animals and the vegetables—of whom Man, by reason of a built-up process of offense and defense, is supposed to be the overlord—what other incentive or incentives do you find there? Love? For the propagation of the species, the progeny of the individual

—yes. But for anything other than the progeny of the individual of the species as against the welfare of the individuals and the progeny of all other species? No. And as for understanding of how or why—to what end? Does anyone know what other creatures apart from Man apprehend or understand?

What we plainly see is birth and death—the result of chemic and electrophysical processes of which at bottom we know exactly nothing. And beyond that—murder, the chase, life living on life, the individual sustaining himself at the expense of every other, and wishing not to die. And then beauty, beauty, beauty, which seems to derive as much and more from this internecine and wholly heartless struggle as from any other thing. And yet, beauty, beauty, beauty—the entire process, to the human eye at least, æsthetic in its results if by no means entirely so in its processes.

On the other hand, if I turn from this to the physicists and biologists—or to science *in toto*—I am at once and almost equally confused and confounded. For here, while I find a world whose assertions, if not thoughts, are based (in so far as possible) on previously verified experience in the physical or chemical worlds, or in that third world jointly erected out of the two of them—the biological realm—I am still, at bottom, sunk in mystery. For, as I have said, here is no *Why*, only a *How*—and the ultimate basis of the *How* not known! Instead, only a chemico-physical process which requires endless observation and correlation but with no least belief that it can lead to more than a very limited knowledge of *How*—which, should sufficient ever be known, is to abolish *Why*.

But let me say here that I have no intention of becoming too technical—or rather, attempting to become so. My intention is solely to present my reactions to a world that is as yet completely immersed in mystery—physicist or no physicist, biologist or no biologist. And as for astronomy, history, geology, sociology—well, we gaze or observe and attempt to set down certain laws, but little more. For we have but five weak little senses and with these during the past few thousand years we have begun to perk and pry—the mystery and the æsthetic beauty of it all luring us on. But the wonder to me is that Man is not even more astounded and dumbfounded than he appears to be each hour of his presence here; that he is not more withdrawn from his so-called necessities than he really is, in order to sit beneath a tree, Buddha fashion, and gaze in wonder and astonishment upon the wholly inexplicable world about him.

For here I am, as I now choose to inform you, at the corner of Broadway and Fifty-seventh Street, in New York. And the world, or at least a typical portion of our very human American world as it is to-day, is marching or rolling by—busses, street cars, autos, men and women, boys and girls. All, however, human beings, of the seemingly favored *homo sapiens,* who in the wasteful and yet possibly shrewd processes of nature have either succeeded or failed, or half succeeded or half failed. At any rate, here they are.

And now what I wish most particularly to point out in connection with this is that this scene taken as a whole is scintillant, brisk, interesting, forceful. And yet, as I here and now once more ask myself: "For what reason, unless it be that each of these individuals thus hurrying here and there—to work, to pleasure, to acts of duty, virtue, crime, or what you will—achieves a somewhat of something which he or she thinks of as pleasure, here and not elsewhere; and, so thinking, actually at times achieves? Apart from that *here,* what is all this about? What else can it possibly concern? A possible future state entirely different from this?"

Impossible. These creatures that I see here and now have little capacity for imagining, let alone sensing, any such entirely different state, assuming such a one to exist. Their reactions relate to what they see, hear, feel, taste, and smell *here*—not elsewhere. And except for various vague and curious and, in addition to that, all too terrified, thoughts as to how such a different state might—and worse—is certain to dispose of them, they have no interest in any other state. It does not exist here. Possibly there is no such other state? Yet in the face of much pother and blather on the part of self-seeking religionists or theorists with this and that quack nostrum as to the why and how elsewhere, after death—these creatures know all too little as to the significance of good and evil here (and try to find the ultimate difference!) and are all too willing to contribute something toward the support of these same nostrum venders, lest, in the strange and unbelievable welter and mystery of things, there may be something to what they say—a God or Devil or supervisory (and therefore more or less inimical) Ruler sitting or moving above Man.

The greatest factor in all this is, as you see, the fear of annihilation. For here, now, is one walking with you. He is tense, alert, strong, charming, alive. Then for a very little while, maybe, he is gone from your presence. And then of a sudden that ever appalling word—dead. He is dead. He or she was alive and now is no more. The look, the feel, the voice, the temperament, the dreams, the plans—all gone. No word, no sound. No trace. The effective and valuable and always amazing body that you knew—dissolved. You stand—astounded—but without answer. No word of truth in regard to it all from either science or religion—but with science arguing eternal dissolution and religion barefacedly lying as to the what and how of the future. But no absolute truth. And struggle and contest and fear stirred in with a little pleasure for those who remain.

A dour credo?

It is all I have to offer. All I have ever intelligently accepted.

Let us now approach the chemical and physical combinations and processes which make the individuals and parts of this scintillant scene. And what a mystery! For here we have —what? Bricks, stone, glass, wood, plaster, paints, and what you will of the surrounding buildings. But representing what? In the last analysis, electrons, protons, quantums of energy in some amazing and constantly shifting arrangement of atoms and molecules which makes it possible for man, responding as he must to his instincts, pleasures, or necessities, to arrange them in this fashion.

And yet, when you go further and ask: "What is Man?"— behold, you are informed that he also is a diversified arrangement of molecules or atoms or electrons, protons, quantums (I am using the current scientific lingo for these amazing mysteries)—but in him masquerading as blood, gray matter, liver, kidneys, muscles, viscera, bones, hair, cartilage, and all their attendant powers, emotions, duties, etc., yet each constructed of the primordial cell, in numbers; which cells in turn are composed, in the last analysis, of molecules, atoms, electrons, protons, and finally (the last word of to-day) quantums. But all finally and inexorably, as the physicists see it, electrical—so that someone has already said that God is electricity. In other words, and to go back to the sentient Greeks, He is Jove with his bolts!

But then, what is electricity? Atoms.

And what are atoms? Electricity.

Wonderful!

But then, as I say, here I am, still looking at the passing crowds at the corner of Broadway and Fifty-seventh Street, and now asking why should electricity, or primordial energy, or what you will, wish to form itself, via electrons, protons, quantums, into atoms, molecules, and eventually cells—in other words, into such a troublesome and mysterious, if varied and æsthetic, scene as this? And why again, composed though we may be of this, that, and the other proton, electron, etc., etc., why should we not in some way be able to sense why we are as we are—assembled as we are of the same ultimate atoms and doing as we do? Why? Good God—surely in the face of all this sense of aliveness and motion and this and that, there should be some intimation of *Why*. But no—none.

And, furthermore, there is no intimation as to why these several electrons, protons, atoms, etc., should wish, assuming they could do so, to combine and recombine—via the long and voluntary or involuntary process of evolution—into wood and stone, heat and cold, snow, water, air, blood, bones, hair, teeth, viscera, etc., in order and at last, say, to make an individual who has to hurry to an office in a shabby suit to earn a meager wage; or a multimillionaire who thinks that the combining of one hundred and twenty-one minor banks into one large one is a great and even wonderful achievement. At best, whatever man does is something that can only prolong the struggles and worries and for the most part futile dreams of those with whom he finds himself companioned here in this atomic or cellular welter, and which in the last analysis may be just nothing at all—a phantasmagoric or cinematic shadow play. Signifying what? A momentary belief in being? Or happiness? Oh, Jehovah! Osiris! Jesus! Jove!

This—nothing less and nothing more—is the significance of the scene at Broadway and Fifty-seventh Street. And as for myself on this bright, sunny morning, I find it pleasant and good, myself a living, if not exactly worthy, part of it.

But now let us shift the scene to the Congo, where, likewise, is a panorama composed of electrons, protons, quantums, or let us say, atoms and cells. And all busy with the work or pleasure, as you will, and whether willing or not, of constructing an amazing succession of species or growths—such as the deadly snake, the killing fly and spider, the savage tiger and lion; in short, such a world of predatory beasts and flowers and trees and vines, poisonous or the reverse, as should be sufficient to lay forever the notion of a kindly directive force or intelligence in the universe. And yet each bent upon the apparently difficult and nearly always miserable labor of sustaining it or himself at the expense of every other. And for how brief a period! At best, from half a minute to a few years. And with seemingly no more knowledge of *Why* than we ourselves—unless sex, the chase, hunger, and the satiation of hunger be *Why*. In short, a kind of electronic or molecular hell, yet atomically no different from that which prevails—or at least produces the scene—at Fifty-seventh Street and Broadway, say, or the body of the Pope, or that of the Archbishop of Canterbury, or Mahatma Gandhi, who is assumed to irradiate only the kindliest and most helpful of thoughts toward all.

And yet—so springs the thought in me at the moment—perhaps, in order to obtain so colorful a scene as this, it is quite necessary to have this angry show of contest and death. Perhaps there can be no true color or zest this side of it. Very well; but why, then, religion or a fixed moral code? Why not rather the Darwinian survival of the fittest, or a man-made series of rules governing the game here and not elsewhere?

As for myself, I see life—for most, at least—as a very

grim and dangerous contest, relieved at best and but for a very little while by a sense or by an illusion of pleasure, which is the bait and the lure for all to all in this internecine contest.

Still, as I so often ask myself, can this be what the universe is for? Not really! For here are immense suns, hot or cold or dead, shouldering each other in space; minute planets spinning like moths humbly and meaninglessly—if this is all the meaning there is. And upon this particular and most minute of planets—ours no less, and the same quite invisible in space, I am told—robbery, oppression, false witness, cruelty, vanity, gluttony, sodomy, and what not else, and all seemingly fortified and entrenched—the weak or deficient, as in the jungle, preyed upon by the strong; the strong fortified by the weakness of the weak and their own strength, and motivated by what lunatic and ever-elusive dreams of happiness. In short, each seeking to establish his dreams for himself—and by whatever methods he may—and then rejoicing in the still more lunatic fanfare which his success in downright villainies at times seems to evoke in those who would be like him, the weaklings and dubs beneath him in position and power! Only meditate on the phrase: "God save the King!"—and then consider the departed kings of the world! Lust of flesh, food, show, applause—these seem to be the chief items with which the world I see is concerned. If I am wrong, let me be properly and appropriately flayed therefor!

I am not unaware that there are opposing points of merit that are not to be gainsaid. These merits I have many times and in many ways stated or sung. Rain-dark violets under rain-soaked leaves. Crimson fungus growths under drooping birch twigs. A brown path over a green hill down which streams a westering sun. A girl, arms akimbo, gazing at the sky at dawn.

A sea a-shimmer in the sun. A beautiful gray rain amid the drooping leaves of the year. A seamed and weary face bent low in sorrow. A light-keeled boat upon an enchanted sea.

I am flooded with happiness—divine, demoniac dreams. I am seized with the very sting and tang of energy and desire, however fateful. So motivated, I can indeed front a universe that knows nothing of kindness, pity, wisdom. With the æsthetic principle here indicated at work among the threads and skeins and shuttles which make this amazing pattern we call Life, I can rest content, though I beg or suffer seemingly meaninglessly at the hands of it.

Moreover, there is the interest that attaches to struggle and defeat as well as to success and dominance among the creations of these atoms and cells—an interest that ranges from wonder at the struttings and show of ignorant power and force to the pathetic complaints and defeats of the incompetent; an interest that swings from applause and acclaim —or the enjoyment of it—to the hatred and vengeance that follow defeat. Indeed, the dominant human mind thus far developed, as I see it at least, is at best a petty piece of machinery, in the main registering states or customs of the silliest possible nature. What does my neighbor do? What is he called? How is he paid, acclaimed? Where is he? How does he feel I should act? Is he more or less successful than I am? Am I better-looking than he, or less? Has he more acclaim, or have I? And the more average the intelligence of the organized atoms, the more prevalent these conventional inquiries and thoughts and dreams. But these are deathless, indestructible atoms, please note, that produce these things or effects—eternal energy in eternal action or change. And this is the result here!

But why, as I now repeat, should eternal energy as presented by atoms and cells concern itself with the humdrum and nonsense that we see here on this planet? Is this all it has to do? **Is** it by any chance the best it can do? God!! Actually, as I see it, society or the constructive efforts of these atoms and molecules and cells comes to little more, on this planet at least, than a scheme or method of procedure whereby each form or species or tribe or race of things can, by contributing something—if no less or more than the bodies or lives of a portion of the totality of each—obtain permission to satisfy each itself in turn by feeding on the bodies or efforts of other organized forms that would like to live and flourish on this earth! And if that is true, what a coarse, grim, and even futile procedure, since so small a percentage of true delight is really achieved! And if not that, just what else, exactly, does the grand process of generation and struggle mean?

And yet, in the face of all this, I would not like to write myself down as a total pessimist. Having observed the process here over a period of years, I find that it has, in the main, the quality of interest—taken all in all, a fairly good show, albeit so filled with anachronisms and illusions and lunacies of one type and another as to make it discreditable either as reason or order. Rather, the best I can say is that I have not the faintest notion of what it is all about, unless it is for self-satisfaction in many and varied ways—all more or less achieved by cruelty or greed, as for instance, life living on life; man growing things in order to consume them; men or creatures preying upon the efforts of others in order to feed and maintain themselves with little effort. Think, for one thing, of the butcher shops at every corner. You do not *see* the abattoirs scattered throughout the world, but hourly they serve you, by murder, even though you dress in silks, sniff bouquets, and perfume your hands!

Of course, the anomalous thing in connection with such a

viewpoint as this is that (at least in so brief a paper as this) it begs the question of æsthetics in nature as well as the presence of emotions, which, whether selfish or unselfish, religious, sexual, or purely æsthetic, cast over the innate savagery of life a gossamer veil of beauty which softens or blurs the essential blindness or indifference or one might almost guess (at times, at least) devised cruelty of it all. For here are, to begin with, the æsthetic forms of things, and on every hand. Architecture, flowers, mountains, the seas, rippling streams, silvery lakes, the depths and silences of forests, bird song, love, the beauty of every living and seemingly quiescent or dead form. Snows that are compounded of lacelike and inspiring designs; rains that are like drops of silver or thin, bright chains of steel. The beauty of a butterfly's wings; a snake's or lizard's skin; the flashing hues of birds or insects; the striding and contemptuous dignity of lions or tigers, at once proud and cruel in their power.

It snows, and the receded saps of life in tree and animal, flower and insect, leave only somber and yet moving and even colorful lines that somehow stir the heart with thoughts not only of a change that will not permit permanence, but a somberness which the inmost molecules of our being appear to respond to as charm. Comes spring—mere mechanical and physical rotation of the earth in sunlight—and ash saplings clash their twigs in rippling, flickering winds; a robin's song is heard; dog-mercury and arbutus bud under the dead leaves of an earlier year. A bit more of mere physical rotation, and yellow, full-grained wheat slumbers under a July sun; gold flies whirl and dance for an hour; songs out of bird throats thrill the fields—wood dove, thrush, lark—and cause the heart to faint or bleed the while we marvel at the seeming insensibility and cruelty out of which these same can and do take their rise.

Opposed to this consoling coat of beauty is the phenomenon

of religion, which hourly—aye, from century to century—voices the plaint of man that all is not well here and that only elsewhere can there be satisfaction or compensation, in part at least, for the ills endured here. The fanfare in regard to it all! The temples, towers, prayers, and the profound stupidity that accompanies it! And not only that, but the fear and awe which throughout the ages have induced billions of creatures, compounded of these same universal atoms about which we are talking, to believe almost anything in regard to themselves or the order and rulership of the universe, and to subscribe humbly or stubbornly to anything which any charlatan or misinformed or misinterpreting philosopher or ascetic or dreamer might evolve out of his own fears or ignorance, and then choose to set forth as the truth, telling how this mysterious thing we call Life is arranged or come by. And yet, why should not at least some of these indestructible atoms or electrons in combination, and of which we are composed, know something of the order or meaning of the structures they erect, and so, via emotions communicated to the brain, say, suggest something of the meaning of life to us? Why not? And yet atoms or no atoms—silence, no less; no least intimation of their own significance or what they know—if anything—from them.

As for myself, I continue to be astounded by this fact: that here in all of these creatures who are so ignorantly worshipful, or those who like myself are not, are all of these same atoms or electrons and protons, and with them—if I can believe some biologists—their derivatives, the molecule and the protoplasmic cell, and all erecting, either intelligently or unintelligently, this thing called Man, or in a broader sense, all flora and fauna. And these underlying units a part (albeit a compound or construction or device) of this same sentient or mechanistic but universal energy which is everywhere—and which, if sentient, should know better, or be more kind, say,

THEODORE DREISER

than to erect ignorant, pathetic, and groveling creatures who really know nothing of anything. And then afterward leave them here to develop all sorts of erratic nonsense in regard to what they are and where they came from; and, those failing, as they do and have, then to turn to all sorts of amazing and yet decidedly pathetic laboratories wherein this compound man proceeds to search or peek and perk, in order to learn, if possible, some minute nothing concerning his *howness* and almost next to nothing as to his *whyness*.

What a condemnation, this, of that seeming sentience below or above Man, this creative if blind energy that so condemns Man to this—this complete ignorance which he may not escape! The almost devilish indifference to the fate or state of creatures so erected, if not by its knowledge and will, at least out of its indestructible energy! I once accented and declaimed a "Mood" in regard to this—and here it is:

>Suns and flowers, and rats, and kings.
>Armies and electrons.
>Saints and microbes.
>The bacillus of cholera.
>The prayers and dreams of St. Francis.
>A Shelley singing.
>A Landru murdering his twenty wives.
>Buddha
>And
>The Marquis de Sade.
>A hundred
>Thousand
>Million
>Murderers in their cells
>Or abroad
>And
>A million martyrs and saints
>Singing and praying.

Nero, Mæcenas, Can Grande,
And this rheumy-eyed beggar at my door
Begging for a dime.
And Orion
And
This rushlike flame
By which I write
And space
And this little ball
On which we spin.

Yet I ask and ask, and ask.
I pray—by God—
On my knees.
I lift up my hands to know.
Yet you do not answer.
Or
You will not;
Or
You cannot.
Yet now,
Now,
I implore you.
I call upon you aloud—
Speak, speak!

Are you jesting?
Feigning?
Dreaming?
Raging?
Are you helpless
Like myself?
Do you know?
Plan?
Thrill?
Aspire?
Do you turn and toss?
Dream and wonder?
Do you hate?

Love?
Envy?
Rejoice?
Sigh?
Die, eventually?
Like myself?
Do you?

O you substance of suns, and flowers, rats and kings.

And if we are not so created, but are the result of chance, then what a condemnation of religion in general as an expression of a terrorized state on the part of energy that does not know what it is yet finds itself erected into creatures that without the slightest knowledge of their past, future, or fate in any form, must still struggle (and how bitterly at times) for the continuance of that which they find ill, perhaps, but hesitate to flee from for fear of encountering something worse—or nothingness! And yet, from this point of view, religion proves itself not wholly an evil nor yet an unmixed good, but only an illusion of the rankest character, yet which for the many at least has served as a nervous or emotional escape from a condition much too severe to be endured. In that sense, of course, the illusion has proved to be a medicament of value, however meaningless without the deadly and sensorially unendurable reality out of which it grew. On the other hand, what is to be said of a reality (these same underlying atoms, electrons, protons, cells, etc., either intelligent or unintelligent, and so mechanistic) that must fall back on illusion in order to endure themselves, or the things into which they have made themselves—men, animals, vegetables? Exactly what? Could universal ignorance do worse? Or evil less?

But now as to our so-called intelligence here on earth. Man, differentiated, as he assumes, from all other lower or lesser flora and fauna, asserts (the majority of *homo sapiens,* at least) a higher and selective intelligence which in its uppermost reaches is not to be differentiated from free will. He knows good from evil and is free to choose between them! The mechanist, of course, denies this. And to me also this has ever seemed the most unfounded and unintelligent of all assertions. For, as I personally have observed life, man responds quite mechanically, and only so, to all such stimuli as he is prepared, or rather constructed, to receive—and no more and no less. And by the same token, the range of his intelligence is limited by his five meager senses and the appetites or chemical calls they are compelled to register and later serve, or he suffers and eventually ceases as an organism. Not only that, but this constitutes the sum and substance of his free will and intelligence—responding to these various stimuli which are neither more nor less than the call bells of chemical, or perhaps better yet, electrophysical states which require certain other electrophysical or chemical atoms to keep them in the forms in which they chance to be.

And as one descends lower and lower the electrochemical or physical stair that leads to the cell and the atom, this same obvious and apparently unchanged sensitivity to stimuli—but nothing more—continues and gives the same seeming appearance of either intelligence or mechanical law, as you will, but that which in ordinary human response or exchange we think of as intelligence. Call any number of chemical or physical or biological masters together and ask. Their unanimous report will be that the sensory responses and reactions which masquerade as intelligence or free will in man never cease in protoplasmic matter of however low a state. Only, as they say, they may, and in most instances do, become less and less complicated, the necessary reactions to stimuli fewer and fewer. But complexity for complexity, the quality or degree of intelligence, or intricate mechanical response, as you will, which they insist is no more than the mechanics of physics and chemistry, remains the same.

As for myself, I really view myself as an atom in a greater machine, just as is the cell in the greater body of which it finds itself a part. But as for myself being a free and independent mechanism with a separate "spirit" of its own?— Nonsense! Science knows nothing of a soul or spirit. And I personally have never been able to find any trace of one, in me or any other. When I am dead, as I see it, I shall be dissolved into my lesser constituents; I shall then be, if anything, a part of universal force, but merged and gone forever. More, I cannot even think of a desirable continuance for myself as I am here, and therefore ask for none.

Enough that my meager electrochemical and physical content as it shows here must remain an indestructible trace maybe of the all in all—to be a part (however minute—scarcely a trace, say—but possibly that) of all light, heat, energy, planets, suns, flowers, rats, kings. To what extent I shall function, if at all, it will be with all that is; and with the poet (Thomas Hood, I believe) can truly say: "If my barque sink, 'tis to another sea."

The only additional point I would like to make or perhaps re-emphasize—for I have probably made it before—is that in spite of all this mechanistic response which disposes of the soul or entity, and in spite of obvious cruelty, brutality, envy, hatred, murder, deceit, and what not else, I still rise to testify to the æsthetic perfection of this thing that I see here and which we call Life. For look you! Here is this great, this enormous force, which as we plainly see, can and does evolve suns, planets, immensities of all kinds and descriptions, to say nothing of such animalcula as rats, bedbugs, flies, and lice.

Still, at the same time it can and does achieve an æsthetic whole—beauty no less—and via the same elements that are in lice and bedbugs as well as in the most distant suns or sidereal systems—in fire and flowers, in Shelley and Christ. You and I may argue that rats and flies and bedbugs are not æsthetic and join no æsthetic whole, but examine more closely with a lens and the concentrated interest of the mind its response to organization and effort, and then judge.

Let us, indeed, witness a contest between animals or slum dwellers, a murder, a rancid pond or neighborhood, the seamed and hoary face of age, want, decay, the rocking and shouldering elephant, the awkward baboon, the pelican or kangaroo, as opposed to the swan, egret, heron, or bird of paradise. Is beauty wanting? To the eye and the mind, is the æsthetic sense lacking therein, not as fully satiated with the wonder of anachronism as well as with that of synchronism? I rise to inquire.

But let me close, and in doing so offer a briefer credo which I once prepared at the request of another editor. Here it is:

I cannot make any comment on my work or my life that holds either interest or import for me. Nor can I imagine any explanation or interpretation of any life, my own included, that would be either true, or important, if true.

Life is to me too much of a welter and play of inscrutable forces to permit of any significant comment. One may paint for one's own entertainment, and that of others perhaps.

As I see him, the unutterably infinitesimal individual weaves among the mysteries a floss-like and wholly meaningless course—if course it be. In short, I catch no meaning from all I have seen, and pass quite as I came, confused and dismayed.

In order to offset the almost harsh and fatal finality of that, let me add two things out of my personal volume, *Moods*,

which, to me at least, seem sufficiently expressive to qualify the
above. The first I have entitled "For Answer," and reads:

> The dark,
> The rain,
> The wind,
> And these too cold regrets
> That now,
> Without,
> Within
> My soul
> Clatter and mourn and squeal
> Against my life—
> Its follies,
> Its defeats.
>
> And yet,
> This misery ended,
> Rain no more,
> Nor sun,
> Nor mood,
> Nor hope,
> Nor pain,
> Nor life—
> Where then shall I—
> Where then shall I—
> Again
> To make my heart to know its beat,
> My soul itself,
> My life its lust—
> Where then shall I,
> Where then shall I
> Find rain
> Or wind
> Or dark
> Or moods
> Or vain regrets
> To whip
> And mourn

>   And squeal
>   And make me live?

And now the second, "Related," which reads:

>   This exquisite moment
>   Of pulsating relationship
>   Here—
>   Now—
>   To bird,
>   Rock,
>   Flower,
>   Tree,
>   Beast,
>   Rain,
>   Calm,
>   Sound,
>   Heat,
>   Cold—
>   This companionship
>   Here and now
>   With wind
>   And sun
>   And sea,
>   Gases,
>   Forces—
>   This integrality
>   In variety
>   And perfect balance,
>   Sentience of union with all
>   From moment to moment,
>   Hour to hour,
>   Generation to generation;
>   This changing
>   Yet not changing beauty,
>   Drama.
>   This responding,
>   You—
>   I—

All static or moving
Things,
In joy,
In pain,
In elations,
Despairs;
Each and all,
As in a song,
As in a dirge,
As in a great cry of elation,
As in a great sob of misery
Or sigh of indifference,
Or contest;
You,
I,
All things—
To what future?
In what forever?

My apologies for this I fear not too articulate or illuminating summation of my lack of beliefs and faith; but none the less, my compliments and regards.

VI.
H. G. WELLS

It has exercised my mind a lot to find out how much I could tell you of my credo in a few thousand words. Because I suppose that means telling what I think I am, why I exist, what I think I am for, what I think of life, what I think of the world about me, and things like that. These are questions to which I have given innumerable hours—in conversation, in reading and writing, in lonely places, and particularly in that loneliest place of all, the dark stillness of the night. Anyhow I am going to try.

In the perfume factories of Grasse, in Provence, they show you little bottles of concentrated extract. In this little bottle, they tell you, they have condensed the scent of half a million roses; in this, acres and acres of jasmine. In this brief paper I shall try to give you the gist of many thousands of nights and days of thought. I shall try to make myself as clear as possible, but you must forgive me if now and then I have to be more concentrated than explicit.

I can say best what I have to say by talking first about immortality. I shall open my matter with a question. Here I am, setting down my thoughts; and there you are, reading them. We are having mental intercourse, sharing our ideas. Our mental lives are in contact. The question I would put is this: how far can we consider this mental life we are sharing to be immortal? And more particularly I would ask you a question I have often asked myself. What is this H. G. Wells who is now thinking before you and with you?

Now what do you suppose our little conference amounts to? What is happening now? You are Mr. So-and-so, or Mrs. So-and-so, or Miss So-and-so, and someone called H. G. Wells is talking to you through the medium of print. That is what most people will call self-evident fact. That is what will pass muster as the truth of the matter. But is it altogether true? Let us go into things a little more precisely. I will talk about my side of the discussion, which is H. G. Wells, but what I have to say will apply quite as well to your side also.

This H. G. Wells is a person who was born in the year 1866 and who has since gone here and there and done this and that. His words are here, some thought that may be considered to be his is here, but are you sure that all of him is present? May I point out that, far from all of him being present in this discussion, very much of him is not present anywhere. The greater part of him is no longer in existence. It is dead. It is past and forgotten. He is already, for the most part, as dead as his grandfather.

Let me explain a little more fully what I mean by this. Consider the childhood of this person. I will tell you of one incident in it. In 1867 he was a small and extremely troublesome infant. He felt things vividly and expressed himself violently. He had, one day, a great and terrible adventure. It must have seemed like the end of the world to him. He was lying on a sofa and he rolled about upon it and fell off. He must have been scared by that fall. But also he fell on a glass bottle. It broke. He was cut very dreadfully about the face. This body I have with me to-day still bears a scar over one eye. No doubt he was frightened and hurt, taken up and soothed. The doctor came and sewed him up.

What a storm of feeling, what a fuss it must have been! Yes, but what do I know of all that now? Nothing, nothing except what my mother told me of it; nothing else at all. All the fear, all the feeling, all the details of the event have gone out of my conscious existence. All that is quite dead. Now, can I really say that H. G. Wells of one year old is here? You will say, perhaps, "Of course he is." There is the scar. And if that child of twelve months old had not existed, how could this present writer exist?

But wait a moment. That grandfather of mine! He was a gardener and he was rather good at growing roses. One day toward the end of the reign of King George III he stood in the sunshine in a garden at Penshurst and budded a rose. I know that for a fact, just as completely as I know for a fact that H. G. Wells fell off a sofa in 1867. And also, be it noted, if my grandfather had not existed, the present writer could not exist. My nose and my eyes would not be the shape and color they are. If the scar is H. G. Wells of 1867, the eye is Joseph Wells of 1828. So, by the same test, if that infant H. G. Wells is alive here, his grandfather is alive here, and so far as one is dead and forgotten, so is the other. There is the same physical continuity; there is the same forgetfulness.

Now this idea that the H. G. Wells who writes this is not all of H. G. Wells is a very important idea in my credo. It is not only that I who am speaking am not in any real sense that baby of 1867, but it is also that I am not a certain ill and angry young man of twenty who lived in 1886. He was struggling in the world under what he thought was an unjustly heavy handicap, and he talked and he wrote. I have photographs of him as he was then; I have stuff that he wrote. And for the life of me I cannot identify my present self with him. I have left him behind almost as completely as I have left my grandfather behind. On the other hand, I have recently been collaborating with one of my sons. We share many ideas and we have very similar mental dispositions. I feel at present much more closely identified with him than with that young H. G. Wells of 1886: or even with the H. G. Wells of 1896, who I find from a photograph wore side whiskers and a cascade mustache and rode about the countryside on a bicycle.

And now let us turn to another aspect of this curious inquiry. This train of thought which is talking to you now is something very much less than H. G. Wells, who is, from my point of view, already very largely dead. But also it is also something very much *more* than H. G. Wells. You and I are thinking about what is immortal in ourselves. Now H. G. Wells never started that topic. It came to him. He heard people talking about it and preaching about it. He read about it. People who died in Egypt five thousand years ago and whose names and faces and habits and sins are utterly forgotten were talking about it. Plato, Buddha, Confucius, St. Paul have all had something important to say on the matter. That discussion came into *our* lives as we grew up. We may participate in it, change it a little, before we pass it on. It is like a light passing through a prism which may test it, refract it perhaps, polarize it perhaps, and send it on again *changed*. We are the prism. The thoughts existed before we were born and will go on after we are finished with altogether.

Now here, you see, is something more—and something very fundamental—of what I am trying to say to you. Either this will seem the most lucid of realities or the most fantastic of speculations. But first let us have what I am putting to you plain. Here, I say, is this H. G. Wells who is talking, and he is —I have tried to show—so far from being immortal that the greater part of him is already dead and gone forever. I will not presume to apply the obvious parallel to you. That is *your* affair. But also over and above this H. G. Wells is something, a living growth and a continual refining of ideas, a thought process which is bringing our minds together. And this thought process has lived already thousands of years ago and may, so far as we know, passing from mind to mind and from age to age, continue its life forever. We are mortal persons responding to the advance of perhaps immortal ideas. We are not ourselves only; we are also part of human experience and thought.

I hope I have made my meaning clear thus far. You may not agree with me exactly, but I hope you have understood me, so that I can go on to the next light in my credo.

A second very fundamental question which man has been debating with himself for many centuries, and which comes to most of us in due time and perplexes us, is the question of what is an individual. It is a question that joins on very closely to these ideas about immortality. How is the individual related to the species? How is the part related to the whole? How is the one related to the many? How is he or she as a whole related to everything in his or her make-up? A great part of the dialogues of Plato, for instance, consists of experiments and explorations about this group of questions.

I agree that to a lot of people this sort of discussion will seem hairsplitting, tedious, and unmeaning. They will fail to see what it is about and what good it is. They feel sure they are individuals, and that is an end to the matter. They will say that they do not want to bother their heads about it. Quite a lot of people seem to live now chiefly to escape having their heads bothered about anything, but most of that kind have probably stopped reading this quite a while ago, if ever they began. To many, however, these questions are full of meaning, and to some of us they are among the most important questions in the world. They are so to me, and I cannot explain what I believe at all without discussing them.

I suppose the ordinary and obvious answer to this question of what is an individual would be to say it is a living being detached from the rest of the world. It is born or hatched as a definite, distinctive self; it maintains itself for a certain time against the rest of the universe, and at last it dies and comes to at least a physical end. But is that an impregnable statement? If one pries into descriptive biology or into modern psychology, one finds first one curious fact and then another coming up to weaken and undermine this idea of the complete integrity of individuals. They are not so definitely marked off as we are disposed to think.

Go first to the biologist. He will agree that men and cats and dogs are very individual creatures. He will probably say that they are strongly individualized. But when you ask him if that is true of all living things, he will at once say "No." He will tell you that most plants seem much more individualized than they are. You can take a plant and break it up into a number of plants. Are they new individuals or are they fractions of the old one? You can even take two plants of different species and graft them together. What is the grafted plant—a new individual, or one or both of the old ones? Trees seem to be much more individual than they really are, just as mountains do. It is a disposition of our minds to think of them as individuals. We talk of the Jungfrau or the Wetterhorn as if they were as complete and distinct as pyramids, but really they are only peaks on a general mountain mass.

H. G. WELLS

And it is not only plants and all the vegetable kingdom that is wanting in individuality. The biologist will tell you of innumerable species of lower animals also, of which two sometimes come together and coalesce into one and one will break up into two or many; and again of individuals that branch off others but never separate and so become what are called colonies, a sort of superindividual. If the higher animals could do as the lower animals do, we should have Mr. Lloyd George coalescing with Mr. Snowden into one individual—which I am sure would be a terrible nightmare for the publicists of France —and we should have Mr. Winston Churchill breaking up into dozens and scores of Winston Churchills and writing books, painting pictures, forming governments, commanding and constituting armies and navies, and carrying every aspect of his versatility to the last extreme. I am afraid he would insist upon it.

But the biologist assures us that all the higher animals have lost these powers of combining and dividing and spreading themselves out. They are highly individualized, he says; they are unified and drawn together, they are cut off from the rest of the universe into themselves, to a degree no other creatures have attained. These individualities such as we have are an exception and not the rule among living things. They are not the common way of life.

But though we are highly individualized, says the biologist, our kind of creature is not completely individualized. He will tell you of various curious cases when sheep and cats and dogs and babies have been born with two heads to one body or two bodies to one head. When there are two heads, where is the individual then? And he will bring home to you the fact that a great part of our bodily selves is unknown to us. We do not know what is inside of us until we learn about it from talk and lessons and books, and unless trouble is brewing we do not know what goes on inside there nor how it feels. Our particular individuality, in fact, does not penetrate to our interiors.

And if you will let the biologist run on, he will tell you that in the blood vessels and substance of our body are millions of little beings, which are extraordinarily like some of the smallest, lowest microscopic animals which lead independent lives, and these go about in our bodies as citizens go about in the streets and houses of a city. These little beings, these corpuscles, kill disease germs, carry food and air about, and do a multitude of services. They have minute individualities of their own. We are made up of millions of such minute creatures, just as cities and nations are made of millions of such beings as ourselves. There are, you see, different ranks and kinds of individuality. It is not the simple matter so many people assume it to be.

Now when we turn from the modern biologist to the modern psychologist, we get still more remarkable revelations about this individuality of ours, which seems at first so simple. He tells us of minds split and divided against themselves. I do not know whether you have read of cases of what is called divided personality. They are fascinatingly strange. They are rare, but they occur. There are people who suddenly forget who they are. The individual becomes someone else. That may happen under hypnotism; it may happen in cases of insanity.

But it may also happen without either hypnotism or insanity. In the same brain and in the same body it is possible for first one and then another personality to take control. Perhaps you have read a story of R. L. Stevenson's which was suggested by these cases—the story of *Dr. Jekyll and Mr. Hyde*. That puts these phenomena in an extreme, fantastic fashion and it ascribes the change-over to a drug. But the change in the actual cases occurs without a drug. Quite a number of us go some little way toward such a change. Which of us, indeed, has not a better self and a worse self?

I have had to abbreviate this appeal to biology and psychology, but I think I have at least said enough to show you the support I find in these sciences for my profound doubt whether this H. G. Wells of mine is really the completely independent, separate, distinct being that it is our habit of mind to consider him. Perhaps my individuality, my personality, seems to be distincter than it is. Perhaps it is—how shall I put it?—a convenient biological illusion.

If I had the time, I could produce a great mass of facts to support that belief, to show how individuality has arisen in the course of evolution and how every individual is, as it were, a sort of experiment made by nature to test this and that group of qualities. In collaboration with Julian Huxley and my son, G. P. Wells, I have been trying to present that mass of facts to the general reader in a work called *The Science of Life,* but our utmost efforts to compress and simplify leave us with a large book. So I can only allude to it here as being full of light upon this issue, the sort of light there is no time to give you now, and then turn to another aspect of this question of "What am I?" and "What are you?"

Let us look within. How do you feel about your identity with yourself? Well, anyhow, let me tell you how *I* feel about H. G. Wells. I have already tried to show that as a matter of fact a lot of him is already dead stuff and irrelevant stuff, and I have also tried to show that this *thought* that is talking to you is something very much more than H. G. Wells.

And when it comes to introspection, then I feel, very, very clearly, that I am something very distinct from this individual H. G. Wells who eats and sleeps and runs about the world.

I feel that I am linked to him as a boat may be moored to a floating buoy. More than that, I have to use his voice, see with his eyes, experience the pain of any physical misfortune that comes to him. He is my window on the world and my mouthpiece. I have to think in his brain, and his store of memories is my only reference library. I doubt if I can think or feel or act as an individual without him. But I do not feel that I am he.

I take a great interest in him. I keep him as clean as I can and am always on the watch to prevent him getting sulky, dull, or lazy—not always with success. He has to be petted and persuaded. I like to be told he is good and remarkable, just as I like to be told my automobile is a good one. But sometimes I wish I could get away from him—heavens, how I wish it at times! He is clumsy in all sorts of ways, and unbeautiful. His instincts and appetites are dreadful. He begins to show considerable signs of wear. The reference library in him might be better arranged and the brain cells quicker at the uptake. But he is all I have to keep me in touch with the world. When he goes, I go. I am silenced for ever.

Now there is nothing original in this sense of detachment from myself. Most people get to something of the sort. When we are young, we identify ourselves with ourselves very completely and fiercely. That may be a biological necessity. But as we ripen—or as we age—the separation widens. All through the historical past of our race one can trace this feeling of detachment. They used to call the part that is talking to you now the soul, and the rejected part the body; but that is not quite my point of view.

The H. G. Wells I look down upon is mental just as much as he is physical; he is the whole individualized, self-centered personality. When I read St. Paul and find him talking of the Old Adam and the New Adam, he seems to be saying something very much nearer to the truth than that popular distinction of body and spirit. When he cries, "Who can deliver me from the body of this death?" I find him very understandable. How warmly have I echoed that cry! My feeling is just that sense of being *thought*—a part of a great process of thought—which finds itself entangled, as some young creature may be entangled in its egg membranes, in an overdeveloped, overintense, overlimited egotism.

Now what I am saying here is not, I believe, an orthodox Christian view. Orthodox Christianity insists that we are ourselves forever and ever. Mr. Gilbert Chesterton ought to tell you about that. My credo is much nearer Stoicism. It is, indeed, Stoicism seen in the light of modern biological science. I do not believe in the least that either the body of H. G. Wells or his personality is immortal, but I do believe that the growing process of thought, knowledge, and will of which we are parts, of which I am a part, and of which you are a part, may go on growing in range and power forever. I think that Man is immortal, but not men.

There you have what I believe, given to you as precisely and clearly as I can. Man, I take it—man in us—is more important than the things in the individual life, and this I believe not as a mere sentimentality, but as a rigorously true statement of biological and mental fact. Our individuality is, so to speak, an inborn obsession from which we shall escape as we become more intelligent. And we are under a necessity to escape from it as we become more intelligent, because increasing intelligence brings us more and more clearly face to face with the ultimate frustration of every individual desire in age, enfeeblement, and death. Personality, individuality, is a biological device which has served its end in evolution and will decline. A consciousness of something greater than ourselves

—the immortal soul of the race—is taking control of the direction of our lives.

If I had the time and erudition, I think I could make an argument to show that this idea of the immortal soul of the race in which our own lives are like passing thoughts, is to be found in what Confucius calls the Higher Person, in what St. Paul calls the New Adam, in the Logos of Stoics, in the modern talk we hear of the Overman or Superman. But I cannot pursue these suggestions now.

But if I might say a word or so about the views one gets from this credo, I should insist first that the subordination of self to a higher order of being does not mean the suppression of all or any of one's distinctive gifts. We have to use ourselves to the utmost. We have to learn and make to the full measure of our possibilities. It is a sin to bury the talent, the individual gift which we possess for the good of the master being, Man.

Nor must you imagine that the subordination of self to the immortal being of the race means a subordination of one's narrow self to the equally narrow selves of other people. It is for them also to give themselves to that life and all that increases knowledge and power. I do not believe in the surrender of one jot or one tittle of one's intelligence and will to the greatest happiness of the greatest number, or to the will of the majority, or any such nonsense: I am not that sort of democrat. This world and its future is not for feeble folk any more than it is for selfish folk. It is not for the multitude, but for the best. The best of to-day will be the commonplace of to-morrow.

If I am something of a social leveler, it is not because I want to give silly people a good time, but because I want to make opportunity universal, and not leave out one single being who is worth while. If I want economic change, it is because the present system protects and fosters a vast swarm of wasteful spenders, no better in their quality and much worse in their lazy pretentious traditions than the general run of mankind. If I am opposed to nationalism and war, it is not merely because these things represent an immense waste of energy, but because they sustain a cant of blind discipline and loyalty and a paraphernalia of flags, uniforms, and parades that shelter a host of particularly mischievous, unintelligent bullies and wasters; because they place our lives at the mercy of trained blockheads. Militarism and warfare are childish things, if they are not more horrible than anything childish can be. They must become things of the past. They must die. Naturally my idea of politics is an open conspiracy to hurry these tiresome, wasteful, evil things—nationality and war—out of existence; to end this empire and that empire, and set up the one Empire of Man.

And it is natural that I should exalt science. In the scientific world I find just that disinterested devotion to great ends that I hope will spread at last through the entire range of human activity. I find just that coöperation of men of every race and color to increase Man's knowledge. We can all be citizens of the free state of science. But our political, our economic, our social lives have still to become illuminated and directed by the scientific spirit, are still sick and feeble with congenital traditionalism.

My space is almost up. I was asked to give my credo, and I have given it. I hope I have interested you and I hope I have not offended you. This is how I try to live; and this is how I have got to a certain mastery over the greed, the fears, the passions, and vanities that troubled my earlier days, and rid myself altogether of the fear of death.

It is good to be a part of life. Just as a sun-dial counts only the sunny hours, so does life know only that it is living. Many experiences there are in life, but one there is that we shall never have. We shall never know that we are dead. My creed, I can assure you, is not an unhappy creed. I have found it a good working creed. I wish you—you other fragments of Man —could tell me what you think of it.

VII.

FRIDTJOF NANSEN

IT IS strange how very rarely one hears men explain frankly and clearly their faith, what they actually believe in their innermost selves and in their sincerest moments; what higher powers they admit, if any; what future. Is this because of a kind of shyness, a consideration for the convictions of others which they do not wish to disturb? Or is it because many people have not been able to arrive at any conclusion as to what they actually believe? Perhaps both. When Charles Darwin was asked about his faith, he answered: "What my own views may be is a question of no consequence to anyone but myself. But, as you ask, I may state that my judgment often fluctuates. . . . I think that generally (and more and more as I grow older), but not always, an Agnostic would be the more correct description of my state of mind."

But although a man's faith is, to some extent at least, his private affair, nevertheless it may have a great effect upon his actions and conduct, and may thus be of importance to his fellow men. It is especially urgent to examine the beliefs of the remarkable age in which we are now living, for in spite of the tremendous advances made by science and the constant evidence of the continuing ability of the white race—portents which might be expected to give confidence, buoyancy, and hope—one often hears the anxious question: Whither mankind? What is the future of Western civilization? The war may have contributed greatly to this gloomy foreboding of some catastrophe to come, but the real cause lies deeper. The real cause lies in the fact that the thinking world is now in a difficult transitional period: old, established truths are shaken and overthrown, old creeds and dogmas are largely abandoned, and there are no new ones ready to take their place.

Whether there are absolute truths we cannot prove or disprove. But having got the capacity of thinking, we ought certainly to use it in deciding those questions which are of most importance in our whole conduct of life, and we must let our reasoning be guided by what we recognize to be the truths of our time. To allow our faith, our views of existence, to be tyrannized by the commands—whether illogical or not—of some other person, "a prophet of God," has nothing to do with morality or goodness. The command "thou shalt believe" is not moral; if we can force ourselves to obey it, we do so not because we are convinced that it is the naturally good and right thing to do, but for fear of displeasing some divine power, and of thus exposing ourselves to punishment. This is the contrary of morality, for we make ourselves subject to an alien despotism in order to gain something by it. Commands such as this are remnants from times when people believed in war gods, gods of vengeance and reward, like the Yahweh of Israel. In our day it might be expected that we should have outgrown such superstitions, and that we should consider it our duty to try, as best we can, to bring our views of life, our faith, our principles of morality, into harmony with our reasoning, and to base our conduct of life on principles which we consider to be right and just.

When we try to form our view of existence and of the system of the world, we have nothing to be guided by but our observations—that is, our scientific research—and our logical thinking. We are thus led to assume that the whole universe—the inanimate as well as the animate world, the physical as well as the spiritual sphere—is ruled by what we, with a general term, call the laws of nature, and that these laws determine the past and the future. We can discover no fundamental difference between inanimate and animate matter, or between the physical and the mental processes. They are all parts and processes of nature. Organic life is a form of energy, and is subject to the same laws that determine the motions of electrons and of heavenly bodies. We do not know yet how organic life and its forms first came into existence on our planet; but that does not prove that we can never know. We know that it must once have begun here, and that it will some day cease, when the sun is cooled so much that the temperature at the earth's surface sinks below a certain level. This is an inevitable process in the endless circulation of the universe. Furthermore, we know that organic life is inseparably bound up with forms of matter and is sustained by supplies of energy, and that it ceases with the destruction of those forms and with the lack of that energy. We can sterilize matter and destroy all life. It is therefore hardly logical to assume that organic life is something fundamentally different from the processes of inanimate matter: they are both produced by physical or chemical energy.

And now the soul? It is an inseparable part of all forms of organic life—animals and plants. We cannot really imagine any living form without a soul, or a soul without a living form. Where life begins the soul begins, and where life ends the soul ends. We can speak about an unconscious and a conscious soul, but we cannot possibly draw the line where the individual, conscious soul begins in the ascending scale of organic forms from the lowest plants and animals to the highest mammals and man, any more than we can in the development of the individual man from the ovum to the adult. When is the individual soul of a man created? Is it at conception? I believe it is. If so, it cannot originally be an indivisible entity, for it arises from two primary components, the spermatozoön and the ovum, and it derives its specific qualities from both sources. But then we have the development of some eggs—for instance, those of bees—without sexual fertilization. This does not detract from my thesis. The processes which constitute the elementary soul are transferred with the sexual cells from the parental forms to the offspring, and the sexual cells are differentiated and set aside at the earliest stages in the development of each individual. The soul may thus be considered as continuous, like life itself, through all generations, but it grows "self-conscious" in the development of each individual of the higher animal forms.

Closely connected with this question of a conscious soul is the old postulate of its *immortality*, which arises from our fear of annihilation, or rather from our desire to live. The claim that the soul should continue to exist after the decay of the body and its organs—by the processes of which it was produced—is so contrary to all reason that it cannot be dealt with as a scientific problem. The question naturally arises: at what stage in the development of the animal forms is it assumed that the immortality of the individual soul was introduced? Is it a prerogative of man only? But if so, had the Neanderthal man, or the Pithecanthropus an immortal soul? Has a gorilla, or even an elephant, a dog, a tiger, a chicken, a serpent, a fish, a lobster, an oyster—has each of these an individual, immortal soul? Where can we possibly draw the line?

And where in space are these enormous quantities of individual souls continuing their immortal existence? The Mohammedans are perhaps the most exclusive, claiming that immortality is a prerogative of the human males, and that not even the human females possess it; but against this our modern champions of women will probably make a violent protest.

The soul in its higher forms is impulses, feelings, memories, conception, consciousness, will, thoughts. We cannot imagine these activities to be attached to solitary electrons or atoms; we must rather assume that they arise by a coöperation of electrons or atoms in an immensely complicated system. Our investigations prove that these activities of the body and the soul are based on the supply of chemical energy. When the body and its organs are destroyed, and the parts of the complicated system forming the seat of the soul are scattered, these mental activities must cease, and the individual soul can no more exist as such; if it continues, it must be something entirely different, deprived of all the characteristic qualities of the individual soul that was a part of the body. And what is our individual soul really? It is inseparably bound up with every part of our body, not only with the brain and the nervous system, but with every functioning organ, every muscle. Alterations not only of the brain, but of other parts of the body— the sexual and other glands—may entirely change the nature of a man's soul, of his whole character, and make him a very different personality, good or bad, moral or immoral. For example, by an operation a hopeless sexual criminal may be made a fairly decent and moral person. The specific qualities of the soul can be cut away slice by slice from the brain, until nothing but the mental activity of a low animal is left. Notice the gradual degeneration of the soul of a man attacked by general paralysis. Which soul is going to survive?

For numbers of people it may be a consolation to think that

the soul is immortal, and that there is a life after this where there may be some compensation for the sufferings and shortcomings of this earthly existence; but certainly it is a less selfish, nobler, and a more wholesome faith to believe that our life is *here* and *now,* that we are passing links in the continuous chain from the past to the future, that we survive only in the effects of our thoughts and acts, and in our descendants, and therefore that we have to do our very best in this one life. This view is apt to strengthen the feeling of solidarity, and it forms a sounder basis for our conduct of life and for the progress of the community than obsolete illusions and postulates, and a doctrine based upon the selfish idea of the salvation of the individual in another life.

Inseparably bound up with these questions is the old problem of free will. When everything that happens is subjected to the laws of nature, when all our actions, great or small, are determined by the endless series of causes and effects in the past, there is, of course, no room for a free will, and there cannot really be any responsibility in the manner in which we generally understand it. All the ingenious attempts which have been made by great thinkers to get round this simple fact, seem more or less futile. The laws of nature are inexorable, and admit no more of a free will than of an absolute cause, whether we call this cause "will" or "God." The whole personality of an individual—his qualities, his character—is determined by birth and environment, by inheritance and education. It may perhaps be said that a strong man can more or less educate himself and shape his own character by his own will. But this will is not free and independent. It is itself a quality which has been inherited and may have been strengthened or weakened by education and environment; its functioning at any moment is determined by previous causes. In reality, therefore, an individual can no more shape his own character than a tree can shape its branches. Whether a man becomes what is called good or bad, moral or immoral, and what views he holds, depend entirely on his inherited qualities and how they have been influenced and developed by education and environment.

Those people who fear that this doctrine may wipe out the feeling of responsibility, which is so important for all social life, may find consolation in knowing that in the moment when we act, we all of us believe that we are free to decide. Even the most positive determinist acts under the illusion that when he is doubtful about what to do, his final decision depends on himself and not upon the workings of previous causes. This idea, even if it is an illusion, seems to be necessary for the welfare of the community, and it is hardly possible to exterminate it in practice from the conscious soul of which it is a part—a soul whose existence is determined by previous causes.

Closely connected with the doctrine of determinism is the question of purpose. If everything is determined by the laws of nature, how, then, can there be any purpose of the whole? The truth is that the eternal laws are because they are, and can serve no purpose outside themselves. Some people argue, however, that if there is no purpose, then the whole universe becomes meaningless. But this proves nothing. Who has any right to say that the universe must have a meaning? Meaning and purpose—are they not really egotistical ideas belonging to our little organic world? Can they be applied to the universe and its endless circulation?

When on a starlit night our eyes are lifted to the heavens and wander far into infinite space toward other Milky Ways, and we are inspired by the wonderful grandeur of the whole, by the sublime majesty, we get a feeling that it is, always was, and always will be, and demands for meaning and purpose dwindle into petty impertinence. Once, a long time ago, our organic living world arose and developed on this little planet, and some day it will again disappear. Is it not to ask too much that it should also have a meaning, a purpose, outside its own changing processes? We may say that the purpose of the grain growing on our fields is to provide food for human beings, since grain-growing is a specialty of ours, but it would be ridiculous conceit to say that the sun is shining in order to make our grain grow, or to think that the purpose of matter and energy is to make our existence possible on this planet.

To many people it may seem even harder to give up the idea of a purpose of existence and a wise scheme of things, than to have to accept the doctrine of determinism and to abandon the idea of a free will, though the one is an inevitable consequence of the other. But just as in the instance of free will, we do not act according to theory: in practice we all act as if there were a purpose in our lives. We can no more get away from this idea than from that of a free will; it is too deeply rooted in human nature, being determined by previous causes.

It is obvious, however, that as the so-called materialistic views of life, mentioned above, spread and pervade the thoughts of the common people, their whole philosophical and religious conception of existence is radically shaken. Old creeds, old religious systems, dogmas, and superstitions, which formed the mainstay of their views of life, can be upheld no longer; and there are hardly any adequate and satisfactory new doctrines ready to take their place. Worse than this, however, is the fact that the idea of morality was hitherto generally bound up with religion, that the current moral rules had their origin chiefly in superstition, and one had to obey them in order to please some supernatural beings, or to obtain some reward

Fridtjof Nansen

here or in another life. People who discover the fallacy of their old superstitions and throw them overboard, may, therefore, be likely to throw their moral rules overboard too, without being able to find new ones. Thus they lose their mental balance, their foothold on life. Their moral and social ideas fall prey to the winds, or disappear in the melting pot. This state of things will inevitably create unrest, uncertainty, confusion, aberrations, often spreading in wide circles, like some forms of communism, and it has an unfortunate effect upon all social life and on the welfare of the community. It paralyzes the hope of a better future.

But nevertheless we dream of a new era for mankind, a time of a better life, of lasting peace, of brotherhood and good will between individuals, classes, and peoples, of mutual confidence and coöperation. Can this dream be realized? Some people think that a better world can be created by sudden improvement, by dictatorial commands, by force, or even by revolutions. It was people of this frame of mind who proposed to wage a "war to end war," but all they reaped was destruction. The old proverb that Beelzebub has to be driven out by Beelzebub is a dangerous one: the use of evil will create more evil, war more hostile feelings, and the use of force more need of force. The lasting betterment of the world cannot be reached by short-cuts of this kind; it must come by gradual growth from within. It can only be attained by education, and time is needed.

It helps nothing to say that men have first to seek the Kingdom of God, unless we know what God it is, and whether He can satisfy modern requirements. No longer can the God be a despotic, supernatural being, giving commands which we have to obey, whether we find them reasonable or not. He has to be the principle of good, the code of ethics which should guide our whole activity and conduct of life.

Moral rules cannot be expected to be any more absolute or everlasting than any other ideas of men. What is considered to be moral will naturally change with time and circumstances. Many moral commands still proclaimed to-day are flagrantly out of date and even harmful. Let us take as an example what is considered to be sexual morality. According to one code, the object of sexual intercourse is to produce children. It is therefore moral to get them and immoral to prevent conception, even if the children will inevitably be born to spend their lives in misery and bad health. This is cruelty and not morality.

Again, let us think of the nationalistic moral code. When a man acts for his country, he has to give up his own private moral principles; if he can gain something for his nation by this surrender, it is supposed to be his moral duty to lie, betray, steal secret documents, rob, and murder. And if he succeeds, he is highly praised as a great patriot and benefactor of his country. If a man is ordered to go as a spy into a hostile country, it is his moral duty to go and to do his best to discover by trickery the secrets of the enemy. If he is caught, he has to be shot, and the soldiers who get the order to shoot him are morally obliged to do so, even though they may be convinced that he is really an excellent man of high moral qualities.

It is necessary to build up a new, sound moral code in harmony with modern views, freed as much as possible from superstition, and based on the old principles of solidarity and love. It should be clearly understood that moral rules are not commands which have to be obeyed through fear—the lowest instinct in man—but they are good in themselves, because their observance furthers the welfare of men in this life, and has nothing to do with the egotistical idea of an individual salvation in another world. As a general rule it may well be said that moral acts are those which in their final effects do good to the individual as well as to the community, while immoral acts are those which finally do harm to the community or the individual, or to both.

If we really hope to be able to approach a better future for mankind, the first condition is to have courage and not to be dominated by fear. We need courage to throw away old garments which have had their day and no longer fit the requirements of the new generations; we must work calmly and with confidence to lay a new and safer foundation for the ethical life of the individual as well as the community. Above all, we must not allow fear to keep alive the distrust and hostile feelings between classes and nations which are the most serious threat of the future. Nations fear each other and think that in order to safeguard their future it is necessary to be armed against every neighbor. We see that some of them even think that armament increases their ability to keep a potential enemy in subjection, but to an impartial spectator this method must seem to have just the opposite effect. It is obvious that as long as views of this kind prevail among nations, there is no hope of securing a lasting peace. If nations could overcome the mutual fear and distrust whose somber shadow is now thrown over the world, and could meet with confidence and good will to settle their possible differences, they would easily be able to establish a coöperation which would secure a lasting peace to the benefit of every one of them, and would further the welfare of the whole world.

Another distressing fact is the lack, up to the present, of almost any kind of morality in international politics and in the conduct of nations toward each other. Whatever they may have professed with their lips, there has in practice been a perfect anarchy which gave a nation the right to do anything, if only it had the necessary power. It may be said that since the establishment of the League of Nations and the Permanent Court of International Justice at The Hague, this condition, at least to some extent, has changed. But perhaps these institutions were established not so much from love of justice as for the sake of security. We have yet to see the Powers which sponsored them make any worthwhile reduction of their armaments.

Now as to class warfare, it is indeed difficult to understand why all these strikes and lockouts are still necessary and why the classes have not yet been able to find any more rational means of settling their differences. It is evidently the result of a deplorable lack of the feeling of solidarity on both sides. By all modern inventions and progress in science, by better hygiene and medical care, it is certainly possible to improve materially the conditions of life for all classes, to make life fuller, richer, healthier, and happier for all citizens, and greatly to reduce the difference between the poor and the rich. By modern improvements in architecture, lodgings can be made much better and, for the poorer classes, more comfortable. The greatly improved transportation systems—automobiles, motor busses, tramways, railways, and so on—make it possible for people to live farther apart, instead of being crowded together in narrow streets. Radios, movies, phonographs, and other contrivances make it possible for almost everybody to get entertainment. With the cheap clothing procurable, most people can be fairly well dressed. We have thus the means to create a brighter, more satisfactory existence for all men. It is left to us to use them. We should, therefore, have reason to look with confidence and hope upon the future.

Social problems can no longer be solved by class warfare any more than international problems can be solved by wars between nations. Warfare is negative and will sooner or later lead to destruction, while good will and coöperation are positive and supply the only safe basis for building a better future.

If all classes meet in perfect confidence, equally anxious to cooperate for a lasting betterment of the social condition of their whole people, then, and only then, can an arrangement be attained which will benefit all parts. Citizens will have to examine calmly the natural possibilities of their country, what trades they condition, and how these trades and their profit can be divided among the classes and among the people in the fairest manner.

But this, of course, involves the determination of each class to make the sacrifices necessary for the attainment of the desirable end. What is needed is the feeling of solidarity and love pervading all our actions and thoughts. And we should always remember that love and tolerance are the most beautiful trees in the forest.

VIII.
SIR JAMES JEANS

Quite frankly, my point of view is that of a scientist—an astronomer. In brief, this means two things. First, because I am a scientist, I am apt to see human life as a chain of causes and effects; the life of to-morrow will be what we make it to-day; as we sow, so shall we reap. Second, because I am an astronomer, I am apt to see the problems of to-day set against a background of time in which the whole of human history shrinks to the twinkling of an eye, and to think of these problems specially in relation to man's past history on earth.

Our ancestors of a century ago read their origins in the Book of Genesis, with 4004 B.C. printed in the margin against the account of the creation. To-day we trace our origins back to a far greater antiquity. We believe that the earth is merely a tiny fragment of the sun, which got splashed off, almost by accident, something like 2,000 million years ago. For hundreds of millions of years it remained uninhabited until at last life arrived, and after passing through many forms—protozoa, fishes, reptiles, mammals—culminated in man. The upward ascent was a devious one; life, it seems, followed many dead-ends before finding its final road which led to man. Also we know that man is an absolutely new arrival on earth; he has possessed and governed it for less than a thousandth part of its existence.

Most of us still think of ourselves as the final triumph of biological evolution; we are convinced we have come to stay as rulers of the earth. I wonder why. A being watching us from another planet might see things very differently. Gigantic reptiles, dinosaurs, ruled the earth for millions of years, but failed to retain their supremacy. Then huge mammals, terrible in their weight and strength, but almost brainless, governed for many million years more. Man has ruled only for a fraction of one million years. Why should he suppose that he has come to stay? Rather it seems to me he must still establish his claim to be the permanent governor of the earth. His own acts will decide whether he is fit to rule in perpetuity or not. We must maintain our position by fighting for it.

We have fought against the wild beasts which once overran the earth and won; human intelligence prevailed over brute strength. But we have not yet conquered the microbe; we are still so ignorant of the causes and modes of operation of certain classes of diseases that they may yet exterminate our race. We have also to fight against famine, against vice, against disruptive social tendencies and against bellicose tendencies to self-destruction. These fights have not yet been won; the issue is still in doubt. We have no right to take it for granted that they will all end in our favour, or that we must inevitably go on to higher and higher things: the dinosaurs and dinoceras of past ages might have thought the same in their day, yet the fate in store for them was decay, defeat and extinction.

They could not have escaped their fate. We can. We face

the future with a weapon in our hands that was not given to earlier rulers of the world—I mean scientific knowledge, and the capacity for increasing it indefinitely by scientific research.

It is a new weapon. No doubt the men who first discovered the uses of fire, who first replaced stone weapons by bronze, or bronze by iron, were scientists in their own way. So also were those shepherds and herdsmen who first noticed that a healthy, vigorous offspring came from healthy and vigorous parents, and *vice versa*. Yet in those early days science entered life in such small doses as to be negligible. To-day, thanks to science, we advance more in a few years than our ancestors did through the whole duration of the Stone Age.

It is our use of this weapon that will mould the future of our race for good or for ill. We no longer believe that human destiny is a plaything for spirits, good and evil, or for the machinations of the Devil. There is nothing to prevent our making the earth a paradise again—except ourselves. The scientific age has dawned, and we recognise that man himself is the master of his fate, the captain of his soul. He controls the course of his ship and so, of course, is free to navigate it into fair waters or foul, or even to run it on the rocks.

It is important to choose the course with care, for we know that we have embarked on a very long voyage. The early Christians believed that the world would end in their lifetime; their Founder had said so. Quite rightly, then, they devoted their whole attention to the living generation. To-day, few, even of our religious teachers, expect the world to end in our time. The earth was in existence millions of years ago, and in all probability will still be in existence millions of years hence. For more time than we can imagine, it is likely to remain in much the same physical condition as now, and so will provide a suitable home for the human race. Whatever our views on a future life in another world, we recapture the old

Jewish concept of an immortality in this world—or something which is effectively as good as immortality—enjoyed not *by* us but *through* us, by our posterity. Our problem is no longer merely to muddle through for a few more generations. We see ourselves as the architects of a tremendous future, with science giving us the power to build for good or evil, to make or to mar.

We have hardly yet realised how grave a responsibility this casts upon us. Amongst other things, I think we shall in time come to see that we must recast a large part of our code of social morality. Virtues and vices have frequently changed places as life moved on through the ages. Witch-burning used to be a virtue, and lending money at interest a vice. And to-day humanitarian acts which appeared wholly virtuous while we were, so to speak, sitting about waiting for the last trumpet to sound, may appear thoroughly vicious in view of their effects on a long posterity. If we are to make the earth a paradise again, it seems to me that our first duty is, at all costs, to prevent the moral, mental and physical wreckage of to-day from reproducing itself, and starting a new sequence of unhappy lives trailing down through endless generations. To encourage this stream of misery becomes a vice; to check it a virtue.

The racing man knows he cannot get a good racing stable by breeding from his slowest horses; the farmer will not get a good dairy herd by breeding from the cows which yield least milk. The teacher knows that, generally speaking, clever parents produce clever children. It is now known, as a scientific fact, that both physical and mental qualities are inherited. For this reason, I do not believe that we shall get a happy and successful nation unless we replenish our stock mainly from the more happy and more successful members of the community. Good education, good physical conditions, good environment are all valuable and necessary, but they will never make a "born-tired" or moral weakling pull his weight in the world. Neither will they give him a happy life. We want something more than good environment—we want good raw material in the form of children born from the best possible stock.

Our unsentimental ancestors achieved this in a very simple way: they just allowed the weaker and less successful to go to the wall. Two hundred years ago three-quarters of the babies born in London died in infancy—three out of every four. Those few who survived must, on the whole, have been abnormally strong, or else born of successful parents, who were able to give them every care. Thus, it was natural for the English race to become strong and successful; the process was almost automatic.

To-day we are heading in precisely the opposite direction. There is no weeding out of the unfit, we save nearly all our babies indiscriminately—good and bad, strong and weak, healthy and diseased. It would not be so bad if this meant that all types contribute equally to the future population of England. Unhappily it does not mean this: in actual fact the largest contribution comes from the most miserable and least successful classes. In the professional and other successful classes late marriages and small families are almost the rule; many of their men spend the important parts of their lives in India or the colonies, abroad or at sea. The result is that these classes are not even maintaining their present numbers; they are on the road to extinction. The same is true of the skilled artisans. Thus it is the most valuable elements of the nation, and not the unfit, that are now being "weeded out," to use an inappropriate word. Meanwhile our present system of doles, grants and subsidies makes marriage easier, and parenthood less of a responsibility, in the least successful classes of the community. In this way, it increases the population in precisely those classes which are even now overpopulated and unable to find employment. It is in these classes that the birth-rate is highest to-day; it is from these classes that the majority of our criminals, paupers and ne'er-do-wells come.

By political action we are, I fear, deliberately pushing our unborn babies into the wrong places. Too many are born, often unwanted, into slums instead of into comfortable homes; too many inherit their physical, mental and moral characteristics from the less vigorous and less successful members of the community. We rob too many of their birthright of health, energy, competence and happiness before they are born. We of to-day are building the England of to-morrow. And I fear it will consist far too largely of hospitals, prisons and lunatic asylums. Its population will contain too many unemployed, and too many unemployables. This is the price our children will have to pay for our irresponsible humanitarianism and sentimentalism; these have held almost undisputed sway in recent years. I believe there is a vigorous reaction against them in the rising generation, but the real irresistible reaction is yet to come, I think. It will come with overwhelming force as soon as the average hard-working, self-respecting citizen begins to realise how great an incubus the unfit and defective, the unenterprising and incapable, form on the prosperity and wealth of the nation, how they make his wages lower, his food dearer, and the risk of unemployment greater.

If we cannot strike a juster balance between the claims of sentimental humanitarianism and those of future generations, it seems to me that the average quality of our population must progressively deteriorate, and I can feel but little hope for England's future. It is, I think, as serious as that. If we are to

> build Jerusalem
> in England's green and pleasant land,

we must, I think, reverse our present policy. We must in some way contrive to secure that as many as possible of our future citizens shall inherit not only a healthy mind in a healthy body, but also those special qualities which make for success and happiness. In this way—and I think in no other—we may hope to establish a nation in which life shall be overflowingly worth living for all, and not merely for a fortunate few.

Yet if I am a democrat, I confess it is mainly because I cannot find anything else to be. The actual achievement of democracy is that it gives a tolerably good time to the underdog. Or, at least, it honestly tries; and it is, I think, for this reason that most of us accept it as our political creed. My objection to it is that, as I think, it forms a barrier to further upward progress. True progress—to better things—must be based on thought and knowledge. As I see it, democracy encourages the nimble charlatan at the expense of the thinker, and prefers the plausible wizard with quack remedies to the true statesman. Democracy is ever eager for rapid progress, and the only progress which can be rapid is progress downhill. For this reason I suspect that all democracies carry within them the seeds of their own destruction, and I cannot believe that democracy is to be our final form of government. And indeed, there is little enough of it left in Europe to-day.

We are still at the very beginning of civilisation. Ordered government has a past of some thousands of years behind it, but a future of millions of years before it—at least, we hope so. The historians of the remote future will, I imagine, see democracy merely as one of the early experiments tried in that age of repeated upheavals—our own—in which mankind was still groping its way to a rational mode of life. It may be that democracy—like teething—is a state through which we have to pass on our way to higher things. Anyhow, it is a restless, feverish state, and I hope it will soon give place to something better. I wonder what. Possibly, in future ages, the power to vote and govern will not be regarded as a right, but as a distinction, to be acquired by service or merit. This may suggest that I have but little respect for the sacred principle of equality. Perhaps so. If I had to choose a one-word motto I do not think it would be "Equality." I might choose "Excelsior"—let us get on to higher things. And a traveller will not get far towards higher things if he is ever afraid of putting one foot in front of the other.

For similar reasons, I feel very little sympathy with socialism. If I think of democracy as a juvenile ailment, I think of socialism as a definite disease. The cause of this complaint seems to me to be poverty and hard times. I am not thinking of the abstract academic socialism of Karl Marx, or of our own intelligentsia; this no longer seems to me to have much practical interest or importance. I have in mind the real, live socialism of the man who finds times hard, employment scarce and wages low, and so wants to levy toll on the wealth of his more successful neighbours, the type of socialism which flourishes in the poorest and most miserable parts of England, and in the most backward and hard-hit countries of Europe. By discouraging thrift, hard work and enterprise, this socialism lessens the wealth of a country, and so makes the poor still poorer. But experience shows that it can get no foot-hold in a prosperous country, so that the cure for it is better trade, better times, and, I think, better education.

If not cured, it kills. Our socialist orators tell us much in glowing terms about the hypothetical socialist future, or at least about their dreamy visions of the socialist future. Why do they tell us so little about the socialist and communist experiments of the past, in which their theories were really tested? It is, I think, because these experiments all ended in failure. The truth seems to be that no socialist state ever endures for long—as such. Thus I do not picture the future government of the world as either socialistic or democratic.

I have often wondered how far, if at all, it is possible to foresee the future state of society. It is commonly supposed that heavy manual labour will gradually give place to machinery, and that in the end electricity will do all our hard work for us like a sort of fairy godmother. All this depends, of course, on whether our descendants succeed in finding some new sources of power. The world's supplies of coal, oil and forests will soon be burnt up, and it may be that nothing will be found to replace them. Nothing appears to be in sight at present, and after we have burnt up the earth's accumulated store of fuel in a few hundreds of years, our posterity may be compelled to return to a much simpler life for their many million of years on earth. They may have to be content with the comparatively small amount of power they can extract from rivers, waterfalls, tides and winds.

It is true that science points to one interesting alternative. The sun and stars pour out light, heat and power in stupendous profusion, and we now believe that they obtain it by annihilating their substance. They turn their atoms into power. It may be that the scientists of some future age will discover how to transform the atoms of our earth into power. If they do, mankind will be able to obtain practically unlimited power with almost no effort. Then the annihilation of a spoonful of sea water will suffice to keep a big ship going at full speed for a year; annihilating a barrow-load of clay will keep England supplied with light, heat and power for several years. If ever this vision is realised, even partially, the curse which fell on Adam will be lifted, and heavy manual labour will almost disappear from life.

The last century has seen science progress enormously on its physical side—it has ushered in the electrical and mechanical age, and has produced so many new scientific devices and inventions that we have, I think, got a bit drunk with them. I do not believe this condition is permanent. One hears frequent reference to the disintegrating effect of telephones and motor-cars on our lives. I agree as to the present, but I think we shall soon learn to make the telephone and motor-car our servants and not our masters. I have often thought that, just as the mechanical side of science has advanced in the past century, so the next century may see a similar rapid and sensational development on the biological side. And this may change the state of society more than we can imagine. To take only one instance, suppose science shows us how to fix the sex of unborn children—so that parents can choose whether their next child shall be a boy or a girl. The first tendency would, I suppose, be to equalize the number of the sexes, so that every woman should find a mate. But would it stop there? Or would women want to reduce the numbers of their sex still further, so that every woman would be greatly sought after? Or would they perchance want to increase their numbers, so that by sheer weight of numbers they would rule the earth?

Far be it from me to prophesy what they might or might not do. I will only suggest that greater biological knowledge may, before long, alter the whole structure of society. Those who think that the life of the future will be like that of the present, only more so, are likely, I think, to be wrong.

For this kind of reason, I do not think we can foretell how large the future population of the world is likely to be. Obviously, the increase must stop sometime and somewhere. The population of England more than trebled in the last century. About eight centuries more of increase at the same rate would see the inhabitants of England packed like sardines—there would literally be standing room only. For myself, I am inclined to think that England is already overcrowded; I rather

Sir James Jeans

suspect that a less thickly populated England would be a happier England, I should like to be able to think of the England of the future as one in which there will be room as well as opportunity for every human being to live in dignity and comfort. I hope every family that wants it will be able to have a garden of its own. I hope, too, that there may still be left wide stretches of countryside and open spaces uninhabited by man.

So much for the temporal world of things which are seen. What of the things which are not seen which religion assures us are eternal? There has been much discussion of late of the claims of spiritualism or psychical research to provide proof of the survival of the dead. Speaking as a scientist, I find the alleged proofs totally unconvincing; speaking as a human being, I find most of them ridiculous as well.

Any approach of science to the unseen world must, I think, be along very different lines. Fifty years ago, the universe was generally looked on as a machine: it was said that the final aim of science was to explain all the objects in the world, including living bodies, as machines, as mere jumbles of atoms which would perform mechanical dances for a time under the action of blind purposeless forces and then fall back to form a dead world. Modern science gives but little support to such materialistic views. When we pass to extremes of size in either direction—whether to the cosmos as a whole, or to the inner recesses of the atom—the mechanical interpretation of Nature fails. We come to entities and phenomena which are in no sense mechanical. To me they seem less suggestive of mechanical than of mental processes: the universe seems to be nearer to a great thought than to a great machine. Such, at least, is the view I feel inclined to take at present, while fully conscious that at any time the pendulum may swing back again as our scientific knowledge increases.

Are we free to take the next step, and assert that the universe is, in its essence, a universe of thought, and that the material objects in it, atoms, stars and nebulæ, are merely creations of thought—not, of course, of your individual mind or mine, but of some great universal mind underlying and coordinating all our minds? As a speculation, yes; but certainly not yet as a scientific fact. We ought not, I think, to say more than that scientific knowledge seems at present to be moving in this direction. For myself, I find almost any system of idealistic philosophy preferable to the materialistic and mechanistic views held two generations ago, but who knows how things may look two generations hence?

It will be thought that all this provides a very hesitating, uncertain and shifting point of view. Yes, it does; and there is a reason. We on earth have been thinking seriously about these things for, shall we say, 3,000 years. After three million years our descendants will still probably be thinking about these things. If they make equally good use of their time they ought to know a thousand times as much then as we know now. Yet even then, so far as we can foresee, human life on earth will only be in its infancy. Our race cannot expect to understand everything in the first few moments of its existence. To-day, it is in the position of a new-born baby which has, just in the last minute, opened its eyes to study the outer world. Its first impressions are, no doubt, vague and imperfect; they probably contain many errors, but also a germ of truth. Even if the baby has only discovered that the world is a very large place and begun to suspect that babies are not its only content, it has discovered something. Its new point of view will be better than the vague, introspective, self-centred dreams in which it indulged before it could properly focus its eyes on external objects. But it would be absurd to expect the baby to understand everything. For a long time to come it must guide its conduct by instinct, by practical hand-to-mouth considerations, by its inborn moral sense, if it has one. Except in the very simplest of matters its newly awakened intellect is not yet a very safe guide.

With this in my mind, I do not worry overmuch about abstract philosophical problems, nor do I trouble much about questions such as finding a logical or rational basis for ethics or morality. Sayings of Christ—"It is better to give than to receive," and "What shall it profit a man if he gain the whole world and lose his own soul?"—take one into regions where logic and science are at present unable to provide any guidance.

We of the present age know very little—almost nothing; we are rather pioneers setting out to explore a new country. We have the thrill of ever-changing views, now and again we reach a ridge or summit which opens up new and unexpected vistas—of necessity our point of view must continually change. Those who come after us will live in a very different world, which they will understand far better than we understand our world to-day. They may find it more wonderful than anything we can imagine; on the other hand, it may prove unspeakably dull. In either event, they will not know the thrill of the pioneer. And, unless human nature changes vastly in the meantime, we may be sure they will regret the "good old days" in which we are now living. They will think of our age as the Golden Age, the glorious morning of the world. And I, for one, do not regret that fate has cast my life in it.

IX.

IRVING BABBITT

[*Irving Babbitt, Professor of French Literature at Harvard, has devoted many years to tracing Rousseau's influence on modern literature and society, and has therefore deemed it appropriate to set forth his own beliefs in connection with a study of this influence.—Ed.*]

Rousseau is commonly accounted the most influential writer of the past two hundred years. Lord Acton, indeed, is reported to have said, with a touch of exaggeration, that "Rousseau produced more effect with his pen than Aristotle or Cicero or Saint Augustine or Saint Thomas Aquinas or any other man who ever lived." At all events this saying needs to be interpreted in the light of the saying of Madame de Staël that "Rousseau invented nothing but set everything on fire." His leading ideas were abundantly anticipated, especially in England. These ideas made their chief appeal to a middle class which, in the eighteenth century, was gaining rapidly in power and prestige, and has been dominant ever since.

The Rousseauistic outlook on life has also persisted, with many surface modifications, to be sure, but without any serious questioning on the part of most men of its underlying assumptions. To debate Rousseau is really to debate the main issues of our contemporary life in literature, politics, education, and above all, religion. It is not surprising, therefore, that his reputation and writings have from the outset to the present day been a sort of international battle ground. One cannot afford to be merely partisan in this strife, to be blind to Rousseau's numerous merits—for example, to all he did to quicken man's sense of the beauties of nature, especially wild nature. Neither should one forget that there is involved in all the strife a central issue toward which one must finally assume a clear-cut attitude.

Regarding this central issue—the source of the fundamental clash between Rousseauist and anti-Rousseauist—there has been and continues to be much confusion. A chief source of this confusion has been the fact that in Rousseau as in other great writers, and more than in most, there are elements that run counter to the main tendency. Rousseau has, for example, his rationalistic side. On the basis of this fact one professor of French * has just set out to prove that, instead of being the arch-sentimentalist he has usually been taken to be, "the real Rousseau is at bottom a rationalist in his ethics, politics, and theology."

Again, there are utterances in Rousseau quite in line with traditional morality. Another American scholar has therefore set out to show that it is a mistake to make Rousseau responsible for a revolution in ethics. Still another of our scholars has managed to convince himself on similar lines that Rousseau is not primarily a primitivist in his "Discourse on Inequality."

Most remarkable of all is a book that has just appeared,† the author of which covers with contumely practically all his

---

*La Pensée de Jean-Jacques Rousseau par Albert Schinz; 2 vols., Smith College, 1929.

† The Meaning of Rousseau, Ernest Hunter Wright; Oxford University Press, 1929.

predecessors in this field on the ground that they have been blinded by partisanship, and promises to give us at last the true meaning of Rousseau. Yet this writer does not even cite the passage that, as Rousseau himself correctly tells us, gives the key to his major writings. It is to this passage that every interpreter of Rousseau who is not academic in the bad sense will give prominence: for the thesis it sums up has actually wrought mightily upon the world. It has thus wrought because it has behind it an imaginative and emotional drive not found behind other passages of Rousseau that might in themselves have served to correct it.

The passage to which I refer is one that occurs in Rousseau's account of the sudden vision that came to him by the roadside on a hot summer day in 1749 in the course of a walk from Paris to Vincennes. This vision has an importance for the main modern movement comparable to that of St. Paul's vision on the road to Damascus for the future development of Christianity. Among the multitude of "truths" that flashed upon Rousseau in the sort of trance into which he was rapt at this moment, the truth of overshadowing importance was, in his own words, that "man is naturally good and that it is by our institutions alone that men become wicked."

The consequences that have flowed from this new "myth" of man's natural goodness have been almost incommensurable. Its first effect was to discredit the theological view of human nature, with its insistence that man has fallen, not from nature as Rousseau asserts, but from God, and that the chief virtue it behooves man to cultivate in this fallen state is humility. According to the Christian, the true opposition between good and evil is in the heart of the individual: the law of the spirit can scarcely prevail, he holds, over the law of the members without a greater or lesser degree of succor in the form of divine grace. The new dualism which Rousseau sets up—

that between man naturally good and his institutions—has tended not only to substitute sociology for theology, but to discredit the older dualism in any form whatsoever.

Practically, the warfare of the Rousseauistic crusader has been even less against institutions than against those who control and administer them—kings and priests in the earlier stages of the movement, capitalists in our own day. "We are approaching," Rousseau declared, "the era of crises, and the age of revolutions." He not only made the prophecy but did more than any other one man to insure its fulfillment. There are conservative and even timid elements in his writings; but as a result of the superior imaginative appeal of the new dualism based on the myth of man's natural goodness, the rôle he has actually played has been that of arch-radical. In one of the best balanced estimates that have appeared, the French critic, Gustave Lanson, after doing justice to the various minor trends in Rousseau's work, sums up accurately its major influence: "It exasperates and inspires revolt and fires enthusiasms and irritates hatreds; it is the mother of violence, the source of all that is uncompromising; it launches the simple souls who give themselves up to its strange virtue upon the desperate quest of the absolute, an absolute to be realized now by anarchy and now by social despotism."

I have said that there has been in connection with this Rousseauistic influence a steady yielding of the theological to the sociological or, as it may also be termed, the humanitarian view of life. One should add that there enters into the total philosophy of humanitarianism an ingredient that antedates Rousseau and that may be defined as utilitarian. Utilitarianism already had its prophet in Francis Bacon. Very diverse elements enter into the writings of Bacon as into those of Rousseau, but, like those of Rousseau, they have a central drive: they always have encouraged and, one may safely say, always will encourage the substitution of a kingdom of man for the traditional Kingdom of God—the exaltation of material over spiritual "comfort," the glorification of man's increasing control over the forces of nature under the name of progress.

Rousseauist and Baconian, though often superficially at odds with one another, have coöperated in undermining, not merely religious tradition, but another tradition which in the Occident goes back finally, not to Judæa, but to ancient Greece. This older tradition may be defined as humanistic. The goal of the humanist is poised and proportionate living. This he hopes to accomplish by observing the law of measure. Anyone who has bridged successfully the gap between this general precept and some specific emergency has to that extent achieved the fitting and the decorous. Decorum is supreme for the humanist even as humility takes precedence over all other virtues in the eyes of the Christian. Traditionally the idea of decorum has been associated, often with a considerable admixture of mere formalism, with the idea of the gentleman. Humanism and religion in their various forms have at times conflicted, but have more often been in alliance with one another. As Burke says in a well-known passage: "Nothing is more certain than that our manners, our civilisation, and all the good things that are connected with manners and with civilisation, have, in this European world of ours, depended for ages upon two principles; and were indeed the result of both combined; I mean the spirit of a gentleman and the spirit of religion."

All the points of view I have been distinguishing—Baconian, Rousseauist, Christian, humanistic—often mingle confusedly. From all the confusion, however, there finally emerges a clear-cut issue—namely, whether humanitarianism, or, if one prefers, the utilitarian-sentimental movement, has supplied any effective equivalent for Burke's two principles. As for the "spirit of a gentleman," its decline is so obvious as scarcely to admit of argument. It has even been maintained that in America, the country in which the collapse of traditional standards has been most complete, the gentleman is at a positive disadvantage in the world of practical affairs; he is likely to get on more quickly if he assumes the "mucker pose." According to William James, usually taken to be the representative American philosopher, the very idea of the gentleman has about it something slightly satanic. "The prince of darkness," says James, "may be a gentleman, as we are told he is, but, whatever the God of earth and heaven is, he can surely be no gentleman."

As to the spirit of religion, though its decline has in my opinion been at least as great as that of the spirit of a gentleman, it is far from being so obvious. In any case, everything in our modern substitutes for religion—whether Baconian or Rousseauistic—will be found to converge upon the idea of service. The crucial question is whether one is safe in assuming that the immense machinery of power that has resulted from activity of the utilitarian type can be made, on anything like present lines, to serve disinterested ends; whether it will not rather minister to the egoistic aims either of national groups or of individuals.

One's answer to this question will depend on one's view of the Rousseauistic theory of brotherhood. It is at this point, if anywhere, that the whole movement is pseudo-religious. I can give only in barest outline the reasons for my own conviction that it *is* pseudo-religious. It can be shown that the nature from which man has fallen, according to Rousseau, does not correspond to anything real, but is a projection of the idyllic imagination. To assert that man in a state of nature, or some similar state thus projected, is good, is to discredit the traditional controls in the actual world. Humility, conversion, decorum—all go by the board in favor of free temperamental overflow. Does man thus emancipated exude spontaneously an affection for his fellows that will be an effective counterpoise to the sheer expansion of his egoistic impulses? If so, one may safely side with all the altruists from the Third Earl of Shaftesbury to John Dewey. One may then assume that there has been no vital omission in the passage from the service of God to the service of man, from salvation by divine grace to salvation by the grace of nature.

Unfortunately, the facts have persistently refused to conform to humanitarian theory. There has been an ever-growing body of evidence from the eighteenth century to the Great War that in the natural man, as he exists in the real world and not in some romantic dreamland, the will to power is, on the whole, more than a match for the will to service. To be sure, many remain unconvinced by this evidence. Stubborn facts, it has been rightly remarked, are as nothing compared with a stubborn theory. Altruistic theory is likely to prove peculiarly stubborn, because, probably more than any other theory ever conceived, it is flattering: it holds out the hope of the highest spiritual benefits—for example, peace and fraternal union—without any corresponding spiritual effort.

If we conclude that humanitarian service cannot take the place of the spirit of religion and that of a gentleman—Burke's "two principles"—what then? One should at least be able to understand the point of view of those who simply reject the modern movement and revert to a more or less purely traditionalist attitude. Dogmatic and revealed Christianity, they hold, has in it a supernatural element for which altruism is no equivalent. Religion of this type, they argue, alone availed to save the ancient world from a decadent naturalism; it alone can cope with a similar situation that confronts the world to-day.

But does it follow, because one's choice between the religious-humanistic and the utilitarian-sentimental view of life should, as I have said, be clear-cut, one is therefore forced to choose between being a pure traditionalist or a mere modernist? At bottom the issue involved is that of individualism. The Roman Catholic, the typical traditionalist, has in matters religious simply repudiated individualism. In this domain at least, he submits to an authority that is "anterior, superior, and exterior" to the individual. The opposite case is that of the man who has emancipated himself from outer authority in the name of the critical spirit (which will be found to be identical with the modern spirit), but has made use of his emancipation, not to work out standards, but to fall into sheer spiritual anarchy. Anyone, on the other hand, who worked out standards critically would be a sound individualist and at the same time a thoroughgoing modern. He would run the risk, to be sure, of antagonizing both traditionalists and modernists; of suffering, in short, the fate of Mr. Pickwick when he intervened between the two angry combatants. This hostility, at least so far as the traditionalist is concerned, would seem to be ill-advised. The true modern, as I am seeking to define him, is prepared to go no small distance with him in the defense of tradition.

At all events, anyone who seeks to deal in modern fashion —in other words, critically—with the religious problem, will be brought back at once to Rousseau. He will have to make his clear-cut choice, not between dogmatic and revealed religion, on the one hand, and mere modernism, on the other, but between a dualism that affirms a struggle between good and evil in the heart of the individual and a dualism which, like that of Rousseau, transfers the struggle to society.

Let us ask ourselves what it is the modern man has tended to lose with the decline of the older dualism. According to Mr. Walter Lippmann, the belief the modern man has lost is "that there is an immortal essence presiding like a king over his appetites." This immortal essence of which Mr. Lippmann speaks is, judged experimentally and by its fruits, a higher will. But why leave the affirmation of such a will to the pure traditionalist? Why not affirm it first of all as a psychological fact, one of the immediate data of consciousness, a perception so primordial that, compared with it, the denial of man's moral freedom by the determinist is only a metaphysical dream? The way would thus be open, as I pointed out in my *Forum* review of *A Preface to Morals,* for a swift flanking movement on the behaviorists and other naturalistic psychologists, who are to be accounted at present among the chief enemies of human nature.

This transcendent quality of will—which is the source of humility and is, at the same time, immediate and intuitive—has often been associated traditionally with the operation of God's will in the form of grace. For this higher immediacy, Rousseau—at least the Rousseau who has influenced the world—tended to substitute the lower immediacy of feeling, thus setting up a sort of subrational parody of grace. In order to make this substitution plausible, he—and, in his wake, the sentimentalists—have resorted to the usual arts of the sophist, chief among which are a juggling with half truths and a tampering with general terms. For example, in their use of words like "virtue" and "conscience," they have eliminated more or less completely, in favor of vital impulse (*élan vital*), the equally vital principle of control (*frein vital*)—in short, the dualistic element that both religion and humanism require.

The half truth that has been used to compromise religion in particular is that, though religion is in itself something quite distinct from emotion, it is in its ordinary manifestations very much mixed up with emotion. I give an example of this error in its latest and fashionable form. In a very learned and, in some respects, able book,* the Reverend N. P. Williams seeks to show that St. Augustine's experience of grace or, what amounts to the same thing, his love of God, was only a "sublimation" of his "lust." St. Augustine was a very passionate man and his passionateness no doubt entered into his love of God. But if it could be shown that the love of God was in St. Augustine or any other of the major saints merely emotion, sublimated or unsublimated, religion would be only the "illusion" that Freud himself has declared it to be. The psychoanalytical divine, who is, I am told, a fairly frequent type in England, is about the worst *mélange des genres* that has appeared even in the present age of confusion.

Another example of prevailing misapprehensions in this field, and that not merely from the point of view of dogma but of keen psychological observation, is the standard treatment of Rousseau's religion by P. M. Masson, a work which has been almost universally acclaimed by scholars and which has, as a matter of fact, distinguished merits as an historical investigation. M. Masson admits that this religion is "without redemption or repentance or sense of sin," and then proceeds to speak of Rousseau's "profound Christianity"!

Religion has suffered not only from the Rousseauist but also from the pseudo-scientist. If the Rousseauist gives to emotion a primacy that does not belong to it, the pseudo-scientist claims for physical science a hegemony to which it is not entitled. A science that has thus aspired out of its due place runs the risk of becoming not only a "wild Pallas from the brain" but, in connection with its use in war, "procuress

---

* *The Ideas of the Fall and of Original Sin* (Bampton Lectures for 1924). See p. 331.

to the Lords of Hell." Mr. Walter Lippmann seeks to persuade us in his *Preface to Morals* that if one becomes "disinterested" after the fashion of the scientific investigator, one will have the equivalent not only of "humanism" but of "high religion." Certain scientific investigators are busy in their laboratories at this very moment devising poison gases of formidable potency. What proof is there that, so far as the scientific type of "disinterestedness" is concerned, these gases will not be pressed into the service of the will to power? In seeking to base ethics on monistic postulates, Mr. Lippmann has simply revived the error of Spinoza, who himself revived the error of the Stoics. This error becomes not less but more dangerous when associated with the methods of science. The question involved is at all events that of the will and finally of dualism. One cannot insist too often that "the immortal essence presiding like a king over man's appetites" is transcendent—in other words, set above "nature," not only in Rousseau's sense, but also in the sense that is given to the term by the man of science.

This higher will is felt in its relation to the impulses and expansive desires of the natural man as a will to refrain. In the great traditional religions, notably in Christianity and Buddhism, the will to refrain has been pushed to the point of renunciation. The modern movement, on the other hand, has been marked since the eighteenth century and in some respects since the Renaissance by a growing discredit of the will to refrain. The very word "renunciation" has been rarely pronounced by those who have entered into the movement. The chief exception that occurs to one is Goethe (echoed at times by Carlyle). Anyone who thinks of the series of Goethe's love affairs prolonged into the seventies is scarcely likely to maintain that his *Entsagung* was of a very austere character even for the man of the world, not to speak of the saint.

One must admit that genuine renunciation was none too common even in the ages of faith. As for the typical modern, he is not only infinitely removed from anything resembling renunciation, but is increasingly unable to accept the will to refrain or anything else on a basis of mere tradition and authority. Yet the failure to exercise the will to refrain in some form or degree means spiritual anarchy. A combination such as we are getting more and more at present of spiritual anarchy with an ever-increasing material efficiency—power without wisdom, as one is tempted to put it—is not likely to work either for the happiness of the individual or for the welfare of society. That the drift toward spiritual anarchy has been largely a result of the decline of dogmatic and revealed religion is scarcely open to question. It does not follow that the only hope of recovering spiritual discipline is in a return to this type of religion. Both naturalists and supernaturalists have been too prone to underestimate the value of the third possible attitude toward life which I have defined as the humanistic.

The humanist exercises the will to refrain, but the end that he has in view is not the renunciation of the expansive desires but the subduing of them to the law of measure. The humanistic virtues—moderation, common sense, and common decency—though much more accessible than those of the saint, still go against the grain of the natural man—terribly against the grain, one is forced to conclude from a cool survey of the facts of history. Such, indeed, is the difficulty of getting men to practice even humanistic control that one is led, not necessarily to revive the dogma of original sin, but to suspect that the humanitarians, both Baconian and Rousseauistic, are hopelessly superficial in their treatment of the problem of evil. The social dualism they have set up tends in its ultimate development to substitute the class war for what Diderot termed

Irving Babbitt

in his denunciation of the older dualism the "civil war in the cave."

One reason that Rousseau gave for his abandonment of his five children was that he had been robbed by the rich of the wherewithal to feed them. The ease with which multitudes have been persuaded to follow Rousseau in this evasion of moral responsibility puts one on the track of a human trait that one may actually observe in oneself and others, and that gives some positive justification to the theological emphasis on the old Adam. This trait may be defined as spiritual indolence, a disinclination to oppose to one's expansive desires any will to refrain, and then to shift the blame on something or somebody else for the unpleasant consequences.

It is evident that in the eyes of anyone who believes in the existence in man of a higher will, with reference to which he may be a responsible moral agent, the characteristic modern malady is not plain and unvarnished materialism but sham spirituality. The remedy would seem to be in a reaffirmation in some form of the true dualism rather than in the merely cynical and "hard-boiled" attitude so prevalent nowadays among those who have become convinced of the final inanity of the humanitarian type of idealism. Joubert wrote over a century ago: "To all tender, ardent, and elevated natures, I say: Only Rousseau can detach you from religion, and only true religion can cure you of Rousseau." I have already made plain that in my judgment one may not only oppose Rousseau on humanistic as well as religious grounds, but that, while making abundant use of the wisdom of the past, one may come at humanism itself in a more positive and critical fashion than has been customary heretofore.

I can scarcely hope, within the limits of an article, to make entirely clear what I mean by a positive and critical humanism. This, to judge by certain current misunderstandings of my position, is a feat I have been unable to accomplish in a series of volumes. I may, however, touch briefly on a few of the main issues. A consideration of Rousseau and his influence will be found to converge on two main problems—the problem of the will, of which I have already spoken, and, of lesser though still major importance, the problem of the intellect. That Rousseau is at the headwaters of an anti-intellectualist trend extending down to James and Bergson and beyond is generally recognized. This trend is prefigured in his saying that "the man who thinks is a depraved animal." At bottom the protest of this type of anti-intellectualist is against the mechanizing of the world by a scientific or pseudo-scientific rationalism. He seeks to escape from mechanism by the pathway of romantic spontaneity. This means practically that he is ready to surrender to the naturalistic flux in the hope of thus becoming "creative." Unfortunately this surrender involves a sacrifice of the standards and the conscious control that are needed to give to creation genuine human significance.

It is above all in dealing with the problems of the intellect and the will that I have sought to be positive and critical. As against the Rousseauistic emotionalist, it seems to me imperative to reëstablish the true dualism—that between vital impulse and vital control—and to this end to affirm the higher will first of all as a psychological fact. The individual needs, however, to go beyond this fact if he is to decide how far he is to exercise control in any particular instance with a primary view to his own happiness: in short, he needs standards. To secure standards, at least critically, he cannot afford, like the Rousseauist, to disparage the intellect. One needs to turn its keen power of analysis to an entirely different order of experience from that envisaged by physical science.

To have standards means practically to have some principle

of unity with which to measure mere manifoldness and change. There is a power in man, often termed imagination, that reaches out and seizes likenesses and analogies and so tends to establish unity. The unity thus apprehended needs, however, to be tested from the point of view of its reality by the analytical intellect—the power that discriminates—working not abstractly but on the actual data of experience. The fraternal union that the Rousseauist would establish among men on the basis of expansive emotion is found, when tested in this way, to involve an imaginative flight from the reality of both the human and the natural order, and so to exist only in dreamland. An inspection of all the facts of human experience, past and present, would seem to show that what unity a man may achieve either within himself or with his fellow men must be based primarily, not upon feeling, but upon an exercise of the higher will.

One's conception of the constant and unifying factor in life will appear in one's use of general terms. It is plain that the humanist and the Rousseauist clash radically in their definitions. As a result of his elimination of the dualistic element, the Rousseauist has, as I have remarked, set up a "virtue" that, in the eyes of the humanist, is not true virtue; and so likewise for such terms as "justice" and "liberty," and above all (at least in its application to man) "nature." If there is to be a reintegration of the dualistic element into these words, there would seem to be needed an art of inductive defining somewhat similar to that which Socrates brought to bear upon the sophists. It is precisely at this point that the keen discrimination of which I have spoken would have its fullest play. At all events one may say that the standards that result from the coöperation of the imagination and the analytical intellect, and that are reflected in one's definitions, are finally pressed by the humanist into the service of the higher will with a view to imposing a right direction upon the impulses and expansive desires of the natural man.

The humanist is rather distrustful of sudden conversions and pistol-shot transformations of human nature. Hence his supreme emphasis on education. If the humanistic goal is to be attained, if the adult is to like and dislike the things he should—according to Plato, the ultimate aim of ethical endeavor—he must be trained in the appropriate habits almost from infancy. Occasional humanists may appear under present conditions, but if there is to be anything resembling a humanistic movement, the first stage would, as I have said, be that of Socratic definition; the second stage would be the coming together of a group of persons on the basis of this definition—the working out, in short, in the literal sense of that unjustly discredited word, of a convention; the third stage would almost inevitably be the attempt to make this convention effective through education.

The mention of education brings the whole discussion home to America. Our educators are more completely and more naïvely Rousseauistic than those of almost any other country. For example, there is an important survival of the religious-humanistic conception of education in France and Germany and, above all, England; whereas the assumption is all but universal among those who control our educational policies from the elementary grades to the university that anything that sets bounds to the free unfolding of the temperamental proclivities of the young, to their right to self-expression, as one may say, is outworn prejudice. Discipline, so far as it exists, is not of the humanistic or the religious type, but of the kind that one gets in training for a vocation or a specialty. The standards of a genuinely liberal education, as they have been understood, more or less from the time of Aristotle, are being progressively undermined by the utilitarians and the sentimentalists. If the Baconian-Rousseauistic formula is as unsound in certain of its postulates as I myself believe, we are in danger of witnessing in this country one of the great cultural tragedies of the ages.

Moreover Rousseauism not only dominates our education but has been eating into the very vitals of the Protestant religion. Practically, this means that Protestantism is ceasing to be a religion of the inner life and is becoming more and more a religion of "uplift." The result of the attempt to deal with evil socially rather than at its source in the individual, to substitute an outer for an inner control of appetite, has been a monstrous legalism, of which the Eighteenth Amendment is only the most notable example. Those Protestants who have allied themselves with an organization like the Anti-Saloon League have been violating one of the most necessary of Christian precepts—that which warns against confounding the things of God with the things of Cæsar.

The multiplication of laws, attended by a growing lawlessness—the present situation in this country—is, as every student of history knows, a very sinister symptom. It may mean that our democratic experiment is, like similar experiments in the past, to end in a decadent imperialism. Nothing is farther from my thought than to suggest that we are on a fatal descending curve. I do not believe in any such fatality, and am in general skeptical of every possible philosophy of history—of the Spenglerian variety most of all. The all-important factor that the Spenglers are wont to overlook or deny in favor of collective tendencies is the moral choices of individuals. For example, the majority in the United States seems just now to be careless of the higher cultural values, to desire nothing better than a continuation of the present type of material prosperity based on the miracles of mass production. Individuals, however, are already standing aside from the majority and assuming a critical attitude toward its "ideals."

Whether this remnant will become sufficiently large to make itself felt in an important way, remains of course a question. At all events, there is an increasing number of persons in this country who can at least see the point of view of the rest of the world. This point of view may be defined as a curious blend of admiration for our efficiency and of disdain for our materialism. The foreigner is, however, far too prone to make America the universal scapegoat for the present domination of man by the machine.

Though the utilitarian-sentimental movement may have triumphed more completely in America than elsewhere, it has been extending its conquests over the whole of the Occident and is now invading the Orient. The issues it raises are, in short, international. That the peripheral merits of this movement are almost innumerable I should be the first to admit: indeed, almost everything in it seems plausible until one penetrates to its very center, and then one discovers an omission that unless corrected vitiates all the rest—the omission, namely, as I have been trying to show, of any reference to a higher will or power of control.

Without making any pretense to a prophetic rôle for which I am not qualified, I am yet willing to express the conviction that unless there is a recovery of the true dualism or, what amounts to the same thing, a reaffirmation of the truths of the inner life in some form—traditional or critical, religious or humanistic—civilization in any sense that has been attached to that term hitherto is threatened at its base. I speak of the interests of civilization, though my own prime objection to Rousseauism is that it is found finally not to make for the happiness of the individual.

X.

SIR ARTHUR KEITH

DEEP in my heart I find a strange reluctance to set down here my innermost beliefs concerning God, man, and the universe. My birth in Scotland and my Presbyterian upbringing may be to blame. The fact that I have passed the sixty-third milestone in life and have acquired some degree of worldly wisdom may also have something to do with it. The real explanation, however, lies deeper: it is fear—or cowardice, if you will.

By nature I am one of the common herd. I fear ostracism. And I court it—perhaps deserve it—when I break the seal of my inner sanctuary and expose the beliefs which rule my conduct and dominate my outlook. Such an act is both sacrilegious and dangerous, for these innermost beliefs of ours are charged with the fierce fire of feeling and of passion. They have become parts of ourselves; we cannot discuss them openly and candidly without committing an assault on men and women whose love and comradeship we desire to retain. Hence most of us choose to be silent; wrangling is painful and the paths of peace are pleasant.

But in these pages I have thrown prudence to the winds. I am resolved to be absolutely and resolutely honest with myself and with my readers. I know I shall shock many, but I hope my confession may bring comfort to others.

I am not alone. At this moment there are some 1,750 millions of us making the journey of life. There are millions who, like myself, have set out with a heritage of goodly beliefs, but, by reason of what we have seen, heard, felt, thought, and learned, have shed them one by one. With me there has been no sudden revolution, no dramatic revelation such as befell Saul of Tarsus; it simply dawned on me, as one day's experience followed another, that I was walking less and less by faith and more and more by reason.

No two human beings have made, or ever will make, exactly the same journey in life. The same events may occur, but their sequence and combination cannot be the same. Every human life is a unique adventure. And if our stock of beliefs depends on the early pilgrimage we make, then there must be in existence to-day just as many shades of belief as there are human beings.

As long as man remains an inquiring animal, there can never be a complete unanimity in our fundamental beliefs. The more diverse our paths, the greater is likely to be the divergence in our beliefs. Most men and women have to take the way in life which happens to be open to them. They have neither the leisure nor the inclination to mark and digest the experiences which come their way. Only a few are free to select their paths and choose those which yield the richest harvests of experience.

The church attracts inquiring youthful minds; it offers them, or seems to offer, the most likely road to a knowledge of ultimate realities. The priest may glean the best that has been revealed or thought concerning the ways of God to man.

In his flock he can study the ways of man to God and assure himself that in the hearts of all men there is an insatiable craving for a settled and abiding creed.

The attractions of the church are of old standing, but those of science are recent. The number of young people who are devoting their lives to the increase of knowledge grows at an astonishing pace. The boundaries of time and space become ever wider as these scientific travelers go farther afield in search of knowledge. We cannot neglect the harvests such searchers bring home. For can they study the works of creation without formulating schemes to explain what they have seen and measured? Without doubt the men who have chosen these novel paths in life have suffered the greatest mental change. They can no longer cling to the orthodox conceptions concerning the governance of the world of matter and of mind.

This is particularly true of men like myself who have spent their days in the study of living matter—especially if that matter has a human shape. My own path in life has given me opportunities which fall to few; it has taken me where I could examine at first hand all important discoveries concerning the pre-history of mankind. It has permitted me to study the most and best that is known of the living human body and brain. My sole right to take part in this series of living philosophies rests on the special experience which my life's work has brought me.

Presently I shall unburden my heart to my readers, but before I begin I should like to lay before them still another explanatory matter. I have said that of the thousands of millions born into the world, no two make identical journeys in life. It is also a fact that no two human beings have ever set out with identical equipment in mind and body. Every face is stamped with individuality when it issues from the womb.

Every baby brings into the world a pattern on its finger tips never seen before.

What is true of its fingers and its face is also true of its brain, but variety in this organ has an infinitely greater significance. Within the brain there are some 18,000 millions of microscopic living units or nerve cells. These units are grouped in myriads of battalions, and the battalions are linked together by a system of communication which in complexity has no parallel in any telephone network devised by man. Of the millions of nerve units in the brain not one is isolated. All are connected and take part in handling the ceaseless streams of messages which flow into the brain from eyes, ears, fingers, feet, limbs, and body.

This mighty but silent traffic begins at birth and never ceases until death. The stream of traffic which is received and elaborated by our brains constitutes our experience, and out of this experience we earthly wayfarers build up our beliefs concerning the past, present, and future.

I have laid before the reader the conception which most inquiring biologists have arrived at concerning the structure of the brain and the nature of mind and thought. Such a conception bears in upon and alters the foundations of their creeds. Certainly the years of labor I have given to the human body and brain have compelled me to abandon many beliefs which are still widely held by the orthodox.

But it was not to explain my heterodoxy that I introduced at this point a brief dissertation on the complexity of the human brain. I mentioned these physiological considerations as a plea for tolerance. If nature cannot reproduce the same simple pattern in any two fingers, how much more impossible is it for her to reproduce the same pattern in any two brains, the organization of which is so inconceivably complex! Every child is born with a certain balance of faculties, aptitudes, inclinations, and instinctive leanings. In no two is the balance alike, and each different brain has to deal with a different tide of experience. I marvel, then, not that one man should disagree with another concerning the ultimate realities of life, but that so many, in spite of the diversity of their inborn natures, should reach so large a measure of agreement.

Having made these preliminary explanations, I have cleared the way for my confession. I shall state, as concisely as I can, the beliefs which I now hold, tracing the circumstances which led me to accept them.

My parents were religious in thought and deed. I was brought up on the Bible. Twice every Sunday the sounds of a "Free Church" bell came across a rural valley to our home in Aberdeenshire, Scotland, and summoned all of us to service. We listened to a clergyman who was sincere, fervid, and learned. He preached the doctrine of salvation through Christ; if we believed in Him, and accepted unreservedly the revelation of the New Testament, then our safety in the next world was assured.

At that time I had no doubt that the existence of a "next world" was a well-ascertained fact. The dead whom I saw conveyed to the quiet of the churchyard were, I was convinced, really on their way to appear before the Great Judge for sentence. Heaven was in the glory of the clouds, and Hell lay within the flaming brimstone bowels of the earth. Both were geographical realities. I earnestly desired to gain the one and avoid the other.

I was told it was easy: I had only to believe. Even then I stumbled as I pressed forward. I frequented evangelical meetings, hoping to catch the ecstasy of faith which suffused the lives of those who had "found Christ." Try as I would, I could not convince myself that mere belief in the divinity of one who died on the cross so long ago, and in a country so remote from Scotland, could save me from the bottomless pit. Such a way of salvation seemed too easy to be true.

In my youth I had no doubts about the Old Testament; for me it was literally true from end to end. It was an authentic history of the world: God created the earth, Adam was the first man, and Eve the first woman. I cannot remember ever questioning the justice of the sentence passed on Adam for eating the forbidden apple.

There were certain Biblical terms I found difficult to picture mentally. "Sin" was one—particularly "original sin." "Spirit" was another; when I read that "God is a spirit, infinite and eternal," no visual image materialized in my mind. But when I read of God the Creator, God the Father, the God of Abraham, the God who spoke face to face with Moses on Mount Sinai, then the result was different. Such a God I could picture, although I fashioned Him, I fear, too much on human lines.

His existence, power, and righteousness I accepted as truths beyond question. The third person of the Trinity—the Holy Ghost—I never could encompass. Even now, when I hear those two words drop from the lips of a clergyman, I try in vain to grasp the image he has in mind.

Such were the bare and crude elements of my creed when I became a student of medicine in the University of Aberdeen. I entered on my studies at a time when Darwinism was capturing the professoriate of Britain. New vistas were opening up; a new history of the earth was being written.

I became enthralled in the study of anatomy and have remained a student of the human body ever since. For it seemed to me then, as it seems to me now, that if man's destiny can be deciphered at all, it will only be deciphered by those who can read the hieroglyphics imprinted on the human body and mind. It soon became apparent to me that I had to give up my beloved Old Testament as a reliable guide to the origin and nature of man. So we younger men abandoned the Bible as a textbook of science.

In the eighties of the last century geologists were unloading in the markets of science harvests of evidence gathered from the rocks. As the evidence accumulated, the evolutionary origin of all living things became a certainty. Then as now, zoölogists were searching for the *way* of evolution—the manner in which transformation is effected in plants and animals; and although there is much concerning the machinery of evolution which remains unknown, yet as early as the end of the nineteenth century zoölogists had agreed definitely on one thing: creation did not happen as pictured in the Bible. The Creator did not stand outside of living things and mold them once and for all. Indeed, creation did not work from without but from within. Creative power began to be thought of as inherent in all living matter.

Like other conservative-minded men, I tried to empty the new knowledge of science into the time-revered Biblical bottles. I know that many have succeeded, and still succeed, in doing so; but to my eye, the Biblical bottles, when modified to hold the wine of modern science, bear no resemblance to the Scriptural originals. To say that they are the same is to prostitute truth.

Yet, between the men who made the old Scriptural bottles and we who make the new there is one thing in common. The wise men of the ancient East felt, just as the men of science now feel, that a rational explanation must be sought and found for the beginning of things; for the heart of man has always craved an explanation of ultimate realities. The Biblical writers were familiar with only one kind of creative power—that manifested by human beings. Therefore, in seeking to explain how life and man came into the world, they conceived a Super-being endowed with human attributes. This Creative Power or God, they believed, worked on matter much as a potter works on clay—that is, he worked from without.

As I have indicated, the modern man of science is also looking for an explanation, but he finds the creative force pervading all matter, living and dead. It is as extensive as space and time. New worlds are coming into existence; others are dying. The machinery of the universe is automatic; the forces which control its movements are inherent in the constitution of matter. To discover how matter became thus endowed is beyond the scientist's reach, but he must take facts as he finds them. It is enough for him to know that the earth, life, and man are still in the throes of creation.

Certainly the creative power which is at work bears no resemblance to the personal God postulated by the Hebrews, and the modern man of science cannot fit Him into the scheme of the world as he knows it. He has to try to reconceive God, and when he has done so, nothing but an unsatisfying abstraction is left. It is unsatisfying because even the greatest men of science, although they may possess the intellects of giants, have still the hearts of children. And children cling to that which is endowed with a human shape and has been given the warmth of living flesh.

By the absorption of this new knowledge my youthful creed was smashed to atoms. My personal God, the Creator of Heaven and Earth, melted away. The desire to pray—not the need—was lost, for one cannot pray for help to an abstraction. And prayer becomes an impossibility for those who are convinced that the natural course of events cannot be altered by calling upon a supermundane power to interfere. I became convinced that the course of human history is determined, not by what happens in the skies, but by what takes place in the hearts of men.

These changes in my beliefs passed silently. I pursued my medical studies, and while still young went to reside in Siam. I went with the pride of the West in my heart and confident of my white superiority. I was thrown into intimate contact with the villages of a remote, jungle-covered province. They were followers of Buddha. In Scotland I had been taught that if we had been deprived of the Bible, we would have remained pure savages. In Siam I found myself among peasants who had never heard of Christ, and yet they were more law-abiding than we were in Europe. They led unselfish, considerate, charitable, and happy lives.

I left Siam with my creed still more tattered and torn. I had become less certain than ever that the truth as revealed and taught in Palestine was really the only truth. Apparently there had been other revelations in other lands, since there were clearly other ways of virtuous living besides the Christian way.

I envy those men and women who know how to keep their creeds intact and unchanged throughout the entire journey of life. Their path is peace and their hope is sure. There are millions, however, who cannot rest until they can make their creed fit the facts of life, or the facts of life fit their creed. I am such a one.

Among my later experiences are those which came to me through my interest in explorations revealing the earlier histories of Egypt, Babylonia, and Palestine. For example, on the site of Palestine, archæologists are exposing the foundations of cities which were laid many centuries before Joshua led the Israelites into the promised land. In the hills of Judæa, and particularly in those on the western shore of Lake Galilee, caves are being explored. They are found to be rich in the records of pre-history, carrying our knowledge of man in Palestine back to an antiquity of at least twenty thousand years. We know from a study of their fossil remains that the men who then lived on the shores of Galilee were quite unlike any now living: they were more primitive in form and more apelike in feature.

Now, such tidings from Egypt, Mesopotamia, and Palestine cannot flow in upon us and leave our regard for the Bible untouched. In the light of this knowledge the Bible appears as a patchwork made by many hands and at many dates. Men were inspired in ancient Palestine; but was the inspiration in any way different from that which now moves our great reformers? When Jeremiah prefaced his message to the Israelites with "Thus saith the Lord," he spoke according to the psychological beliefs of his time; had he known more of the human brain and how thoughts arise within it, he would have used more guarded language.

Thus my belief in the divine inspiration of the Bible became undermined. It remained for me a book of books, still divine—but divine in the sense that all great books are divine which teach men how to live righteously.

At every available opportunity I have pursued another inquiry which has left its mark on my creed. It is one thing to read of the discoveries of fossil man; it is quite another to handle and examine the fossil bones, the skulls, the casts of their brains, to compare them, to realize their place in time and in their evolutionary sequence. When we add to such evidence the many and striking approaches which great apes make to man in structure, and the parallel courses pursued by ape and man during their development, the Darwinian con-

Sir Arthur Keith

ception of man's origin becomes, to men situated as I am, no longer a theory but an actuality.

We have to face the fact that we are the descendants of apelike ancestors. The truth, at first sight, is often ugly and repulsive to our personal feelings, but when it *is* the truth, its ultimate effects on us are always salutary. The sooner men realize their humble origin, the better it will be for their happiness. Perhaps they will then understand the true nature of those faults of the flesh known to good churchmen as "original sin."

The faithful priest accounts for man's inborn tendency to sin by tracing his descent from Adam. The modern biologist regards "original sin" as man's inheritance from the jungle. It must not be thought that evolution has diminished man's inheritance of animal propensities; on the contrary, it has strengthened the evidence. But at the same time evolution proves that there has mercifully taken place a great expansion in those regions of the brain which give man control of himself and the power to choose. The fight between good and evil, which is waged daily in the breast of every man, woman, and child, is the struggle for mastery between the old inheritance and the new.

Of all my studies, that which has touched my creed most closely has been my search into the nature of man's mental life. Beyond a doubt our thoughts, feelings, longings, aspirations, and passions are manifestations of the brain. When it is narcotized, destroyed, or dead, consciousness disappears. Man's brain does not stand as a thing apart; it is the culmination of an ascending series. There is no part of it and no function manifested by it that cannot be traced to humble beginnings lower in the animal scale. And what we postulate for man's brain we must in all justice apply to that of the ape, the dog, and all other beasts.

Now, when physiologists study the living brain of an ape, they have no grounds for supposing that they are dealing with a dual structure. The brain is not a tenement inhabited by a spirit or soul. The "spirit" or "soul" is but a name for the manifestations of the living brain. The leading neurologists of the world are agreed that the same is true of the human brain. It was only when they abandoned the dual conception—an inheritance from the dark ages of medicine—that they began to understand the disorders of man's mind and how to treat them.

Modern medicine thus strikes at the very root of Christian doctrine. For if man is truly mortal, if death ends all, if the human soul is but the manifestation of the living brain, as light and heat are the manifestations of a glowing bar of steel, then there can be no resurrection of the dead. Man has the seeds of immortality in him, but the gift is for the race, not for the individual.

Thus the orthodox creed of my youth has been shattered by the impact of modern science. And since no man can live on a creed of pure negation, one may ask if it is possible to build a satisfactory way of life out of the wreckage. In all humility I believe a way is possible. That which at first seemed a curse has turned out to be a blessing. For if men believe, as I do, that this present earth is the only heaven, they will strive all the more to make heaven of it. To feel that we are mere birds of passage, only temporary probationers, is not conducive to the best conduct.

Once we have accepted our humble origin and the heritage it has brought us, we are prepared to discipline ourselves and to behave with tolerance, sympathy, and charity to all others. We have to be resolutely self-reliant, not casting on the cross burdens which we ourselves ought to bear.

The natural span of man's existence contains enough to make this life a prize worth living. I have within me—as have all living beings—a greed of life, an urgent craving for immortality. That longing, which lies at the very root of the Christian religion, I look upon as a sin of the flesh—one to be conquered and suppressed. It is a vice akin to avarice. With its suppression comes a peace which only those who have felt it can realize.

A way of life is possible for man under the new dispensation of knowledge—but what of the ultimate meaning of life? How has life been called into existence? Why has it culminated in a human form? For what final purpose have we been called into existence? Surely man is part of a great whole!

The human brain is a poor instrument to solve such ultimate problems. We have to recognize its limitations. Yet it perceives how well-ordered all things are and how wonderful are the inventions of nature. Design is manifest everywhere. Whether we are laymen or scientists, we must postulate a Lord of the Universe—give Him what shape we will. But it is certain that the anthropomorphic God of the Hebrews cannot meet our modern needs.

I cannot help feeling that the darkness in which the final secret of the universe lies hid is part of the Great Design. This world of ours has been constructed like a superbly written novel: we pursue the tale with avidity, hoping to discover the plot. The elusiveness of the chase heightens our ardor, until the search becomes part of our religion. For the secret of secrets recedes as we run. The ultimate reason for man's existence is the only fruit in the garden of life which he can never hope to pluck.

Clearly, then, my creed is imperfect. It is not final. No creed is final. Such a creed as mine must grow and change as knowledge grows and changes.

XI.

JAMES TRUSLOW ADAMS

[*Mr. Adams has chosen to expound his beliefs in connection with his answer to the question: "Why Be Good?"—Ed.*]

WHAT is "morality"? Perhaps our cavemen ancestors discussed the problem as they sat around the fire at night while the sabre-toothed tiger snarled without, a hundred thousand years ago. To-day it is almost as unsettled as ever despite *The New Oxford Dictionary*. For our present purpose I choose to define morality as that portion of human thought and conduct that stems from and is controlled by "I ought" as contrasted with either "I want" or "I must." I am not here concerned with discovering where this feeling of "ought" came from or with analyzing it philosophically. It has existed in the best specimens of *homo sapiens* for many millennia past, and for the moment I accept it as an original datum.

I have no hesitation, you will note, in conceding that it belongs to the emotional rather than the rational portion of man's nature. Man is a creature of impulse, emotion, action rather than reason. Reason is a very late development in the world of living creatures, most of whom, as far as we know, get along admirably in daily life without it. Indeed, as we consider attentively the world about us—its business, its journalism, its habits and customs, its loves and hates—we may well ask whether reason is an innate part of human nature or merely a useful tool that has been discovered, like fire. Perhaps it is quite as dangerous to play with; I am not sure that people should not take out insurance against its careless use. However that may be, its discovery has fascinated man. Having unexpectedly found a key that unlocks many doors, we have come to insist that it shall unlock all, and have acquired a sneaking feeling that it is rather disgraceful not to be able to "give a reason" for anything and everything. So strong has this feeling become that we are even inclined to deny the very existence of whatever we cannot easily rationalize, obviously an absurd procedure which could be tolerated only by the shallow intellectualism in which we splash about so much these days.

Morality is real, account for it as we may or may not.

The study of my own mind and a reasonable study of other peoples' tell me that for every human being there are two laws, two imperatives (leaving out mere desire): the civil law of his social group, tribe, or nation, and the moral law. The first tells him "you must," and the second "you ought." Not attempting to rationalize for the moment, but merely to report what we find, I think we must admit this to be true, and also that we instinctively recognize the moral law as having a validity and an authority superior to the civil. Here in America to-day we have illustration of the two kinds of law, and their relative superiority, in the question daily asked by thousands of people: "*Ought* I to obey the Prohibition laws or not?"

Many of our (somewhat pseudo-) scientific friends try to

dodge this problem of the categorical imperative, this sense of "ought" which is as uncomfortable as a pin in our trousers, by resolving it into its origins. They try to explain it away and invalidate it by the inconsequential method of showing how it evolved. They are, however, by no means agreed as to its origin, nor do I think it would make the slightest difference if they were.

In 1930 A.D. I am a creature with legs, sexual organs, a body, arms, a head with ears, eyes, nose, mouth, and a brain that occasionally functions logically—an instrument capable of receiving impressions through five senses from an otherwise unknown universe. A very limited equipment for the Lord of Creation, but the best we can do yet. My ancestor of several million years ago was not even so well off. I understand that at one stage he had gills, and perhaps fins instead of legs. I have no wish to return to that previous state. Indeed, aside from my inability to do so, it would seem a pity to waste the development of those millions of years. If I do not wish to return to his physical body, why should I to his stage of "love," "beauty," "morality"? If I tried to look at the *Night Watch* of Rembrandt with the eyes of a much later ancestor, even a relative of the chimpanzee, I would merely be wasting a million years or so of Nature's time and effort to make me what I am.

When we try to see the universe whole, which, of course, includes its scientific aspect, it seems to me that we have got to account for its evolution and also for its present state. There is no use denying the existence of the moon simply because a certain number of million years ago it was probably a mere protuberance on the surface of the earth. In the same way, there is no use denying that a certain animal called man has a sense of the beautiful and, at least in the more highly developed individuals of the species, a sense of moral obligation, and that the latter sense has been utilized by Nature in such a way as greatly to facilitate his social development.

In other words, there has been a Something—call it what you will—in the universe which has developed a moral sense out of emotion in the same way that it has developed stars out of nebulæ, and in our description of the universe we have to find room for morals as well as for stars. Man's life has been greatly enriched by his being able to live in large social aggregates of great complexity of organization. He could not have done so, according to all experience, unless the conduct of the innumerable coöperating individuals had been governed in one sphere by the civil law and in another, not amenable to that, by what we call the moral law. The moral law is thus a reality which has played its part in raising man to a higher level. It has been an essential part of the evolutionary process.

If society depended solely on its code of civil laws or on a complete individualism in morals, it would not be found hanging together to-morrow morning. The fact would seem to be sufficiently obvious, although to a good many so-called thinkers it apparently is not, that when vast numbers of human beings live in extremely complex relations with one another it is essential that they be able to count definitely on certain modes of behaviour in each other, at least within broad but well-developed limits. When, for example, we greet a friend by holding out our hand, we expect instinctively that he will shake it. If, instead, he should vigorously kick us in the stomach life might be very exciting and individual but, with that degree of unpredictability, would soon become quite impossible for busy people. In the same way we have to count upon normal people obeying the civil law, on their not repudiating a written contract or burning down a house as soon as we have built it.

But there is a vast field of human conduct not controlled by instinctive reaction or by the civil law, and yet in which a certain broad predictability of action is essential if human society is to function. In this field we need something to guide decision and action. A simple example will suffice. In daily life it is needful in general that we shall be able to rely upon the truth of statements made to us. The civil law, however, can do nothing to prevent people from lying. Unless it runs the risk of doing more injustice than justice it has to limit its control to clear-cut, provable cases. It can thus punish perjury but can never reach the infinite possibilities of less formal perversions of the truth. We have to trust to the working of the moral law which says it is wrong to lie except in the rarest of cases.

In the field of morality, the rules become expressed in time in moral codes, which both in themselves and in their influence upon society vary greatly from place to place and age to age. Because they so differ, however, it would be as foolish to claim that morality does not exist as to deny the existence of beauty because of the different exemplifications of it in, say, the drawing of a wave by Hokusai in Japan, the modelling of a bust of Nefretete in Egypt, or a portrait by Rembrandt in Holland.

Let us consider for a moment the family life of the Trobriand Islanders as pictured by Malinowski. A man and woman marry and live together as husband and wife. She is not dependent on him economically but on her brother in another village. The husband owes support not to his wife but to his sisters. It is the wife's brother, not the husband, who possesses disciplinary authority over the children. The father is their playmate, whereas the disciplinarian is an uncle who appears in the village only at intervals—a rôle played by the father with reference to *his* nieces and nephews. The children are free to indulge in sexual practices, except between brother and sister, unhindered by outward regulation or inner inhibition, until the age of puberty, when their love affairs, although even yet not permanent, become somewhat more lengthy and serious. Finally comes a marriage, which is binding, and after that the couple must—and, in practice, do—remain faithful to each other.

However extraordinary this framework of family life may appear to us, there is nothing lax about it. There are all sorts of definite regulations between the sexes, and prohibitions concerning intercourse and marriage between certain people; and the Trobriander, however his inclinations may rebel, is expected to keep to the rules as strictly as are members of a European family. In both systems, of course, there are occasional lapses, but they are regarded *as* lapses, and as such are reprehensible. The point is that in all societies, no matter how different in structure, certain codes of conduct are considered moral and requisite if society is to function at all.

These codes, formed unconsciously, almost instinctively, through long periods of time and closely fitting the needs and mode of life of the peoples employing them, may come to be out of date and maladjusted to the requirements of a changed condition of life. If the change in conditions comes about very gradually, the code will alter almost imperceptibly, just as we can watch it changing among the Hebrews from the time of Moses to that of Christ. In such a transformation certain specific alterations will occur in the code, but there will be no questioning of the code as a whole or of the obligations of morality. If, on the other hand, the change in conditions is abrupt, then the people will face a crisis of terrific import:

and in the period between the sudden breakdown of the old code and moral system, and the formation of a new one (if such a new one *is* formed), the degeneration is swift and may be permanent, as we have seen over and over in the contact of alien races.

The moral and social degradation of the Pacific races is due largely to the insistence of the white man and his missionaries upon a too sudden change in the moral beliefs and codes of the natives. In the same way, we are to-day facing a moral crisis of immeasurable magnitude, caused in part by a change in living brought on by the Industrial Revolution, and in part by the breakdown of the old religious sanctions for our formal moral code. Our danger is similar to that of the Trobrianders. Such dangers, arising out of the conflict of racial cultures, are clearly described by Pitt-Rivers in that classic of ethnology, *The Clash of Culture and Contact of Races*.

But a similar clash may also occur within the framework of a single society when the comparatively small groups of genuine intellectuals and the great mass of the emotion-motivated workers form almost different races. It might well prove that the former, in trying to destroy too rapidly the moral sanctions and codes of the latter, would be found to have brought about the same unfortunate result of breaking down without ability to build up which has been that of so many missionary efforts in foreign lands.

Unfortunately, because of the fact that the moral law by its very nature cannot be enforced by physical or political power (which is precisely why its field is different from that of the civil law), the problem of providing a sanction for it is one of extreme difficulty. In the past, the sanction for the moral law has usually taken two forms: one for the few and the other for the many. In practically all periods and among all races, we find a certain élite among the people—individuals to whom the moral law appears as a thing of beauty, who would feel the same disgust for an immoral act that they would for a repulsive one æsthetically, or a bestial one physically. They have the same instinct for morality that the artist has for beauty, or the gentleman for his code of honour. For them there is no need of a sanction involving compulsion, either physical or psychological. They have, so to speak, the moral gift, as poets and painters have the artistic gift. In the same way that great artists and poets have led men to see beauty, so these moralists have led men to see morality; and just as human life would be infinitely less rich and full without the legacy derived from æsthetic genius, so would it be impoverished without the legacy derived from moral genius.

With the great mass of mankind, however, it has been different, and a sanction with power behind it is required to make people conform to both the moral law and the civil law. The difficulty of providing a sanction for the former is, as I have said, very great. Civil law and political force cannot be invoked. The sanction must be psychological and it must be powerful.

Reason is psychological, but it is not powerful as a compelling motive to conduct in most men and women. For that we have to rely upon instinct and emotion. Instincts change slowly and are therefore useless for this purpose. So we have to return to the emotions, and of those the most powerful are love and fear; and, in the past, the needed sanctions for popular morality have been love for the character of some great moral leader, or love and fear with reference to the supernatural.

The leadership of humanity has temporarily passed to two new types—the super-business man, who has replaced in power the former statesman (who by long practice had at least some knowledge of the psychological needs of the society he ruled), and the scientist, who has largely replaced in mental influence the artist, moralist, and religious leader. And not only did the scientist replace them, but, until very recently, he often sought to demolish them.

One group of new leaders, the super-business men, have to a large extent failed to see that the need for morality in the people they practically govern is greater than ever, because social relations are infinitely more delicate and complex in adjustment than heretofore. The other group, the earlier scientists, to a great extent sought to invalidate the conception of a moral law and to undermine the foundations of its sanctions. Both greatly aggravated a crisis that was already one of the most momentous in the history of Western civilization.

We are now floundering in a morass. Considerable numbers of both clergy and scientists are beginning to show signs of panic, while the super-business men vaguely sense that something must be done to make society "safe." They themselves are powerless to lead in person. To make matters worse, a large part of the Protestant clergy have sought to reinstate a specific and partly outworn "moral code" by giving it the impossible sanction of the civil law, thus further undermining an understanding of and respect for the "moral law." On the other hand, many scientists and modernists have, with equal lack of understanding of human nature, sought to bolster up newly devised codes of conduct with the sanction of scientific reason. Both experiments are bound, in my opinion, to be futile, if not to end in disaster.

It may be that man is capable of great change and development in his nature, as Dewey avers. Unquestionably he is, but these improvements require long periods of time. It may be that, millenniums hence, reason will be a more powerful motive of conduct than instinct and emotion. It is not now, and it is not likely to be during the lives of the next few generations. To depend to-day upon reason as a sufficient guide in the whole field of conduct not governed by the civil law is like trying to take shelter under an acorn instead of an oak tree in a storm. The simple fact is that we cannot count upon the great mass of men in this industrial civilization of ours in the year 1931 basing their conduct, and basing it rightly, upon reason and scientific knowledge.

For another thing, it is becoming obvious that the present situation cries aloud for some code, whatever it may be, by which men may guide their own daily lives and on the observance of which other men may count in dealing with them. But the scientists and the modernists are hopelessly at variance as to the details of any such code. Scientific knowledge itself is constantly changing. A discovery of one year receives confirmation another, or is thrown aside. We are learning all the time, but we certainly do not know enough yet to undertake the remodeling of society and morals on a basis of scientific knowledge.

One recalls the story of the showman who, when nudity on the stage was daring, produced a woman in the garments of Eve on the platform of a small town hall, claiming she was "The Naked Truth." A countryman, after craning his neck and examining her carefully, called out, "She ain't Truth. She's Molly Mullins." That is the trouble with so many of the ethical systems suggested as scientific. I do not mean for a moment to blink the fact that there has been a perilously severe dislocation between the old moral code and the new type of life forced on us by the Industrial Revolution. Our traditional morality, which has had practically no new axioms added to it for two thousand years, required adjusting in many parts. But that adjustment cannot be made effectively in the cold light of reason and by the aid of a most inadequate store of scientific knowledge of human nature.

Even in the much cruder and simpler domain of civil law, the great object lesson of prohibition is teaching us that a mere fiat of the civil power is not sufficient in itself. It has got to be in harmony with a whole mass of psychological factors having not the remotest relation to economic efficiency or scientific reasoning.

The danger of the crisis for us is its suddenness, as it was for the Trobriand Islanders. That danger is the breakdown of all morality: we are bidden to discard the old moral code without being able to accept another in its place. The danger has been enormously increased, as I said above, by the breakdown in traditional popular sanctions coincident with the strain on the code. It is useless to prophesy, but we may at least indulge in a few guesses.

Looking over the situation, I think we may divide the people into groups. First, there are those whom I have mentioned above—the men who have the same instinctive appreciation of and love for morality that artists have for beauty, the class from which the moral leaders of mankind have always arisen. They will be untouched by the crisis, and may provide the leader we need. Second, there is the group which will "rock the boat" as wildly as they can—the group for whom a little knowledge is a dangerous thing, and who love novelty and excitement, mistaking it for progress. Third, there is the group, happily steadily increasing as the world goes on, for whom reason is not a dangerous but a useful tool, and who, appreciating to the full all that science has given us, and at the same time the part that the emotional and the irrational play in social development, will mediate for us between the two. Lastly, there is the vast herd which has no more of an instinctive love of morality than it has of beauty, which has lost that emotional, irrational, religious sanction for morality that formerly kept it in order, and which is as innocent of reason as a tabloid newspaper.

It is this last group which forms the crux of the problem. Within any appreciable period of time to expect it to reason like John Dewey is as irrational as to expect it to carve like Phidias or paint like Rembrandt. It will be guided by its desires and emotions. The intellectuals, particularly the younger ones, immensely overestimate the influence of reason and the scientific enlightenment. A thousand years hence, who knows? But we are dealing with the present—the present, when, in spite of science, twenty thousand persons in a day visit the grave of a Catholic priest near Boston to be healed by touching his tomb!

Meanwhile the responsibility rests upon the instinctive moralists and upon all those—scientists, intellectuals, plain people—who have not lost the ability to see life whole. We must not expect the longshoreman, or the bricklayer, to become a John Dewey overnight. That will take time—a jolly good bit of it. A moral law is as essential as the civil law. Such a law, unpopular as the doctrine is, seems to be embedded in the evolutionary process. It is inoperative without sanctions. For the average individual in society those sanctions, for countless generations yet to come, and in spite of high schools, are bound to be emotional. They will be based on heaven and hell, on a belief in God and a future life, on a fervent admiration and whole-hearted following of some adored leader, or on some other emotion—not on reason.

Intellectuals, as well as missionaries, may ruin the civilizations they attempt to make over by narrow views of human nature and by being in too much of a hurry. Changes have got to occur in parts of the moral code, but society cannot

JAMES TRUSLOW ADAMS

abrogate the moral law. It would cease to cohere if every man, in that large field of conduct outside the scope of the civil law, should substitute with infinite variety his personal "I want" for the more universal "I ought."

This may be bad news, but it seems to be the truth.

A good many impulsive and expansive natures object to moral codes on the score that they are repressive, that they consist of "Thou shalt nots." There are two comments to be made on this objection. The first is that negative commands are in general far less limiting than positive ones. Take, for example, the commands to an athlete in training. He must not eat this or drink that. He must refrain from many things if he is to become fit. But these "negations," as our restless moral rebels are so fond of calling them, are less limiting, really less coercing than the positive commands of the trainer. It is less restrictive to be made to abstain from mince pie and a glass of beer than it is to be made to spend hours daily exercising the muscles.

This is equally true in the moral sphere. Consider the much abused Ten Commandments of the Jews. Is there not a much larger sphere of free action left to us by "Thou shalt not steal, or bear false witness, or commit adultery" than by Christ's "Thou shalt love thy neighbour as thyself"?

In the history of the race there have been innumerable moral codes. A code has, of necessity, to be somewhat generalized, but every code of every race has deeply imbedded in it both a sense of the values of life and a realization of the complexity of human nature.

There are innumerable things and acts that have value, many of the simplest and lowest forms of which have value for animals as well as for ourselves—such as warmth, food, shelter, sexual satisfaction, and so on. There are others which come only with the higher organization and civilization of man, such as wealth, social consideration, all the tools provided by ascending degrees of knowledge, intellectual enjoyment, and the satisfaction of the various highly developed emotions in art, love, and morality. As a rule, the free play of man's powers, emotions, and functions gives him satisfaction, whereas the inhibiting of them gives a sense of pain or vague frustration. Life is activity, hence the deep-seated objections to negations.

On the other hand, if self-expression is a good, it also became evident to what we may call "the subconscious wisdom of the race" that it must have limits or it ceases to be a good, both for the individual himself and for his fellows in society. Food is a good; but to express oneself by gorging for days at a time is not good. Up to a certain point, the free expression of the emotions is a good; but if it goes so far as to end in murder, it is not a good. It becomes clear that if we are to get the good out of self-expression, we must introduce somewhere the negations of self-restraint. Limits begin to appear in what would otherwise be an unbounded welter of self-expression. In some cases these limits have to be placed because of the effects of the individual's acts on himself; in other cases, because of the effect they have on other people, man being a social animal.

These limits will vary with different types and planes of civilization. The problem of just where they shall be placed so as to insure the maximum good to the individual and to society, with the minimum pain due to an excess of the "good," is perhaps the most subtle and difficult one facing mankind at all times and in all places. It is obvious, however, that not only must they be set somewhere, but that every individual must, for his happiness and convenience, have some general rough notion, at least, as to the line of demarcation. In the first place, owing to the complexity of human nature and of even the simplest, as we would call them, of savage societies, no individual has either the requisite knowledge or judgment to stake out all these limits for himself, to say nothing of the period of childhood when habits are formed.

How, then, do the limits get placed? As far as we can see, by a gradual development through a long period of trial and error. Little by little they establish themselves as tribal customs and ethical codes.

There is, however, a further problem with which we are already becoming entangled. It is not simply a question of a vast number of goods in life which at certain limits change their character and turn into evils, but of a measuring of the comparative values of these infinitely varied goods. The choice, whether conscious or not, begins in the animal world. A fox can lie in the warm sunshine and go hungry, or bestir himself, make a raid on a farmer five miles off, and have a chicken dinner. He cannot have both goods at once.

For man, the possibilities of choice become almost limitless, not only because of the complexity of his society, but even more because of the complexity of his own nature.

No one can live a satisfactory life who has not established for himself some scale of values. If a man spends a thousand dollars on a week's debauch, he cannot have a car with the same money; if he buys a car, he cannot have a trip to Europe; if he spends it on anything, he cannot have the peace of mind of knowing it is in the bank. The more I consider the restless, discontented, and far from happy life which, in spite of our so-called prosperity, we lead to-day, the more it seems to me that the root of our trouble is in our having, for a while at least, lost our scale of values. We are bewildered by the tremendously increased range of choice among unfamiliar novelties opened to us by the sudden substitution of our modern machine civilization for that which had developed through all preceding ages. Not knowing what is worth most to us, besieged to have everything, we exhaust ourselves in the attempt to choose; and, in spite of colossal effort and colossal possessions, we find life profoundly unsatisfying.

The fact is that the average man of to-day—who has cut himself off from the past, due to a changed material life and the new intellectual atmosphere—is essaying an impossible task.

Given a complex nature and a complex environment, no man can depend solely on his own desires and thought to lead him through life with satisfaction. To an extent that we little dream of, we have to rely upon the accumulated wisdom and experience of those who have gone before us.

Where the range of choice in things and conduct is almost limitless, it is evident that there must be a scale of satisfactions and values or the individual will end in frustration or disaster. Such a scale must be based on a multitude of considerations. It must take into account the whole length of a man's life and not the gratification of the moment. It must consider the abiding satisfaction as well as the intensity to be derived from a good. It must cover all of man's nature in order to understand the effect a satisfaction of one portion of it may have on another. It must know all his nature in order to estimate how a good will develop that nature so as to be able to enjoy other goods, or vice versa.

All of this and more is too much for any one man to work out for himself in tired evenings. Whether we like it or not, we have to accept a great deal from the past. Otherwise we shall wreck ourselves.

I am a deep believer in individualism and have fought elsewhere against merely standardized lives. What I call "the subconscious wisdom of the ages" has itself been built up from the innumerable essays, in this direction and that, of countless individuals in the past. Ethical systems and codes can guide us only in general. Here and there in our lives there are always cropping up individual situations in which we have to decide what our conduct shall be. But to say that the systems can only guide us in general is very different from saying that they can be scrapped *in toto*.

Morality is not an edict. It develops slowly, and from time to time gets itself expressed in systems or codes. These, as I have frequently said, have varied greatly in minor detail, but as mankind rises higher and higher they tend to weld together.

Although they come to us connected with some great personality, they are really the result of slowly accumulating racial wisdoms. Confucius, Buddha, Plato, and Christ would have understood one another perfectly in their ideals. Christ, of course, should not be confused with the Christians any more than Plato with the Platonists. It must be remembered that an ethical system is different from the religious system to which it may or may not be bound. In an age of faith the latter may give powerful support to the former as a sanction, but the two are different. These ethical systems—the outgrowth of racial wisdom—are closely fitted to the needs of the races among which they arise.

The needs of Western European civilization, springing largely from Greece, have been fed by Greek philosophy, the teachings of Christ, and the Roman Stoics. Taken together, these form a great body of ethical doctrine, of which, for the great mass of people, the most appealing is that derived from Christ. *Some* body of such doctrine is essential if we are not to drift into moral anarchy. To say that a great mass of hundreds of millions can dispense with the old ethics and rule themselves according to science is, if I may say so, the sheerest drivel. Whatever may be said of some sciences, those of man and society still have to have their diapers changed every hour or so. To expect the mass of our populations to guide their lives according to the latest pronouncements of a Freud or any single "modern" is to have lost all contact with reason.

Is the old body of ethical doctrine of Western Europe so outworn that it can no longer suffice? I do not think so. Personally, I believe the Stoic rather than the Christian or Platonist doctrine gets me through the tight places in life, though all help at different times. But they all have one thing in common. They all insist upon a scale of values, rising from the basest of the material to the highest of the spiritual, and they all insist on the need of a certain amount of self-sacrifice and self-discipline. Has the need for these things disappeared?

Americans are getting incredibly soft, and the mere multiplicity of goods calls for self-denial. Good things are hard, and the new philosophy and ethics being taught in many quarters can end only in bankruptcy of the spirit. It is hard to learn to play the violin and "a cinch" to turn on the radio; it is so much easier to pay a dollar to watch "the Babe" make a home run than to play baseball yourself. So it goes, and because of this and a lack of moral fibre we are becoming not only one of the most uninteresting, but also one of the most discontented races on the earth, in spite of our wealth.

For a few generations ahead, perhaps, the fear of plague or starvation is lifted from us, but we still have need of self-control and self-discipline—the "Golden Mean" of the Greeks, the ethics of Christ, or the doctrine of the Stoics. We cannot discover everything for ourselves in a year. Things have changed a lot in a short time, but human nature has not so completely changed, and the wisdom of the race will help our own momentary vision. We have been a long time working up to the development of those needs that must find satisfaction in something beyond ourselves—such as truth, beauty, goodness—and it is not all to be undone by a few telephones, a motor car, a radio, and a bathroom much inferior to Cæsar's.

In every direction—economic as well as spiritual—we hear the new doctrine of self-expression versus self-restraint being preached. The apostles of this doctrine are all alike in failing to take into consideration both the whole of a man's life and the whole of his nature. They think only in terms of the moment's gratification. Henry Ford, for example, preaches that we should spend, not save; that "use" not "saving" should govern our relation to raw materials and our own income. Mr. Ford, with his billion dollars, may not have to save, but the workmen whom he throws out of employment ruthlessly whenever it suits his purpose may feel at times that his wisdom may not, after all, be quite as great or as disinterested as the accumulated wisdom of the race expressed in homely saws and ethical doctrines.

Take the interminable subject of the relations between the sexes. Everywhere and at all times we find some sort of family as the unit of society, as the cell in the social body. As the family and the home have developed, they have, it is true, taken varied forms, but those forms have been molded by a long process of adaptation to the whole mentality and culture of the peoples among whom they have arisen. For many thousands of years we Western Europeans have worked toward a home consisting of husband, wife, and children. That there have been innumerable lapses is of course true, just as there have been innumerable bank defalcations and murders.

The satisfactions that this family group has afforded have been quite different from those of mere sexual gratification. As man has risen, not only has love become something different from mere appetite, but a life of devotion to others in a family group brings into play a whole range of emotions and satisfactions that cannot be found emerging from a temporary liaison of passion.

Those who claim that a permanent relation must go in order to permit self-expression without repression, ignore a fundamental point. The man and woman who have a dozen lovers in as many years *are* expressing a certain portion of their nature, but not that portion which would have found expression in an unselfish and devoted married life. They are not getting twelve times the results that they would have got from one mate. They are getting something so different as to have no common measure. Like so many self-constituted guides of to-day, the advocates of such self-expression fail to think clearly and to see life whole. You can take your pick between a Virginia reel of lovers or the building up of a life-long relationship. The results of the two are incommensurable. Which, carried out thoroughly and with earnestness, is likely to show the most enduring satisfaction at all periods of life and to produce a higher type of civilized being?

It is indicative of the shallowness of many of the minds so loudly taking part in the discussion of marriage and the home that they appear to see nothing but the marriage bed and the bank account, and are blind to the whole range of higher and enduring satisfactions that a lifelong union loved through, and in a real sense, fought through, brings or can bring. It is as useless to discuss this range with a person who cannot perceive it as to discuss Beethoven with a person who has no ear for music, but the reality is there.

I do not see how we can deny that there are values in life; or that there is a scale of values; or, again, that the scale rises from the purely physical and material to the spiritual. In spite of the Declaration of Independence, all men are not born equal. They will not all find their satisfactions at the same level of the scale. Most will huddle at the lower level; some will rise higher; a few will rise very high. But this does not disprove the scale or the fact that a man who does rise gains more enduring satisfactions and is a higher type. As for the satisfactions, they are, as I have said, often incommensurable.

For example, take Jay Gould and one of the honest men crushed by his power. The latter may have spent years trying to pay his debts, but we obviously cannot compare the satisfactions of the two men in terms of money. As to which gets the higher satisfaction and is the higher type of men, the accumulated wisdom of our race does not hesitate, just as, without "scientific proof," it does not hesitate to place a Beethoven above an ephemeral composer of "sob stuff"; a Confucius above a Chinese river pirate; a Washington above a war profiteer; a Christ above a Brigham Young; a Marcus Aurelius above a Caligula. Why? Science has absolutely no answer, but there is something in the deeps of our own being as evolved through countless ages up to this year of 1931 that tells us so. A system of ethics that is to bring satisfaction to man has got to take more account of the vague and often unconscious stirrings in these deeps than of the contradictory doctrines of scientific or economic efficiency of the passing moment.

Science is rightly stressing the importance of the subconscious. The tiny spot in our nature illumined by reason is nothing as compared with the vast subterranean reservoir of the deeps of our being. It is a stream flowing on through countless ages, and one of the most fatal mistakes that the present is making is in thinking that we can cut ourselves off from all our roots in the past merely because the outer form of our culture has changed so rapidly in a mechanical age, which may after all prove transient and disastrous. No one of us, however learned—and most of us are not at all so, in spite of a smattering of this and that—can devise for himself a complete philosophy of life and a brand-new code of ethics as he looks about at the infinitely complex environment, at society, at his own consciousness, and tries to penetrate to the dark and mysterious depths.

What, then, are we to do? How are we to try to be good —that is, to live a life in which we shall strive for the deepest, the noblest and most enduring satisfactions, and to try to rise to the highest possibilities of our entire nature? It seems to me the most sensible thing to do is to rest heavily for insight and instruction on those great teachers of the past who summed up in their words the wisdom of the race.

As for the code of conduct to be found in these, it is not, I think, outworn. We must, as I have pointed out, have some such code. Here and there our manners and customs may undergo changes in the course of time in order to adjust themselves to new conditions of environment—especially if the latter continue along their present trend. But taking the deeps as well as the surface of human life into consideration, I believe that the code of morals we already possess (I do not mean distortions of it in bigotry or social convention) still form not only our safest but a *safe* guide for daily conduct, and, if followed, would lead us not only to a better but to a much more satisfying life than most of us have been having or than we are likely to gain by a complete discarding of them for a haphazard experimenting with unrestricted yielding to impulse.

> *Play then and sing; we too have played,*
> *We likewise in that subtle shade.*
> *We too have twisted through our hair*
> *Such tendrils as the wild loves wear. . . .*

> *We too have tracked by star-proof trees*
> *The tempest of the Thyades. . . .*
>
> *But the stars keep their ageless rhyme;*
> *Flowers they can slay that spring thought sweet,*
> *But the stars keep their sublime;*
> *Passions and pleasures can defeat,*
> *Actions and agonies control,*
> *And life and death, but not the soul.*

So Swinburne.

Adrift on a tossing sea of impulse, passion, desire, innumerable goods for choice, we come at last to realize that some body of rules is as necessary if we are to make port as are chart and ephemeris for a navigator. For the navigator to throw these away would be to lose his ship. Some day we may be offered a better and more accurate code of ethics than has been used by us for generations; but who offers such a one now? I do not claim that truth is immutable or that morality is transcendental. I see all too clearly the innumerable maladjustments of the present day, but I also see the complete bankruptcy that must follow, both for the individual and society, from every individual's trying to form his own system, to live with no system, or to follow any or every contemporary voice that calls us to start in a hundred different directions, too many of them toward mere will-o'-the-wisps. If morality is a factor in the cosmic evolution of man at the point we have reached, we cannot attempt to be wholly amoral without serious maladjustment to our environment, which will result in pain and dissatisfaction.

If we are to try to be moral, we must have some code. We cannot form an entirely new one, as I have tried to show. We must, therefore, accept and try to follow the old one, remembering that the whole of human nature must be satisfied, the deeps as well as the temporarily troubled surface. In time, certain specific applications of the code may come to be altered; but in order that the alteration may be wise and satisfying, it will have to be consistent with the spirit of the code. It will have to be based on the recognition of a scale of values rising from the physical and material to the spiritual, and will have to take into consideration the whole span of man's life and the whole extent of his complex nature.

Such an alteration is not likely to come about from the mere fiat of any modernist or scientist. It may come about from the results of innumerable experiments by innumerable individuals over a long period of time, which will gradually be taken up into the body of accumulated racial wisdom. But that is a very different matter from the sudden and wholesale abandonment of the whole code and of the theory of a scale of values.

It may be objected here that all I am doing is appealing to authority, and that such an appeal is no longer of any use; that we have to find out things for ourselves. To that I would answer, first, that we cannot, if we would, find out everything for ourselves in our complex moral life, any more than we can wash all past knowledge away in business or science and start afresh. In the second place, the sort of authority to which I appeal is the same sort to which we appeal in every other department of life.

I do not pay attention to the Ten Commandments just because, according to an old story, they were handed by God to Moses on a mountain top; or to the parable and moral concepts of Christ because they are found in a book called the Bible; or to the doctrines of Marcus Aurelius and the other moral leaders in the past because of any supernatural or unreasonable authority of name or book. The reason we can look toward these figures for guidance is that, in the first place, they synthesized the moral experience of the race up to their own times from one point of view or another; and, in the second, that their writings or sayings have been found to be of immense help in all the centuries since to those of either ordinary or of high mentality who have seriously wished to lead a moral life based on a realization of values in life and conduct.

All this, it seems to me, is quite different from that mere "appeal to authority" against which all of us so instinctively rebel in the intellectual atmosphere of our present age. It is not an appeal to anything supernatural or compulsory. It is an effort to avoid both an anarchic individualism and the impossible task of creating an entirely new system of ethics for oneself. It is merely the same sort of appeal to a recognized body of attested knowledge and wisdom that we would make in any other department of life.

This may all sound very old-fashioned, but man's life itself is very old. The fine skull dug up in China recently was said to be a million years old. A great deal happened to mold our subconsciousness before the psychologists discovered that there was such a thing. If the doctrine of this essay appears old-fashioned, it also appears to me—though I may be prejudiced—a good bit like common sense. It is not going to be easy after cavorting all over the place with no standards, scale of values, or codes, to get down to them again, even if our cavorting has not given us that sense of freedom and that joy of life, year after year, which we had expected.

I can only again quote Plutarch: "Good things are hard." And, somehow, easy things do not seem to give that permanent satisfaction that they assuredly would if we had had a say in making the universe.

We didn't.

XII.
H. L. MENCKEN

"Faith," said the unknown author of the Epistle to the Hebrews, "is the substance of things hoped for, the evidence of things not seen."

The definition, in these later days, seems to be pretty well forgotten, especially by those master forgetters, the Christian theologians, for it is common to hear them discussing (and denouncing) the beliefs of men of science as if they were mere articles of faith. The two things, of course, are quite distinct. Belief is faith in something that is known; faith is belief in something that is not known. In my own credo there are few articles of faith; in fact, I have been quite unable, in ten days and nights of prayer and self-examination, to discover a single one.

What I believe is mainly what has been established by plausible and impartial evidence, *e.g.*, that the square on the hypotenuse of a right triangle is equal to the squares on the other two sides, that water is composed of oxygen and hydrogen, and that man is a close cousin to the ape. Further than that I do not care to go. Is there a life after death, as so many allege, wherein the corruptible puts on incorruption and the mortal immortality? I can only answer that I do not know. My private inclination is to hope that it is not so, but that hope is only a hope, and hopes and beliefs, it seems to me, can have nothing in common. If, while the taxidermists are stuffing my integument for some fortunate museum of anatomy, a celestial catchpole summons my psyche to Heaven, I shall be very gravely disappointed, but (unless my habits of mind change radically at death) I shall accept the command as calmly as possible, and face eternity without repining.

Most of the sorrows of man, I incline to think, are caused by just such repining. Alone among the animals, he is dowered with the capacity to invent imaginary worlds, and he is always making himself unhappy by trying to move into them. Thus he underrates the world in which he actually lives, and so misses most of the fun that is in it. That world, I am convinced, could be materially improved, but even as it stands it is good enough to keep any reasonable man entertained for a lifetime.

As for me, I roll out of my couch every morning with the most agreeable expectations. In the morning paper there is always massive and exhilarating evidence that the human race, despite its ages-long effort to imitate the seraphim, is still doomed to be irrevocably human, and in my morning mail I always get soothing proof that there are men left who are even worse asses than I am.

It may be urged that such satisfactions are lowly; nevertheless, the fact remains that they are satisfactions. Would the tinsel world that idealists pant for be better? Would it be really habitable at all? I am ready to doubt it formally. It would be swept, at best, by chill winds; there would be no warming glow of human folly. There would be no Lindberghs in it, to risk their necks preposterously and charmingly; there would be no Comstocks and Wayne B. Wheelers, no Hoovers

H. L. Mencken

and Coolidges; there would be no poets with their pretty bellyaches; above all, there would be no theologians. And maybe no Americans.

One hears complaint that the existing world is being Americanized, and hence ruined. It may be that my steadfast refusal to join in that complaint is patriotism; if so, make the most of it. Here in these States, if we have accomplished nothing else, we have at least brought down all the more impossible varieties of human aspiration to absurdity, and so made life the more endurable. Alone among the great nations of history we have got rid of religion as a serious scourge—and by the simple process of reducing it to a petty nuisance. Alone again, we have rid ourselves of the worst curses that lie in politics—and by the easy and obvious device of making politics comic.

The Fathers of the Republic, I believe, were far cleverer fellows than they are commonly represented to be, even in the schoolbooks. If it was not divine inspiration that moved them, then they must have drunk better liquor than is now obtainable on earth. For when they made religion a free-for-all, they prepared the way for making it ridiculous; and when they opened the doors of office to the mob, they disposed forever of the delusion that government is a solemn and noble thing, by wisdom out of altruism. The bald facts stand before every eye to-day; it is a joyous and instructive business to contemplate them. And it is even more joyous and instructive to contemplate the sad heavings of those who still refuse to face them, but try to get rid of them by the arts of the prestidigitator and the rhetorician.

When I travel abroad, which is no oftener than I can help it, I am always depressed by the gloom of the so-called intellectuals. My acquaintance among them, in most of the countries of Europe, is somewhat large, and so I can't escape their agonies. Everywhere they fret themselves to death over the problem of government. Everywhere they plan to bring in Utopia by turning this gang out and putting that gang in. Everywhere they believe in wizards and messiahs. It seems to me that we in America—that is, those of us who have become immune to rhetoric—have got beyond that naïveté, and that we are the sounder and happier for it. Reconciling ourselves to the incurable swinishness of government, and to the inevitable stupidity and roguery of its agents, we discover that both stupidity and roguery are bearable—nay, that there is in them a certain assurance against something worse.

The principle is surely not new in the world: everyone ought to know by this time that a mountebank, thinking only of to-morrow's cakes, is far safer with power in his hands than a prophet and martyr, his eyes fixed frantically upon the rewards beyond the grave. So a prudent man prefers Hoover to Stalin or Mussolini, or even to Ramsay MacDonald, a Scotsman and hence a fanatic. No doubt Al Smith would have been better, if only on Burke's theory that politics is at its best when it is most closely adjusted, not to reason, but to human nature. But Hoover is natural enough for all everyday purposes; and where his timidity makes him fall short, his failure is concealed by the glorious labors of such corn-doctors as Borah, Jim Watson, Charlie Curtis, Andy Mellon, and Old Joe Grundy.

Here I do not argue that mountebanks are more admirable than honest men; I merely argue that, in such fields as those of politics and religion—to which, of course, the master-quackery of pedagogy ought to be added—they are socially safer and more useful. The question before us is a practical one: how are we to get through life with a maximum of entertainment and a minimum of pain? I believe that the answer lies, at least in part, in ridding solemn ponderosities of their solemn ponderosity, in putting red noses on all the traditional fee-faw-fo-fums.

That enterprise, by the cunning of the Fathers, we have been able to carry further in the United States than it is carried anywhere else. Do strong men blubber against the outrage of prohibition? Then smell their breaths to see how real their grievance is. Are there protests against the clubs of the police? Then compare a few amiable bumps on the head to a quart of Mussolini's castor oil. Do jobholders consume the substance of the people? Then ask the next Englishman you meet to show you his income tax bill. And are the high places of the land held by trashy and ignoble fellows, bent only upon their own benefit? Then take a look at the scoundrels who constitute the state in France.

I have said that the Fathers, by making religion a free-for-all, reduced it to innocuous absurdity. No doubt many a saddened patriot will enter a caveat to that, thinking of Cardinal O'Connell and his effort to make Boston a Dublin slum, and Bishop Cannon and his bold attempt to run the whole United States. But these rev. gentlemen really prove my case. For after all, Monsignor Cannon, even with both White House and Capitol quaking every time he looks up from the stock ticker, has *not* succeeded in forcing prohibition upon the country: all he has succeeded in doing is to make his whole moral system odious and the theology behind it infamous. Nor has His Eminence of South Boston achieved anything better. When he came into his princely dignity, the church he serves was plainly making progress in America, and there was a steady infiltration of intellectuals into it. But now it is headed in the other direction, and every time he arises to denounce Einstein or to launch his janissaries against a new book, its momentum is accelerated.

In this department I have myself been an eyewitness of a large and salubrious change—and it is a pleasure, from the opposition bench, to offer it as a set-off to all the public skullduggery that the tender-minded complain of. That change has to do with the general American attitude toward ecclesiastical organizations, and especially toward the one that Dr. Cannon adorns. I well remember the uproar that followed a polite allegation I chanced to make, now nearly twenty years ago, that the Methodist Church, at least in the South, was operated by charlatans and manned by ignoramuses. The editor of the paper in which it appeared—his dark, innocent eyes wet with tears—stared at me as if I had denounced female chastity or advocated cannibalism. His office was overrun for weeks by prancing pastors, threatening him with disaster. They met in conclave and passed resolutions against him and me; some of them, with their fingers carefully crossed, prayed publicly for my salvation.

Fortunately, they also challenged my facts, and under the pretense of meeting that challenge it was possible for me to renew and reiterate my allegation. But it went down very badly, and for a long while I was under the displeasure of so-called fair men for raising a religious rumpus, and for failing in that respect which, so it appeared, was due to all bodies of believers. Even when, five or six years later, the Anti-Saloon League began running its trails of corruption across the country, and I ventured to point out the patent fact that it was the offspring of Methodism and as anti-social as its parent—even then such charges were generally felt to be somewhat advanced. So again when the Ku Klux emerged from the swamps and began trying to put down civilization. The first article in which I spoke of it as no more than the secular arm of the Methodist-Baptist Inquisition was badly received, and I was widely advised to confine myself to constructive criticism.

This advice made some impression on me: I became, in fact, more or less constructive. But meanwhile Bishop Cannon and his friends went into politics full tilt, brandishing clubs and howling for blood, and before long what had once seemed scandalous became only too self-evident. The Southern editors, for a time, had very hard sledding; they had to discuss politics without mentioning the principal current politicians. But that was soon a sheer impossibility, even to publicists so subtle, and presently they were ventilating the facts with candor, and politics in their dismal section became realistic again, and very lively. To-day they all belabor the Methodist Crokers and Charlie Murphys in a hearty and open manner, and have their say about the whole evangelical camorra in precisely the same terms they use against the Italian Black Hand, the Vice Trust, and the American Civil Liberties Union.

Nor is this new frankness confined to the South. The last presidential campaign brought the subject of evangelical theology into open discussion everywhere, and the result, as I see it, is a great increase in public pleasure, and, to some extent at least, in public enlightenment. With all the old taboos got rid of, that theology is being revealed as what it actually is—a decadent form of Puritanism, preposterous in its ideology and brutal and dishonest in its practices. If the hinds of the farms and villages still cling to it, then certainly it is fast losing its hold upon all the ranks above them. To confess to a belief in it to-day is to confess not only to stupidity, but also to a kind of malignancy—a delight in opposing decent ideas and harrowing honest men.

For that change, so swift and so sanitary, we have to thank Bishop Cannon and his colleagues of the Anti-Saloon League, the Ku Klux Klan, and the Methodist Board of Temperance, Prohibition, and Public Morals. They have gained (at least transiently) a formidable power over politicians even worse than they are, but they have wrecked their church. They have won a battle and lost a war.

The wrecking of such churches as these, whether they be spiritual or secular, seems to me to be an excellent gauge of the progress of civilization. For men become civilized, not in proportion to their willingness to believe, but in proportion to their readiness to doubt. The more stupid the man, the larger his stock of adamantine assurances, the heavier his load of faith.

There is a darky living in the alley behind my house who knows a great deal more than I do, and is far more positive and confident in his kind of knowledge than I am in mine. He knows that he will be snow-white in the life beyond the grave, and that the Twelve Apostles will be very polite to him. He knows that a rabbit-foot carried in his pocket will protect him against thieves, warts, and the police. He knows that the fall of the die may be conditioned by verbal formulas, mainly theological in character. He knows that meeting a black cat on a dark night is comparable, practically speaking, to meeting a locomotive head-on. He knows precisely why the stars were hung in the sky, and how they are kept there, and what their influence is upon the destiny of man. He knows what Moses said to Abraham, and what Abraham said to Pontius Pilate. He is the proprietor of a perfect epistemology, and his cosmogony, pathology, and political science are neat, well-rounded, and completely sufficient for his standards of judgment. To find his match as a wiseacre one must resort to the Rev. Billy Sunday, to Arthur Brisbane, or to the Pope.

Nevertheless, I am iconoclast enough to doubt his whole

stock of wisdom, as I doubt, indeed, that of his three colleagues in omniscience. His certainty that cancer is caused by incantations seems to me to be somehow dubious. I prefer to believe that no one knows what causes it, and to reckon that belief a kind of knowledge.

The common view of science is that it is a sort of machine for increasing the race's store of dependable facts. It is that only in part; in even larger part it is a machine for upsetting *un*dependable facts. When Copernicus proved that the earth revolved around the sun, he did not simply prove that the earth revolved around the sun; he also proved that the so-called revelation of God, as contained in the Old Testament, was rubbish. The first fact was relatively trivial: it made no difference to the average man then, as it makes no difference to him to-day. But the second fact was of stupendous importance, for it disposed at one stroke of a mass of bogus facts that had been choking the intelligence and retarding the progress of humanity for a millennium and a half.

So with every other great discovery in the physical world: it had immediate repercussions in the world of ideas, and often they were far more important than its immediate effect. The long line of glorious workers in medicine are not to be regarded merely as cheaters of the grave, for the grave, in the long run, has cheated every one of them in turn; their service to man was that they dissuaded him from laying vain blames for his ills and making vain and ignominious appeals for aid against them, and set him to examining them, and himself with them, in a rational and self-respecting manner. That medicine saves to-day thousands who must have died yesterday is a fact of small significance, for most of them will leave no more marks upon the history of the race than so many June bugs; but that all of us have been persuaded thereby to turn from priests and magicians when we are ill to doctors and nurses—that is a fact of massive and permanent importance. It benefits everybody worthy of being called human at all. It rids the thinking of mankind of immense accumulations of intellectual garbage. It increases the dignity of every honest man and it diminishes the puissance of every fraud.

To believe in frauds, it seems to me, is incompatible with any sort of dignity. It may be held, by the sorry standards which prevail in certain quarters, to be virtuous, but it is plainly not dignified. Is it a fact that the authors of the New Testament were inspired by God, and compiled a record that is innocent of error? It is not a fact. They were ignorant and credulous men, and they put together a narrative that is as discordant and preposterous, at least in material parts, as the testimony of six darkies in a police court. Is it a fact that believing that narrative is an act of merit, and that its reward is deliverance from Hell and entrance upon an eternity of bliss? It is not a fact. More, it is not even an innocent fiction. For its necessary implication is that the test of a proposition is something unrelated to its truth—that lying is virtuous so long as it brings a reward.

There, it seems to me, pragmatism is run to earth at last and turns out to be, not a lion, but only a fox. I can imagine no self-respecting man haggling for advantage on any such terms. It involves not only a repudiation of every rational criterion of truth; it also involves a repudiation of every sort of decency. Whenever such an idea is unhorsed in the world, the integrity of man increases.

The supply, unluckily, still remains very large. Its reservoir is the mob, uneducable and irrational, and along the banks of that reservoir many enterprising frauds—theological, political, and philosophical—find profitable fishing. There are impatient men who long to heave the whole company overboard at one swoop: they are the fashioners of Utopias. But human progress, of course, can never be so facile. It must be carried on, not with the cosmic engines of gods, but with the puny machinery at hand; and that machinery, as everyone knows, is always breaking down.

The Fathers of the Republic, despite the sagacity that I have been praising, were a bit too confident and impatient. I suppose they believed that by setting religion adrift they had got rid of it, but all they had really done was to make it ready for self-wrecking years after their day was done. Again and even worse, they bent their hardest endeavors to setting up a government of the most sagacious, the most honorable, the most fit—but all they actually achieved was to let in the least fit, and a century and a half afterward we are still struggling to get rid of the Hardings, Coolidges, and Hoovers.

Things would move faster if there were a general agreement as to the goal, but that is too much to hope for. There are men in the world, and some of them not unintelligent men, who have a natural appetite for the untrue, just as there are others who have a natural appetite for the ugly. A bald fact somehow affrights them: they long to swathe it in comforting illusions. Thus one hears from them that it is somehow immoral for an artist to depict human life as it actually is: the spectacle of the real must be ameliorated by an evocation of the ideal, which is to say, of the *unreal*. So Thomas Hardy becomes a bad artist, and the author of *Pollyanna* a good one.

One hears again, and from the same men, that religious faith is a valuable thing *per se,* even if it be faith in propositions revolting to the most elementary intelligence. And one hears that it is an evil business to dwell upon the gross and intolerable failures of democracy, lest the general belief in democracy itself be converted into doubt. The facts, it appears, are nothing; the important thing is to retain a hopeful and pleasant frame of mind. The most valuable philosopher is that one who conjures up glittering universes in which two and two make five, six, or even ten; the most despicable is the fellow who keeps on insisting that they make only four.

Of such sort are the reconcilers of science and religion, the more naïve variety of Liberals in politics, and the various disciples of Hamilton Wright Mabie and Edward W. Bok in the arts. I daresay the first-named were an active and expectant party in the day of Copernicus; if so, they must have given a great deal less comfort to Copernicus than to Pope Paul III. They continue energetically to-day, proving that Genesis and the Darwinian hypothesis are not in conflict, that curved space is still reconcilable with the Book of Revelation, and that, in any case, it is better to go to church on Sunday than to stay away.

The tragedy of such men is that, in the long run, they are bound to find that they are holding empty bags. The Popes, soon or late, always go over to Copernicus, as Dr. Andrew D. White once proved in two noble tomes. The truth, battered and torn, yet survives all the pretty nothings that beset it. Out of the welter of hopes and fears, of cautions and evasions, there always arises in the end the gaunt, immovable figure of a solid fact.

Certainly the Liberals in our midst should have learned long ago how dangerous it is to tackle such facts with no better weapons than hosannas. Is it so soon forgotten that they once believed in Roosevelt? And then in Wilson? And then in the War to End War? And then in a long series of other impostures, ranging from the initiative and referendum to the direct primary, and from woman suffrage to prohibition? There is more here than mere innocence; there is also, it seems to me, a downright libido for the improbable, a thirst to believe what can scarcely be imagined as true.

Certainly something of the sort must be sought in the current Liberal crush upon Holmes, J., an upright judge but no more fit to be a hero of Liberals than his predecessor in their adoration, the limber Borah. I have been vastly diverted of late by reading the volume of Dr. Holmes's dissenting opinions, so conveniently arranged by Mr. Alfred Lief. It shows that his juridic theory, taking it by and large, is hardly to be distinguished from that of the late Mr. Chief Justice Taft, and that not a few of his dissenting opinions have been launched against a more liberal majority! Yet the Liberals, with their craving for unrealities, continue to hail him as one of them, and when disillusionment overtakes them at last, as overtake them it must, they will no doubt turn to some even more impossible hero—maybe even to Mr. Chief Justice Hughes or Old Joe Grundy.

Such is the will to believe. Holding it to be a great nuisance in the world, and worse even than the will to power, I try to keep myself as free of it as I can. On gloomy days I speculate as to the probable state of modern man if it had ever been universal. We'd still be following Pope Paul; nay, not the Pope of that name but the Saint, with his cocksure ignorance and his Little Bethel moral scheme. Perhaps we'd be even further back than that—among the sheiks of the Palestine plateau and the primitive shamans of the Central Asian wilderness. It seems to me that such prophets as Dr. Robert A. Millikan, when they flirt gravely with the rev. clergy, ask us to go back almost that far.

Are the clergy true teachers or false? Is the body of ideas that they merchant true or not true? If it is not true, then I can imagine no prudent and profitable traffic with them. They have a right, of course, to be heard, but they have no more right to be attended to than the astrologers and necromancers who were once their colleagues and rivals.

There is only one man who has a right to be attended to, and that is the man who is trying, patiently, fairly, earnestly, diligently, to find out the truth. I am willing to give him my ear at any time of the day or night, year in and year out. But I am not willing to listen to the man who argues that what might be or ought to be true is somehow superior to what *is* true. One Copernicus, it seems to me, is worth all the Popes who ever lived, and all the bishops and archbishops, and all save a baker's dozen of the holy saints.

The title of this article is far too wide. No man, within the space allotted me, could make anything approaching a complete or even a fair statement of his credo. I must content myself, after the foregoing prolegomenon, with a few random notes.

I believe that religion, generally speaking, has been a curse to mankind—that its modest and greatly overestimated services on the ethical side have been more than overborne by the damage it has done to clear and honest thinking.

I believe that no discovery of fact, however trivial, can be wholly useless to the race, and that no trumpeting of falsehood, however virtuous in intent, can be anything but vicious.

I believe that all government is evil, in that all government must necessarily make war upon liberty; and that the democratic form is at least as bad as any of the other forms.

I believe that an artist, fashioning his imaginary worlds out of his own agony and ecstasy, is a benefactor to all of us, but that the worst error we can commit is to mistake his imaginary worlds for the real one.

I believe that the evidence for immortality is no better than the evidence for witches, and deserves no more respect.

I believe in complete freedom of thought and speech, alike for the humblest man and the mightiest, and in the utmost freedom of conduct that is consistent with living in organized society.

I believe in the capacity of man to conquer his world, and to find out what it is made of, and how it is run.

I believe in the reality of progress.

I—

But the whole thing, after all, may be put very simply. I believe that it is better to tell the truth than to lie. I believe that it is better to be free than to be a slave. And I believe that it is better to know than to be ignorant.

XIII.

JULIA PETERKIN

It is not easy to discover within myself my credo, much less to put into words exactly what I believe concerning nature, or man, or the universe—for the simple reason that my old hopes and many of those pleasant faiths which became a part of my childhood persistently interfere whenever I try to make them stand aside or give place to my naked beliefs. And since my beliefs seem bent on hiding their starkness behind these gentler and more comforting things, it is no easy task to seize them and drag them out into the open. My reason has to make the utmost effort to force them to stand up calmly before me long enough to be seen and then to be adequately expressed.

My span of years up to now has been divided into two distinct halves so far as my beliefs are concerned. During the first half I was taught many most interesting things from the lips of those in whom I had complete trust. Along with the proprieties I was taught to believe that for me to become cultured and cultivated was the end and aim of my life, provided I could be good enough to merit eternal happiness in the life to come. My welfare in the next world was presented to me as a thing of enormous importance. I was convinced that even though I should succeed in gaining this whole world and yet lived so that I lost my soul in the next world, my whole existence would be far worse than futile. I was taught not only to pray but to believe that my prayers could avail much for me, and never to doubt that my happiness on earth and my eternal happiness beyond life depended chiefly on my accepting a multitude of things which I could in no way understand.

I dared not question the things which experts in beliefs and faiths had decided upon. I knew I had many blessings. I was protected from discomfort and ugliness and fear. My days were pleasant. I had no reason to complain of the scheme of which I was a living part, yet I knew that the members of my family who were doctors of medicine were far more interested in combating ills of the body than in the salvation of souls. Discussions which concerned health and disease often took place in my home, yet these discussions were always hushed when I began to listen, for I was a girl child, and girl children were thought to be better off when kept ignorant of certain matters which men—certainly men who were doctors—must inevitably know. I was encouraged to turn my attention toward more graceful interests, such as music or pictures or literature. Ignorance concerning the fundamental facts of life was believed to be better for me than knowledge.

When my brother became a doctor, he often worked in the laboratory with a microscope and glass slides which held him entranced for hours. He was patient with my interruptions and generous enough to show me the difference between the rods and crescents which were patterns of malaria, and the delicate silken threads which were those of tuberculosis, until finally to recognize germs became for me a fascinating game.

JULIA PETERKIN

I shall never forget my thrill of excitement when I gazed through that microscope at a section of a cat's tongue which was cancerous. To me the word *cancer* was surely the most terrible word in the world—a word which was even more mysterious and deadly than *hell*.

One day a friend was extremely ill, and in my distress I followed my brother to the laboratory to ask what he thought about the probable outcome of that illness. He was busy with glass slides and the microscope and did not notice me until with an exclamation he said: "Here they are. Would you like to see them?" I looked and saw on the glass slide pairs of tiny black specks not very different from fly-specks. They were pneumonia germs, and before many days passed the relatives of those germs destroyed the life of my friend. Medical skill could not save him. Prayers did no good. Tears helped nothing. He was dead.

Then a faint suspicion rose in my heart that to the Creator those pneumonia germs were of as much account as the life of the human creature who had perished, and that he as an individual was gone forever, the same as the germs on that glass slide. My whole structure of faiths and beliefs crashed into a confused heap. Those specks which my eyes had seen through a microscope swept away all that I had been taught of theology. Even when a minister stood over the open grave into which all that was left of my friend was lowered and read the beautiful and solemn words, "O death, where is thy sting? O grave, where is thy victory?" they failed to drive from my mind certain cold, hard facts which stood clearly before me.

I resolved to find out as much of truth as I could, and, if possible, to be strong enough not to be crushed by it. My values had shifted and the second half of my life began.

When I came to this plantation to live, my whole physical

world changed completely. My home was no longer in a town made up of paved streets and comfortable houses in neat rows, but was among wide fields which had for years been cleared from the forests. Here everyone was black except the few members of my own household. The current speech was different, the conventions were new and strange. Few of my old rules of living applied.

But although life here was utterly different from the life I had known, I soon discovered that its current was just as strong and that it took no pains to conceal the facts of birth or love or death. People who could not read or write, who were utterly unacquainted with books, whose only use for newspapers was to paste them over the cracks in the cabin walls to hinder the wind as it whistled through, seemed to live quite happily in spite of what I regarded as their ignorance and immorality. They had never heard of germs, and many of them prayed to the sun.

Hester is an old black woman who has been very kind to me, and one afternoon when I found her facing the west and going through the ceremony of her evening prayer to the setting sun, I watched and listened. I went into her cabin, but she did not pause, for the mistress of the plantation was to her as nothing before the sun—the master of the whole world.

I asked her many questions and she gave me very simple answers. She said that if the sun were to hide his face for the span of one short moon's shining, the whole world would grow cold and dark and the life upon it would die; yet perhaps if all the life in the whole world were dead and the sun should shine out again, its warmth and light could make life stir, so that trees and grass and beasts and birds and even men themselves might be born. That was why she prayed to the sun and thanked him every day for life. It sounded reasonable, and to this day I believe with Hester that the sun is the source of life in the world. I differ with her in the matter of praying to him, for I prefer to seek his sunshine instead.

In the matter of free will I also agree with Hester, although it humbles me greatly to think that I cannot make my own choices and have some little power over my own destiny. Hester laughs and points to the smoke which rises out of her cabin chimney and says that if the smoke could talk and I asked it why it climbs always upward and not downward, it would say, "I choose to climb upward and that is why I go up out of the chimney."

Hester says that smoke is born to be smoke and no praying or fasting or trying could ever make it become anything but smoke. In the same way men are men, trees are trees, all things are what they are. And they may as well be willing to stay what they are.

Hester knows the importance of heredity and she carefully saves the seed of her strongest plants for new planting and keeps the eggs of her best fowls for hatching. Since, like Hester, I believe that heredity is a law, I cannot think that strong children are born from weak parents, or good children from bad parents, any more than I can think that fields planted with seed from frail plants will yield good crops. Good bird dogs do not result from the breeding of poor-nosed or gun-shy sires and dams. Nor do children born of feeble, foolish, unhealthy parents become changed into strong, wise, sound children by medical means, education, moral training, or environment. No power has so far been found that can put brains into empty heads or that can make natural weakness into strength.

Men are born to be what they are as surely as automobiles are modeled into different types. If a car is a Rolls-Royce to start with, it must stay a Rolls-Royce for the rest of its existence. It may suffer from lack of proper care, lack of lubrication, be covered with mud, be broken and battered by misfortunes, but it remains a Rolls-Royce. If a car is made a Whippet, then a Whippet it is for the rest of its span of years. No amount of polishing or repainting or oiling can ever change it into a Rolls-Royce, although certainly it may prove a far more useful machine than an ill-cared-for, battered Rolls-Royce could ever be.

I do not believe that the care and pity given by the strong to the weak have helped civilization. If democracy gives morons and defectives an equal economic, political, social, and biological opportunity with better human beings, this fact alone is bound to make democracy destructive sooner or later, for heredity counts in men just as it counts in animals and trees and grass.

Men who succeed usually attribute their success to some special cause, such as hard work—some peculiar necessity or inspiration. They fail to mention where they came by that energy which drives them on, that will to power which they have inherited. Ancestor worship is not an ill-placed religion. Men are what they are by the law that controls the cells of germ reproduction, and not by weight of prayer or education.

And so heredity is a law of life, whether it deals with Presidents or asparagus, setter dogs or princes, and the chromosomes in those germ cells, which in time become adult human beings, inevitably behave according to a law which is as fixed as the law which governs the precision of solar systems; a law which can be influenced no more by hope, or sentiment, or prayer than by the charm worn on a string around the neck of a Gullah Negro.

I have no convictions whatever concerning the origin of the physical universe, and no idea at all how these stable, persistent, law-abiding cells which compose me and other living creatures became endowed with their burden of life. The whole process of creation, the entire creation of the inanimate and animate world, may be merely the outcome of mechanical force and action. I do not know. There is no way for me to find out. It does not seem to matter. It must be none of my affair or I'd be less helpless about my ignorance of the matter. At present my mind is certainly not disturbed over my ignorance. There are too many other interesting things about which I can satisfy my curiosity in some measure, and my days are too full of them to waste one minute over what the wisest of men have not yet discovered. But whatever the source of the universe is, I am sure it has come about through fixed laws.

I have no objection to the notion that matter is the parent of life and mind, or to the theory that electrons and electricity, life and mind, are all manifestations of one universal energy with its origin in the sun.

I cannot think that the beginning of life was an accident or a fortuitous event which occurred some millions of years ago. It is a phenomenon that repeats itself every day. Life creates. As it was in the beginning, is now and ever shall be, world without end, amen. And life does not represent the entrance of a new form of energy into the universe, or a new series of laws, but is a step in the same old evolutionary process resulting from an energy which is limitless and ordered.

Many names have been given to this energy—God, Allah, Zeus, Jupiter, Jehovah, according to the group which has applied the name. None of these names offends me. It is enough to know that I am alive, and that my life, which has already lasted for a good span of years, has existed in an unbroken line from the uttermost depths of the eternity which is behind me. To know that generation after generation the force which animates me has been passed on and on, its form influenced and shifted and changed by every environment it has touched and by countless other causes I can never know or understand.

I feel quite satisfied simply to possess within my individual body this curious spark which has come to me through so many experiences, to accept it and the inheritance which it has accumulated from every forbear behind me. I firmly believe that my only obligation to myself and to society, and to the Great First Cause, whatever that may be, is to be myself as fully and completely and perfectly as I possibly can manage to be. I do feel a certain dignity in the fact that I am alive, while myriads of forms, less able to meet and adapt themselves to circumstances than my ancestors and I have been, have perished from the earth; for my being alive proves that I came from stock with a strong will to live and the hardiness to persist in living and in reproducing its kind. This is no mean inheritance, and even if my forbears made only a poor, groping, uncertain struggle to preserve the life within them, they succeeded, all of them, for a time. So here I am along with the rest of their progeny, and all other progeny; for what is true of me is also true of every living creature.

I regret that the strange urge which takes the form of ambition thwarts so many intelligent men, so many great nations; that legislators and rulers become pitifully confused and enact such a multitude of laws to be kept that no normal person can ever become acquainted with them, much less understand and heed them, instead of turning their talents and energies to discovering those laws which have existed since the beginning. Yet such faith have I in the adaptability of all things which have life that I believe a sheer will to live and to possess certain qualities can, by a patient and persistent determination, fill needs, as the eyeless creatures have developed organs of sight, the legless become runners, and the wingless fliers. All necessary qualities and traits will be achieved as life sees they are needed.

I rejoice that we have achieved in some measure a certain amount of freedom in speech and expression of thought and that the power of ignoramuses, who would like to throttle us for putting our convictions and beliefs into words, grows less and less. We surely must realize the importance of our right to say what seems to us to be the truth without fear of molestation. Not because what we say matters to anyone but ourselves, but because when we fail to speak what we do believe is true—or substitute for what we think is true, words which we think are not true—then inevitably we lose whatever perception of truth we may have achieved. And surely a persistent will to discover the truth is our only means of ever finding out any particle of what it is.

My most comforting faith is that everything in the universe exists under law. Inanimate things, the same as we who try to reason, have their rules of being and abide by them faithfully. Stars and dew, birds and blades of grass, men and clods of earth have to fulfill their destinies.

The drops of water in the slimiest mud puddle know when the temperature reaches the freezing point; and without the slightest hesitancy, but with the most powerful insistence, they step up into ice crystals which are as lovely and perfect as the purest flakes of snow.

Hester is right. All things in the universe are under marching orders. Law is, and we must abide by it. Certainly it is not possible for me to guess why the sun became what it is, or how it cast the earth off from itself, or how the first spark of that energy which we call *life* contrived to clothe itself with a body. I do not know how life came under that necessity which keeps it creating and re-creating, adapting itself to environments, passing on old traits, multiplying into new forms. It is enough for me to believe that life does all this and to feel that the time allotted me for walking in the sunshine is a great experience.

I rejoice that I am under the same laws that regulate my neighbors—Hester, as well as those other neighbors, the worms and the gnats, and the mules which plow the fields. It comforts me to know that nothing is too small or humble to be left outside the charmed circle, and to believe that the smoke rings which float casually out from a burning cigarette are as much a part of the great universe as the rings of Saturn.

XIV.
LEWIS MUMFORD

BETWEEN one's conscious philosophy and the faith that one lives by there is a greater or smaller gap, as the first becomes more deeply integrated with one's nature, and as the second rises to completer expression. In a harmonious life, the intellectual formula and the inner impetus would be one; but such harmony is far to seek. There are professed Christians, perhaps honest in their intellectual convictions, who have never had a single natural impulse to live in charity and peace. In *Androcles and the Lion,* Bernard Shaw confronted one of these creatures with the temptation to exercise his physical strength in combat and overthrew in a moment all his dearly prized beliefs: the powerful Ferrovius had a conscious philosophy which neither emerged from nor properly disciplined the man that he was; the discrepancy was too great, the points of contact too infrequent. The result of holding such a system is either perpetual conflict or perpetual hypocrisy.

Within the norms of society, every man must find his own living philosophy. This is more than the sum of one's beliefs, judgments, standards, axioms, put together in an orderly system: it is rather a resolution of one's abstract plan of living with the circumstances and emergencies of actual existence. An adequate philosophy ought to bring together one's scheme of living, one's conscious reflections, and the inner go of the self. While it faces the evils of existence, it should recognize and consciously multiply the goods. What are these goods? Where are they to be found, and how are they to be embodied?

Most of the ethical philosophies of the past have sought to isolate the goods of life and to make one or another of them supreme: they have looked upon pleasure or efficiency or duty or sacrifice or imperturbability or self-annihilation or decorum as the chief end of a disciplined and cultivated spirit. Since no one goes through the world unhurt, and since violence and injustice have often had the upper hand, they have sometimes sought by a system of supernatural bookkeeping to redress the evils of earthly existence in another sphere; but to seek pleasure or immortality or happiness has been the common goal of these faiths—if not now, then hereafter.

There is no sanction in my philosophy for any single set of ends or goals. The fact that sunshine is beneficial to the body does not make the Sahara an ideal place to live in; and no single principle will produce an harmonious and well-balanced life. Values emerge from life at all its levels: there is virtue, as Plato saw, in the good shoemaker, quite as much as there is in the philosophic guardians of the Republic; and just as a well-organized state would destroy the foundations of its existence if all its members became philosophers, which is very much what happened in our American Brook Farm experiment, so no particular function or good can gather exhaustively to itself all the possibilities of existence. To despise the animal basis of life, to seek value only at the level of conscious intelligence and rational effort, is ultimately to lose one's sense of cosmic relationships; and without this sense a noble consciousness of human destiny, higher and wider than any merely human institution, has never arisen.

Instead of framing our philosophy around an abstract end, and reproaching the universe because it appears indifferent to the particular goal we have erected, it would be wiser to begin with the nature of life itself, and to observe at what point one good or another does in fact emerge from it.

One knows life, not as a fact in the raw, but only as one is born into human society and uses the tools and instruments society has developed through history: words, symbols, grammar, logic, science, art. One finds oneself within a human world of values; and only as a result of persistent inquiry and experiment does one reach such a useful concept as that of a physical universe, considered as self-existent and apart from these values. Logically, one may begin with an abstract system of space-time relations, or with the conception of a lifeless physical universe of matter in motion, and one may build up a succession of steps culminating in human consciousness and value; but in actuality, it is with the complete tissue of experience that one begins, and only by steadily sloughing off personality, myth, human relevance can one descend to a universe from which one has voluntarily abstracted oneself.

This orientation is important. If it is correct, values are not accidental to experience, nor are they merely ornaments added to the brutal body of existence, as in a bad piece of architecture, without affecting either the function or the design: values are, on the contrary, present from the beginning, and they exercise a determining influence over every stage of life and thought.

If the physical universe does not, as a separate concept,

imply life and value, it is nevertheless true that human value implies the physical universe: hence the preoccupation with the stars and with cosmic destiny that pervades almost every religion, even that austere and attenuated form associated with modern positive science. The vague stir within us, which we associate with the beat of our hearts and the expansion of our lungs, requires for sustenance a whole solar system, merely to maintain such elementary relations as the heat of our blood. Similarly, the crudest social existence implies the effort of untold generations of men to differentiate foods from poisons, invent tools, devise shelters, create symbols, signs, and gestures, and build up a body of communicable experience.

Individualism in the sense of isolation is merely a spatial illusion. The more self-sufficient an individual seems to be, the more sure it is that, like Thoreau at Walden Pond, he carries a whole society in his bosom. This fact applies equally to nations. Both physically and spiritually we are members one of another; and we have never been anything else, although the callosities of ignorance and egotism have sometimes made us insensitive to this condition. This sense of cosmic interdependence is both one's ultimate intuition about the universe, and the most direct key to its practical activities: for the cosmic sense probably grew originally out of the realities of social life itself, the oneness of the tribe, of parent and child, of husband and wife. Without this sense, man is a defiant atom, awaiting annihilation—a cruel joke in a mirthless world.

Life begins then with a tissue of inherited values. Only by hard effort and experiment does one reach the matter-of-fact plane: indeed, the sense of a neutral world, untouched by man's efforts, indifferent to his activities, obdurate to wish and supplication, is one of the supreme triumphs of his imagination, and in itself represents a fresh human value.

Thought, social relations, biological activities, cosmic backgrounds—all call for a system of manifold coöperations, and the finer life becomes, the more complicated is this network, and the more highly conscious must one become of one's relations within it. Goethe once put the case admirably in a conversation with Eckermann: "People are always talking about originality; but what do they mean? As soon as we are born, the world begins to work upon us, and keeps on to the end. What can we call ours, except energy, strength, will? If I could give an account of what I owe to great predecessors and contemporaries, there would be but a small remainder." The person who fancies he has made his own career, or the inventor who believes he has the sole right to his invention, or the philosopher who announces a completely new system of thought, is merely ignorant of his sources. Darwin formulated his Origin of Species with the sense of having made a unique personal discovery; before he was finished the similar hypothesis of another young naturalist, Wallace, was brought to his attention; by the time he published his second edition, he had at last become aware that a whole literature on evolution had preceded his announcement. The individual contribution, the work of any single generation, is infinitesimal: the power and glory belong to human society at large, and are the long result of time.

This is the philosophic justification for communism. Since it coincides with the practical reason for communism—namely, that every human being requires approximately the same share of air, water, clothing, food, shelter, and the prevailing material culture, with small differences to allow for climate and occupation—the political institutions of society should be arranged to establish this minimum basis of life. Differentiation and preference and special incentive should be taken into account only after the security and continuity of life itself is assured. This is my fundamental political faith: it corresponds roughly to Plato's. Necessarily, the task of organizing a basic communism is not an easy one, particularly in an industrial world where so many steps intervene between the land and the raw resources of nature and the ultimate products that must be made available. While special societies like monasteries and armies have often achieved a rough measure of communism, the real difficulty is to apply the method to the community at large and still preserve those delicate volitions and intense individual interests which are an incentive to creative activity.

One of the first moves in this direction is to alter by example and education the current scheme of values. In our present Western societies, with the exception of Soviet Russia, pecuniary prestige and property interests come first; life, and the values derived from actual living, exist on sufferance, or are scourged out of existence. Love, art, poetry, disinterested thought, the free use of the imagination, the pursuit of non-utilitarian activities and the enjoyment of non-consumable goods—all these things do not come within the dominant pecuniary scale of values, and are falsified and belittled by any such association. Yet a life that does not enter into their realm is a life that has never fully come to flower: the means and instruments of daily activity, which are sanctified by the existence of these deeper values, are bereft of even their proper significance by being condemned to serve as substitutes for the whole.

While a basic economic communism, which would extend to the whole community the decent practices of the household, seems to me a necessary measure of justice and practical statesmanship, one need not therefore hold, with an older school of revolutionary thinkers, that the evils of life are entirely the work of an ominous capitalist class, or that they are entirely economic in origin and would be abolished under a more humane régime.

On the contrary, I have no more notion of abolishing evil than I have of abolishing shadow in a world of light. Fourier's belief that the ocean itself under a harmonized social order might turn into lemonade, and Spencer's picture of the future society as a sort of polite eternal Sunday afternoon, are merely exhibitions, as it were, of an unfathomable shallowness. Evil and good are phases in the process of growth; and who shall say which is the better teacher? Illness, error, defeat, frustration, disintegration, malicious accident, all these elements are as much in the process of life as waste, nutrition, and repair. The very forces which, if triumphant, would destroy life are needful to season experience and deepen understanding. The virtuous man aims, not at the abstract condition of goodness, but at a life abundant: his success lies, not in escaping evil, as the Brahmin avoids taking life by having even the insects swept out of his path, but by turning it to the account of the vital process itself.

Observing the rôle of evil, the great religions of the past have celebrated almost solely the negative aspects of existence: they have confronted death and extinction in all their forms, and have been concerned above all with the relief of the ailing and the release of the transgressor. In reaction against the superstitious element in these religions, one must not commit the opposite error of ignoring the function of evil in the vital economy. The goods of life have large capacities for mischief: who has not observed the charity that poisons the giver, and the brotherhood that is based upon hatred of the outsider? In fact, nothing needs such constant watching and revision as the practice of the virtues: before one realizes it, as Emerson pointed out in Uriel, goods become evils. But similarly, the evils of life have a large capacity for good; and the mature person knows that they must be faced, embraced, assimilated; that to shun them or innocently hope to eliminate them altogether is to cling to an existence that is both false to reality and essentially lacking in perspective and depth. Like arsenic, evil is a tonic in grains and a poison in ounces. The real problem of evil, the problem that justifies every assault upon war and poverty and disease, is to reduce it to amounts that can be spiritually assimilated.

This doctrine is just the opposite of certain "optimistic" life-denying attitudes and habits of mind that have become popular during the last three centuries: particularly, the notion that comfort, safety, the absence of physical disease are the greatest blessings of civilization, and that as they increase evil will be automatically abolished. The fallacy of this view lies in the fact that comfort and safety are not absolute qualities, but are capable of defeating life quite as thoroughly as hardship and disease and uncertainty; and the notion that every other human interest, religion, art, friendship, love, must be subordinated to the production of increasing amounts of comforts and luxuries is merely one of the dark superstitions of our money-bent utilitarian society. By accepting this superstition as an essential modern creed, the utilitarian has turned an elementary condition of existence, the necessity for providing for the physical basis of life, into an end. Avaricious of power and riches and goods, he has summoned to his aid the resources of modern science and technology. As a result, we are oriented to "things," and have every sort of possession except self-possession. By putting business before every other manifestation of life, our mechanical and financial civilization has forgotten the chief business of life, namely, growth, reproduction, development. It pays infinite attention to the incubator—and it forgets the egg.

Lewis Mumford

Now, the end of all practical activity is culture: a maturing mind, a ripening character, an increasing sense of mastery and fulfillment, a higher integration of all one's powers in a social personality, a larger capacity for intellectual interests and emotional enjoyments, for more complex and subtle states of mind. In part, the interests of culture are served directly by participation in workaday activity, and in part, they emerge from it and independently preside over it. Arrested personalities look back, perhaps, with regret to some temporary fulfillment in youth, as Mark Twain looked back to the happy adventures of Huckleberry Finn; whereas developing personalities accept, without impatience or regret, the next stage in their growth; and by the time they are men, they have no difficulty in putting away childish things.

Growth and culture imply both activity and periods of leisure sufficient to absorb the results of this activity, using it to enrich art and manners and personality. The Athenians were quite right in believing that the final goods of life could not be achieved by anyone who was forced to spend the entire day in some spiritually deadening or physically exhausting task in the shop or on the farm; but it is equally true that the spiritual life itself suffers by complete divorce from the vivid experiences and the salutary restraints of practical activity, and though the Athenians in some measure retained their hold on the fundamental manual and operative realities by participating in sport and war, it is perhaps no accident that their most original mind was a stone-cutter by trade, and the son of a midwife. A society that gives to one class all the opportunities of leisure, and to another all the burdens of work, dooms both classes to a partial spiritual sterility: for one of the main tasks of life is to keep the inner world and the outer, the spiritual and the practical, in constant and rhythmically related activity.

The practical moral to be drawn from this is that servile labor—even if it produces necessities—should be minimized to the utmost, and that leisure must be distributed more universally in the form of a shorter working day, instead of being permitted to exist as the penalizing burden of "unemployment." Without leisure, there can be neither art nor science nor fine conversation, nor any ceremonious performance of the offices of love and friendship. If our Machine Age has any promise for culture, it is not in the actual multiplication of motor cars and vacuum cleaners, but in the potential creation of leisure. But so long as "comfort" and not life is our standard, the Machine Age will remain impotent.

Our higher activities are curbed in society by the present alternations of excessive toil and short periods of sodden release. The fact that the majority of people go to the theater or the concert hall, for example, at the end of a long working day explains in good part the quality of the drama they demand: in a state of physical fatigue, they are unable to face the intense experiences that the great composers and dramatists call forth: they are jaded, and they need stimuli, or they are irritated, and they need sedatives. Except for an occasional musical festival for the leisured, like those at Salzburg or Glastonbury or Bethlehem, there has been little opportunity in our civilization to experience art under conditions which permit sensitive enjoyment, to say nothing of complete rapture. In this respect the traditional religions with their days of rest devoted to contemplation, and their seasonal festivals, were far more favorable to the finer culture of the mind. The effect of leisure in our machine-ridden society is merely to promote other forms of purely consumptive activity; such as the ritualistic vacuity of motoring, or equally banal forms of sport and show.

What applies to the contemplative arts, applies equally to

the arts of action: the dance, gymnastics, above all, perhaps, to sexual intercourse. Without leisure, freshness, energy, they lose their inner impetus, and must be excited to activity by the rivalry of athletic matches, by the negative stimulus of ill-health, or by preliminary bouts of strong liquor. Yet all these arts are quite as central to life as the most beneficent instrumental activity. In so far as many primitive communities have maintained the arts of action in a more consistent and wholehearted way than our Western civilization, we need not boast too loudly about our advantages; for our progress has not been unmixed with lapses and regressions in matters that are much more important to our welfare than the production of cheap pig-iron.

Instead of the one-sided practical activity fostered by the ideals of the utilitarians, and abetted by our modern technology, with its intense specialization, I believe in a rounded, symmetrical development of both the human personality and the community itself. Economics would play a part in that development, but it would not dominate it. That specialization leads inevitably to efficiency is a specious argument; for as there is, in Ruskin's words, no wealth but life, so there is no efficiency except that which furthers life. Moreover, this argument takes no account of the mountains of useless arid work that are accumulated under our present habit of specialization; and it gives to this practice the sole credit for gains that are due to quite another technique, namely, coöperative intercourse and association.

The metaphysical case against specialization is even more overwhelming. We live in a world where no single event exists by itself; but, on the contrary, where every event is organically conditioned by its environment. If one attempts to deal with any little segment in isolation, one is dealing with a temporary abstraction. One begins, indeed, to learn a little about the things that are closest to one's interest only when one has traced out their inter-relationships with that which may, apparently, lie far beyond. While abstract, analytical thinking is one of the great achievements of the race, it is misleading and mischievous unless it takes place in a synthetic environment. The habit of substituting abstractions for the situation as a whole is responsible, for example, for our habit of placing economic needs ahead of esthetic and spiritual ones, whereas it should be plain that they are indissolubly connected from the first moment of infancy when the baby taking milk at the breast responds equally to the esthetic stimulus of the lullaby; and it is only by a systematic and brutal mis-education that these inter-related needs can be sundered. That we have actually achieved this divorce during the last century is only a proof of the overwhelming power of the educational process when it is reënforced by the customs and preoccupations of society at large.

How are we to achieve synthesis in thought and synergy in action? Shall we heap together in a vast mechanical accumulation all our specialist researches, in the fashion of an encyclopedia? Shall we boil down all knowledge and practice into popular outlines? No: the result of such an arithmetical addition would merely be another specialism. While a schematic synthesis is a necessary help to orderly thinking, the place to achieve synthesis primarily is in living itself, in encompassing all the activities that make a full life. This does not mean that we are to disperse ourselves, like the proverbial rolling stone, in a series of inconsecutive and non-related occupations: it means, rather, that once we have found a central purpose and point of view in our own life, we should subject ourselves to every activity that is necessary for a full experience and a complete understanding of life—knowing at first hand both manual toil and esthetic ecstasy, periods of hard routine and periods of adventure, intellectual concentration and the animal relaxation, strict discipline and random activity. We must explore our environment in space and time, and selectively reconstitute its chaotic elements in a related pattern—taking possession of the historic heritage of culture by reëducation, and reacting upon the cities and landscapes and industries we have surveyed by re-planning them for actual functions and humane ends. Both reëducation and re-planning begin at home: a social program that lacks a form of individual discipline is a hollow shell. This form of discovery is ultimately self-discovery; and through coöperative action, it becomes self-fulfillment.

Such a complete mode of living must inevitably carry over into each special situation: only a vicious system of mis-education can prevent it. By ceasing to live in isolated compartments, one avoids the delusive habit of treating the world in this manner, and one approaches each event with an intuition of its wholeness—as not primarily physical or biological or economic or esthetic, but as all of these things together in a certain unique, emergent combination. Temporarily, as a practical convenience, one will not be afraid of using the method of analysis to the utmost; but, weighing, measuring, decomposing one will still be aware of the organic whole in space and time with which one started, and to which, enriched by the processes of analysis and specialized activity, one must ultimately return.

In so far as we fall short of completeness and symmetry in our daily life, we must be doubly aware of the unconscious distortions and falsifications that follow from such a condition. The conceptions of purity and chastity and biological fulfillment, formed by abstemious saints driven grudgingly to admit that it is better to marry than to burn, have very little relevance or efficacy in guiding the rest of the race in the joys and duties of family life; and in general, the intensification of the spiritual life which follows from complete abstention from the normal routine of the mass of mankind, has frequently erected for society goals and duties that arise properly only from such spiritual concentration—and without it work mischief. The peace achievable in solitude gives small clue to the proper guidance of the ego in social situations of strife and rivalry. A living philosophy must face life and society in their complex wholeness; it must avoid those deceptive simplifications which derive from the conscious or unconscious renunciation of the whole.

My faith, for its full consummation, must be embodied in a community; for a well-integrated life is impossible unless the social relations that condition and develop it respond to its needs. How shall I describe such a community? This life does not exist in the past, although every civilization in its best moments gives more than a hint of it, and plenty of guarantee against its being fantastic and beyond reach. Symbolically, this rounded and inter-related life has been expressed in certain works of art, such as *Moby Dick, War and Peace, The Magic Mountain;* and if one were founding a church, instead of summoning up one's intuition of life, one would include in the calendar of saints a Plato, a Blake, a Goethe, a Whitman. Though among men of science this faith has cohered more slowly, partly because the pattern of research has been set by a purely analytical seventeenth century physics, it gets its rational support from science to-day, and would include men like A. N. Whitehead, J. S. Haldane, J. A. Thomson, L. J. Henderson, Jennings, and Wheeler.

For me, the confirmation of my intuitions came through acquaintance with Patrick Geddes, whose long life spans the service of many sciences, from biology to sociology, and many types of activity, from that of the speculative philosopher to the planner of cities. Geddes showed that a conception of life, unified at the center and ramifying in many inter-relations and comprehensions at the periphery, could be rationally lived; that it had not been outmoded by the age of specialization but was actually a mode that might, through its superior vitality and efficiency, supplant this age; that one could practice in one's own person in the germ a type of thinking and feeling and acting which might ultimately be embodied, with fuller, deeper effect, in the whole community; that even on the crude test of survival, a life that was organically grounded and pursued with a little courage and audacity, had perhaps a better chance than the narrow goals and diminished possibilities of our dominant civilization. My utopia is such a life, writ large.

To be alive, to act, to contemplate, to embody significance and value, to become fully human—these ends are difficult of achievement; and they are all the more so at a time like the present when the whole weight of our civilization is thrown in the opposite direction and, as Spengler has profoundly demonstrated, tends towards forms of sterility and death. But these goals are none the worse for being difficult; and even if the battle were doomed to be lost, one would remember that the path of salvation lies not in the victory, but as Krishna tells Arjuna, in the acceptance of battle. "Not tame and gentle bliss, but disaster, heroically encountered, is man's true happy ending"; and in this spirit one can face with equanimity both life itself, and its tragic and ambiguous rewards.

XV.
GEORGE JEAN NATHAN

IN THE exposition of what I myself happen to believe, it is certainly not my purpose to argue or even to hint that this personal set of beliefs is either philosophically or emotionally admirable or that its adoption by anyone else is a consummation devoutly wished on my part. I suspect that what other men believe, though it be often objectionable to me, may stand them in quite as sound service as my own beliefs stand me, and that it may contribute equally to their self-esteem, happiness, bank accounts, worldly eminence and wives' low opinion of them. A man's beliefs, after all, save he be a professional practitioner of letters and hence a racketeer of words, a self-blackmailer and a Judas unto himself, are and should be his private, personal property, as safe from vulgar public scrutiny as his love-making or his underwear. There is something indelicate, even bounderish, in exposing one's most secret articles of faith, a fact appreciated by the relatively gentlemanly among the professional carpenters of letters mentioned, as may be witnessed by the obvious posturings, evasions and mendacities they indulge in when they engage, for hire, to contribute to the public prints. There is about the "beliefs" they expound on such occasions a considerable air of fraud; it is plain that, while they are ostensibly betraying their confidences, they are withholding much that is true of themselves and of their private philosophies, and much that, being true, would be altogether too embarrassing to set down in print. By way of subterfuge, they accordingly offer to the public a bold, forthright, cocksure and impudent front—but with their fingers carefully crossed behind their backs. If we may put any trust in the gossipy records, there never lived a bigger liar than Rousseau. And if I personally out of long association know anything of a number of writers who are in the habit of undressing their beliefs in public, you have my word for it that the ghost of Rousseau still walks.

While I do not desire to appear in the light of an exceptional truth-teller and while frankly confessing that I entertain certain beliefs that a delicacy inherited from an illegitimate great-uncle, together with a skepticism as to the police, forbids me indiscriminately to merchant, there are certain convictions, deeply imbued in me after forty-odd years on this earth, that seem to me legitimately communicable. The first of these is that, of all philosophies governing life and conduct, that sponsored by the Cyrenaic academy, somewhat qualified, is the only one that is eminently satisfactory, eminently workable and productive of any real happiness. In a hedonism that combines the forthrightly egoistic with a modest measure of the altruistic, that governs its pleasures partly by intellect and partly by emotion—depending upon the vagaries and humors of the occasion—and that foams effervescently in the wake of work seriously and painstakingly done, I believe above all other beliefs. To me, pleasure and my own personal happiness—only infrequently collaborating with that of others—are all I deem worth a hoot. It would make me out a much finer and nobler person, I duly appreciate, to say that the happiness and welfare of all mankind were close to my heart, that nothing gave me more soulful happiness than to make others happy and that I would gladly sacrifice every cent I have in the world, together with maybe a leg, to bring a little joy to the impoverished and impaired survivors of the late Afridi raids in India, but I have difficulty in being a hypocrite. As a matter of fact, the happiness and welfare of mankind are not my profession; I am perfectly willing to leave them to the care of the professional missionaries of one sort or another; I have all that I can do to look out for my own happiness and welfare. And so has any other man, unless he happens to be a multi-millionaire, a failure in life who seeks to conceal his failure from himself in devoting himself to worse failures than himself, a gourmand of publicity, or a devout server of God. I happen to be exactly none of these—though, so far as the second catalogue goes, I surely do not view myself as a stunning success—and consequently regard myself as a sufficient problem without looking about me for other problems.

That I am selfish and to a very considerable degree possibly offensive is thus more or less regrettably obvious. All that I am able to offer in extenuation is that so are most other men if you dig down into them and, paying no attention to their altruistic pretensions, get at the hearts of them. In all my experience I have yet to find and know intimately a man worth his salt in any direction who did not think of himself first and foremost. He may drop a quarter into the hat of a beggar (when somebody is looking); he may have gracious manners; he may obey the punctilio on every occasion; he may be genial and liberal and hearty; he may buy the drinks when it comes his turn; he may be scrupulously polite, considerate and superficially lovable. But under it all his first interest, his first consideration and his first admiration are reserved for himself. The man who thinks of others before he thinks of himself may become a Grand Master of the Elks, a Socialist of parts or the star guest of honor at public banquets, but he will never become a great or successful artist, statesman or even clergyman.

Happiness is the goal of every normal human being. As it is given to few men to die happy, the best that man can hope and strive and pray for is momentary happiness during life, repeated as frequently as the cards allow. Pleasure, whatever its species, is the drink in the desert. It is the beautiful, transient reward of travail and pain. There is no other reward, except for those still sufficiently aboriginal to believe in an hereafter. The ambrosia of the gods, the lovely angels, eternal blue skies and peace, the music of golden harps are too far off and dubious so far as my own metaphysic goes. I prefer to trust to the more realistic and visible Grand Montrachet, pretty girls, Mediterranean coast and symphony orchestras of the here and now.

What makes for pleasure and consequent happiness? Each man to his own poison. In my case, a life devoted, both professionally and in leisure hours, to literature, drama, criticism, music and the arts generally, with due and careful heed paid to a moderate but satisfying alcoholic diet, guaranteed by a constantly replenished wine cellar that has complacently decided never to hear of the Eighteenth Amendment, to decently prepared foods, to the society of selfish and hence interesting comrades, to the amiable company of amiable women, and to the avoidance of any and everything that might disturb my annoying equanimity. The life of a writer has always seemed to me to be about as good a one as any low human being could hope for. His office is in his hat; his tools are in his pocket; his boss is himself; he is foot-loose, free, clockless, independent. He can say what he wants to, however inexpedient, injudicious and discommodious, and get paid handsomely for what other working men would promptly get sacked for. He can keep his mind alive and kicking with controversy and enjoy himself in putting his inferiors in their places. He can, with relatively little work and with easy hours —if he has any talent at all—earn a very satisfactory livelihood. He moves in a world not of trade but of ideas. He deals in words, for which he doesn't have to lay out a cent and hence takes no financial risk, instead of in commodities that have to be paid for first out of his own funds. He is rewarded for his fun, like most artists, where other men are rewarded more often only for their misery. Serious or gay, he is a playboy in a world that other men run for him with the sweat of their brows.

As a very humble and lowly member of the craft and as one who still has a very considerable distance to go before he may deserve the name of artist, I can yet appreciate the tremendous advantages over other men that a real artist enjoys. In the first place, he has contempt, that most valuable of human self-wrought and self-sustained gifts. In the second place, he has liberty, freedom and autonomy—more than any other man. In the third place, he can be himself at all times and in all places. He can work when he feels like working, loaf when he feels like loafing, keep superiorly aloof from politics and all other such scurvy diversions of the rabble. He is free always to choose his friends as he will, without the usual man's often necessary regard for their business connections and influence; he may be indiscreet without damage to his work; he can tell the world to go to hell and make the world like it. If any man stands a chance for happiness on this earth, it is the artist who has the choicest position at the post.

Although I myself, due doubtless to defective skill, have to work pretty hard, I do not believe in too hard work. The hardest workers are and properly should be the congenital clerks, bookkeepers, mill-hands and suchlike pathetic incompetents and slaves. The superior man should be able and privileged to take life with relative ease. A life spent in constant labor is a life wasted, save a man be such a fool as to regard a fulsome obituary notice as ample reward. Show me a man who, as the phrase goes, works himself to death and I'll show you an unimaginative dolt. There is a lot of amusement in this world and a man should get his full share of it. There probably never lived but two men who gained importance and honorable celebrity in this selfsame world who did not take considerable time off in which to have some sport, and of the two exceptions one is suspect because of his peculiar taste for communion with birds, while the other finds at least part of his story still scouted by many millions of people.

"Work," airily observed a character in a play of the late Haddon Chambers, "is for workmen." An Englishman, Chambers once remarked to me that he had written the line as an evangelical text for Americans. I believe about work as I believe about drink: it should be used in moderation.

I believe in a college training but not in a college education. The latter, I have learned from personal experience, is worth very little; the former, which imparts a knowledge of the value and uses of leisure, a somewhat superior ease and serenity, and a humorous view of indignation, whatever form the latter may take, is not without its advantages.

I believe in the state of bachelorhood, at the very least up to the age of fifty. Thereafter, a man may conceivably marry to his benefit, but certainly not before. The arguments in favor of earlier marriage, customarily advanced by the presumptively purer of the species, strike me as being peculiarly obscene and, where they are not obscene, hollow. The superior biological and hence inferentially superior amatory qualifications of the younger in years constitute one of the chief of these arguments. While fully conscious of the importance of sex in any contentful marital relationship, such a *plaidoyer* seems to me to be as illogical as it is indelicate, since it contends that two persons possibly ill-suited to each other in every other way—spiritually, intellectually, socially and economically—are to be recommended, endorsed and applauded as life-long companions simply on the ground of their virtuosity in anatomical arithmetic. Another favorite contention is that a man should marry while he is still malleable, that is, before he becomes set in his habits,—in other words, that the moulding of a man's character, his psyche and his future should be entrusted not to himself but to a woman. Up to the age of fifty, a man should be responsible to himself and to his work alone. A wife, however sympathetic, patient and charming, by very reason of her sympathy, patience and charm, would be a too pleasant and agreeable distraction. At fifty, a man has learned himself more or less completely, and has sounded out fully the possibilities and potentialities of his profession and his career. Then and only then should he consider matrimony. It is a rare marriage, negotiated at or after that age, that does not turn out prosperously and satisfactorily. The great majority of marriages that go on the rocks are those contracted in earlier years.

I am against all reforms and all reformers. The world, as I see it, is sufficiently gay, beautiful and happy as it stands. It is defective only to those who are themselves defective, who lack the sagacity, imagination, humor and wit to squeeze out its rich and jocose juices and go swimming in them. With Norman Douglas I agree: "I am not the stuff of which reformers are made; rather than indulge in that variety of meddlesomeness I would sweep a crossing. Nine-tenths of the reformers of humanity have been mischief-makers or humbugs. I have no desire to be added to the list. A man who has reformed himself has contributed his full share towards the reformation of his neighbor."

While I do not care for money and own to the somewhat vainglorious boast of never having consciously written a line with any thought of its marketability in mind, I am neither poseur nor fool enough to affect an air of disdain of it. The man with money in his pocket not only enjoys a power that men without money do not; he is also in a position to do his work in the world more carefully, more independently, more truthfully and more successfully. The best artists living to-day, the men who are doing their finest work, are without exception men who have no need longer to worry about financial matters. They have looked out for that first. A destitute and miserable man may write a good book, or paint a good picture, or write a good piece of music, but the records hint that he seldom, in these days, contrives to do another.

It seems to me that the writers who are loudest in proclaiming their veneration of truth are most often simply vociferous admirers of their own pet fallacies. As for me, while given to an equal esteem of truth, I freely confess that I do not know what the truth, the final truth, about most things is and —like my colleagues alluded to—conceal my doubts and misgivings in self-persuading and, I hope, occasionally more publicly convincing convolutions of the English language, periodically enriched with more or less showy borrowings from the French, German, Italian and Hindu. As with most men, I believe most positively in my own ideas, right or wrong. These, to me, constitute the truth, whatever others may think of them. Once I believe a thing head and tail, no one can alter my conviction.

It also seems to me that the current American literary

George Jean Nathan

school of cynicism as to sentiment, love and romance is cheapjack, fraudulent and silly. The American, as I have on more than one occasion observed, being generically the most sentimental of men, is ashamed of his sentiment and, like a man with thinning hair who drops miscellaneous jokes at the expense of baldheads, seeks to conceal or at least to divert uncomfortable attention from the fact by deprecating it in others. The most cynical writers in America to-day are personally so many honeydew melons, happily and sweetly sentimental husbands and fathers. It is merely that, like uncertain and unconfident men ever, they offer their public protestations of hard-boiled manliness—in the American definition—in order to hide from their womenfolk, laughing up their sleeves, their irresolution, nervousness, weakness and innate childishness. Romantic love is the privilege of emperors, kings, soldiers and artists; it is the butt of democrats, traveling salesmen, magazine poets and the writers of American novels.

My code of life and conduct is simply this: work hard, play to the allowable limit, disregard equally the good or bad opinion of others, never do a friend a dirty trick, eat and drink what you feel like when you feel like, never grow indignant over anything, trust to tobacco for calm and serenity, bathe twice a day, modify the æsthetic philosophy of Croce but slightly with that of Santayana and achieve for one's self a pragmatic sufficiency in the beauty of the æsthetic surface of life, learn to play at least one musical instrument and then play it only in private, never allow one's self even a passing thought of death, never contradict anyone or seek to prove anything to anyone unless one gets paid for it in cold, hard coin, live the moment to the utmost of its possibilities, treat one's enemies with polite inconsideration, avoid persons who are chronically in need, and be satisfied with life always but never with one's self. An infinite belief in the possibilities of one's self with a coincidental critical assessment and derogation of one's achievements, self-respect combined with a measure of self-surgery, aristocracy of mind combined with democracy of heart, forthrightness with modesty or at least with good manners, dignity with a quiet laugh, honor and honesty and decency: these are the greatest qualities that man can hope to attain. And as one man, my hope is to attain them.

I am against snobbery in all its lovely American forms. As a born American, I suppose that I am naturally and unpleasantly infected with some of the bacteria, but I keep about me constantly a large and handy assortment of antitoxins. I am for all religions equally, as all impress me as being equally hollow. The variation is merely one either of external and superficial beauty or hideousness of spectacle. I believe that no man's life is finally complete and rounded—to quote an eminent Hungarian—without a wife, a child, a home, though I have not practiced what I preach and have neither wife nor child and live in that apologetic substitute for a home, a New York apartment. (It looks out on a building given over to shyster lawyers!) I believe, with Nietzsche, though I dislike the banality of dragging him forth on every occasion, that so long as you are praised, believe that you are not yet on your own course but on that of another. And also that it happens sometimes by an exception that a man only reaches the highest when he disclaims his ideal, for this ideal previously drove him onward too violently, so that in the middle of the track he regularly got out of breath and had to rest.

The observation that when a given truth survives it is no sign that anyone has cherished it over a given duration of time, but simply a sign that believers in it have succeeded one another in an unbroken succession—this observation seems to me to be one of the few truths of which a careful man may say without qualification that it is substantially true. Much of what I believed in 1910 I no longer believe, but someone else *does* believe it—some pathetic ass. Thus every truth with any merit in it whatsoever is kept alive. As one crowd of believers goes out, another comes in.

To be thoroughly religious, one must, I believe, be sorely disappointed. One's faith in God increases as one's faith in the world decreases. The happier the man, the farther he is from God.

Politics impresses me as a peep-show the particular low humor of which is derived from the circumstance that the performers have their eyes glued to the other end of the same keyhole that is used by the onlooking customers.

A Socialist, as I see it, is ideally fitted for going to jail. All his ideas are ready-made and quite solid, and so he can risk being alone. Unlike other men, solitude brings him no metaphysical and philosophical doubts, concerns and despairs. Socialism is thus a sort of insurance against insanity, like patriotism and religion. A man swallows it, gives up thinking, and is happy.

I believe that a man's tastes, in essence, change but little. His tastes at fifty are at bottom his tastes of twenty filtered through the gauze of wisdom, prudence and ennui.

I hold that companionship is a matter of mutual weaknesses. We like that man or woman best who has the same faults that we have.

I am always skeptical of the honesty of a man's culture if his library shelves fail to reveal at least a few grotesquely unintelligible volumes. In the heart of every genuinely cultivated man there is a peculiar fondness for certain books that, though perhaps trashy and empty to some of us, are for one reason or another close to his secret fancy.

The true artist, I believe, has no goal, but a dozen goals:

each a milestone on a road whose end is ever some miles beyond the grave into which he is finally laid. It is only the superficial artist who has a goal, and who often achieves it.

The world, I have found, respects the man who smashes its philosophical illusions, but it despises the man who smashes its emotional ones.

I admire J. Pierpont Morgan but not Rockefeller. Morgan is hard-fisted, hard-punching, ruthless, brave, forthrightly avaricious and lacking in all hypocrisy. Rockefeller, a moral coward, wraps himself in the seven veils of church and charity by way of concealing the true golden-yellow color of his psychical epidermis. I respect Clemenceau for his courageous errors and disrelish Wilson for his cowardly exactitudes. I have no patriotism, for patriotism, as I see it, is often an arbitrary veneration of real estate above principles. I believe that one intelligent man is worth ten parcel of beautiful women, but I would rather spend an evening with the beautiful women. I believe that intelligent men should be taken on at lunch. I believe that whiskey and gin are bad for the system and that wine and beer are more beneficial to it than all the drugstore philtres in Christendom. I owe my glowing health to wines and beers, although I occasionally drink whiskey and gin and find that, despite my belief to the contrary, they do not seem to do any particular damage. I believe that Richard Strauss is the only substantial living composer, that Sinclair Lewis is the most significant American novelist, that there is not a living statesman worth serious consideration, that Stephen Phillips is a much greater poet than many think, that the only young serious dramatist in Europe worth talking about is Franz Werfel, that the most beautiful spot in the world is a certain little inn hidden away on the bank of a stream in the Black Forest, that Lindbergh, Coste, Byrd and all that crew are absurd futilitarians, that the best place to eat on earth is, first, Madame Génot's in the Rue de la Banque, Paris, and, second, the Vieux Logis in the Rue Lepic of the same town, that Spatenbräu is the most perfect beer, that the faint cinnamon smell of a carnation is the most gratifying of all flower perfumes, that the only completely original playwright since Ibsen is Pirandello, that the only authentic gentlemen left in the world are the Austrians, that athletic sports, save in the case of young boys, are designed for idiots, that money is meant to be spent and not saved, that since we are all now duly and perfectly aware that America has its full share of Rotarians, Kiwanians and Ku Kluxers, not to mention the Anti-Saloon League, the W.C.T.U., the Y.M.C.A., the D.A.R. and the Methodist Board of Temperance, Prohibition and Public Morals, we may as well stop harping on the subject, that it is occasionally well, by way of making the world more palatable, to indulge one's self luxuriously in a remission of judgment and delude one's self momentarily with illusion, and that, when all is said and done, each and every man's philosophy of life, whatever it may be, is profoundly right so long as it makes him happy.

XVI.

HU SHIH

My FATHER, Hu Chuan, was a scholar and a man of strong will and administrative ability. After a period of classical training in literature and history, he took great interest in the study of geography, especially in the geography of the frontier provinces. He went to Peking and, with a letter of introduction in his pocket, traveled forty-two days to Kirin in Northern Manchuria to see the Imperial Commissioner, Wu Ta-chen, who is now known to European Sinologues as one of the greatest archæologists in China.

Wu received him and asked what he could do for him. "Nothing," said my father, "except let me follow your mission to settle the boundary dispute with Russia, so that I may study the geography of the northeastern provinces." Wu was interested in this scholar who had taken only his first degree in the literary examinations and was almost penniless after the long journey outside the Great Wall. He took the young man with him on his historic mission and found in him a most valuable and hard-working assistant.

One time my father's party lost its way in an immense forest and could not get out for three days. Provisions were exhausted and all reconnoitering had failed when he suggested that a search be made for running streams, which would in all probability flow out of the forest. A stream was found and the party followed its course to safety. My father composed a long poem to celebrate this occasion. When forty years later I used this incident as an illustration in a paper on Professor John Dewey's theory of systematic thinking, several surviving acquaintances of my father still recognized this story, though I had not mentioned his name, and wrote to inquire if I was a younger son of their long-departed friend.

Although Wu Ta-chen had once recommended him to the government as "a man capable of governing provinces," my father never achieved political prominence and, after becoming an official in Kiangsu and Formosa, died at the age of fifty-five when Formosa was ceded to Japan as a result of the Sino-Japanese War.

I was the youngest son of my father and the only child of my mother. He married three times. The first wife was killed in the Taiping Rebellion, which swept over my home district in southern Anhui and reduced it to ashes. By a second marriage he had three sons and four daughters. The eldest son proved to be an incorrigible degenerate at an early age. When my father lost his second wife, he wrote home that he had decided to marry a girl of the good, sturdy stock of the farmer class.

My mother's father was a farmer who also practiced tailoring during the off months of the year. He came from a respectable family which was massacred during the Taiping Rebellion. Being only a small boy, he was made a captive and carried away to serve in the army of the Taipings. To prevent him from running away, four characters—"Tai-ping Tien-kuo" (Heavenly Kingdom of Everlasting Peace)—were branded on his face and remained throughout his life. But he managed to escape and, after terrible hardship, returned to his home only to find it in complete ruins without a single member of his family left alive. He worked hard, cultivating his land and practicing tailoring, which he had learned in the bandit camp. He grew up, married, and had four children of whom my mother was the eldest.

My grandfather's life ambition was to rebuild the family dwelling destroyed by the Taipings. Every morning before sunrise he would go to the riverside, select three heavy loads of stone, and in three trips carry them on his shoulder pole to the site of his ruined house. Then he would start out for his regular work in the field or in tailoring. When he returned home late in the afternoon, he would make three more trips and carry three more loads of stone for his future house before he sat down to supper. All this hard and persevering work was silently witnessed by my mother, who secretly regretted that, being a girl, she was unable in any way to lighten her father's hardship and accelerate the realization of his dream.

Then came the matchmaker who met my grandfather in the field and pleaded eloquently on behalf of my father for the "birth date" paper of his eldest daughter. My grandfather consented to talk it over with his family. But when he told the proposal to his wife in the evening, she was very furious. "Never!" she said. "How can you think of giving our daughter to a man thirty years older than she? And some of his children are older than our daughter! Moreover, people will naturally think that we, in giving our girl to an elderly official, are sacrificing her for the sake of money and respectability." So the old couple quarreled. In the end the father said, "Let us consult the girl herself. After all, it's her own affair."

When the question was placed before my mother she remained silent, as was usual with Chinese girls in a similar situation. But she was thinking grave thoughts. To marry a middle-aged widower with grown-up children meant that the contract money to be paid to the bride's family would be much more than in an ordinary marriage. That would be a great help to her father's building projects. And she had seen my father before and knew that he was revered by everybody in the district. She adored him, and was willing to marry him, partly because of a sense of hero worship, but chiefly because of her filial anxiety to help her toiling father. So when she was pressed by her parents for an answer, she said resolutely: "If you think he is a good man, I'll obey. After all, a man of forty-seven is not very old." My grandfather sighed with relief when he heard it, and my grandmother burst out in great fury: "So you want to be a *taitai* [lady] of a mandarin! So let it be!"

My mother was married in 1889 at the age of seventeen, and I was born in December, 1891. My father died in 1895, leaving my mother a widow at twenty-three. By his death, she became head of a large family with many grown-up stepchildren. The position of a Chinese stepmother is proverbially difficult, and her life from this time on was a long period of patient suffering and painstaking compromise.

My mother's greatest gift was forbearance. Chinese history records that when an Emperor of the Tang dynasty asked the patriarch Chang Kung-i by what principle his family had managed to live together for nine generations without separation or division, the grand old man, too feeble to speak, requested leave to write out his answer, and he wrote a hundred times the word "Forbearance." The Chinese moralists constantly cite this story of the "Hundred Forbearances" as the best example of family life, but none of them seems ever to realize the terrible amount of suffering, friction, suppression, and injustice which have made forbearance an absolute necessity.

Ill-feeling, daggerlike words, hostile looks on the part of the stepdaughters-in-law—my mother bore all this patiently. Sometimes she found herself reaching her limit of forbearance. Then she would stay in bed in the morning and gently weep aloud, mourning the early loss of her husband. She never mentioned the offending daughter-in-law nor the offense. But each time these tears had an almost miraculous effect. I would invariably hear a door open in the room of one of the sisters-in-law, and the footsteps of a woman walking in the direction of the kitchen. Presently she would return and knock at the door of our room. She would enter with a cup of tea and offer it to my mother, imploring her to cease weeping. My mother would take the cup and accept her silent apologies. Then there would be peace in the family for about a month.

Although she could neither read nor write, my mother staked all her hope on my education. I was a precocious child and before I was three had learned over eight hundred characters, which my father taught me every day on square slips of pink paper. A little after three, I was already in school. I was then a sickly child and could hardly climb a doorstep of six inches without assistance. But I could read and memorize better than all the other boys in the school. I never played with the children of the village and, because of my complete lack of child play, I was given the nickname of *Shien-seng* (the Master) when I was five. Fifteen years later, at Cornell University, I was nicknamed "Doc" when I was a Sophomore, and for this same weakness.

My mother would wake me up every day before daybreak and make me sit up in bed. She would then tell me all she knew about my father. She would say that she expected me to follow the footsteps of him who was to her the best and greatest man that ever lived, a man who, she said, was so much respected that all opium dens and gambling houses in the vicinity suspended business during his occasional sojourns at home. She told me that I could glorify him and her only by my good conduct and by achievements in scholarship and in the government examinations—that whatever she was suffering would be rewarded by my diligent application to my studies. I would often listen with half-open eyes, but she rarely gave up this morning sermon except when some lady guest was staying with us in the same room.

When daylight came, she would dress me and send me to school. When I grew a little older, I was always the first to arrive at school and almost every morning knocked at my teacher's door for the key to open the school gate. The key was handed out through the small crevice between the two doors and I was soon in my seat reading aloud my assignments. The school was not dismissed till dusk, when each boy bowed to the big picture of Confucius in crimson rubbing and to the teacher and went home. The average length of the school day was twelve hours.

While allowing me no child play of any kind, my mother gave me every encouragement in my childish attempt to build a temple of worship to the great sage, Confucius. I learned this from the son of my eldest half-sister, a boy five years my senior. He had built a paper temple of Confucius with all kinds of gorgeous color-papers, and it attracted me. I used a big paper box as the main hall of worship and cut a big square hole on its back to which I pasted a smaller paper box as the inner shrine for the tablet of Confucius. The outer hall where I placed the great Confucian disciples was decorated with miniature scrolls on which were written eulogies of the great sage which I partly copied from my nephew's temple and partly from books. Incense sticks were frequently burned before this toy temple and my mother rejoiced in my childish piety, secretly believing that the spirit of Confucius would surely reward me by making me a renowned scholar and successful candidate in the literary examinations.

My father was a classical scholar and a stern follower of the Neo-Confucianist Rational Philosophy of Chu Hsi (1130-1200 A.D.). He was strongly opposed to Buddhism and Taoism. I remember seeing on the door of my uncle's house (which was my first school) a sun-bleached sign bearing the words "No alms for Buddhist Monks or Taoist Priests," which, I learned afterward, was part of the Rationalist tradition left by my father. But my father was dead, my scholarly uncle soon left home to become a petty official in Northern Anhui, and my elder brothers were in Shanghai.

The women left at home were under no obligation to respect this Rationalistic tradition of my father. They observed the usual rites of ancestor worship and were free to worship wherever custom and occasion led them. Kwan-yin, the Goddess of Mercy, was their favorite deity, and my mother, chiefly out of her anxiety for my health and well-being, was a devout believer of Kwan-yin. I remember going with her on a pilgrimage to a temple of this goddess on a mountain, and she, in spite of the bound feet which pained her throughout her life, walked the whole distance of hilly trail to and from the shrine.

I was in the village school, of which there were seven in our village, for nine years (1895-1904), during which time I read and memorized the following books:

1. *The Book of Filial Piety,* a post-Confucian classic of unknown authorship.

2. *The Elementary Lessons* (or "The Small Learning"), a book of Neo-Confucianist moral teaching commonly attributed to the Sung philosopher, Chu Hsi.

3. The Four Books: *The Analects of Confucius, The Book of Mencius, The Great Learning,* and *The Doctrine of the Mean.*

4. Four of the Five Classics: *The Book of Poetry, The Book of History, The Book of Change,* and *The Li Ki.*

My mother, who was always economical in her household expenses, insisted on paying my teacher at least thrice better than the usual tuition fee, which was two silver dollars a year. She paid six dollars from the beginning and increased it gradually to twelve. From this insignificant increase in the fee, I derived benefits a thousand times greater than the numerical ratio stated above can possibly indicate. For the two-dollar pupil merely read aloud and recited by heart, and the teacher never took the trouble to explain to him the meaning of the words memorized. I alone, because of the additional pay, enjoyed the rare privilege of having every word and sentence in the readings explained to me, that is, translated from the dead language into the colloquial dialect.

Before I was eight years old, I could read with very little assistance. At the suggestion of my second brother, my teacher made me read *The General Mirror for Government,* which was in reality a general history of China in chronological form compiled by the great historian Ssu-ma Kuang in the year 1084 A.D. This historical reading interested me greatly and I soon began, as an aid to memory, to compile a rhymed summary of the dynasties, emperors, and chronological eras.

Then one day in a waste-paper box in my uncle's house I chanced upon a torn volume of a part of the great novel *Shui Hu* (The Hundred and Eight Heroes of Liang-shan) and read it through while standing by the box. I ran about the village and soon found a complete set of the novel. From that time on I devoured every novel known in our community and in the near-by villages. They were written in the *pei-hua*, or spoken language, and were easily intelligible and absorbingly entertaining. They taught me life, for good and for evil, and gave me a literary medium which years later enabled me to start what has been called "the Literary Renaissance" in China.

In the meantime, my religious life underwent a curious crisis. I was brought up in an idolatrous environment and accustomed to the ugly and fierce faces of the gods and to the folk-versions of Heaven and Hell. When I was eleven I was one day rereading aloud *The Elementary Lessons* of Chu Hsi, which I had memorized without much understanding. I came upon a passage where the Rationalist philosopher quoted the historian Ssu-ma Kuang in an attack on the popular belief in Heaven and Hell. The quotation reads: "When the body has decayed, the spirit fades away. Even if there be such cruel tortures in Hell as Chiseling, Burning, Pounding, and Grinding, whereon are these to be inflicted?" This sounded like good reasoning and I began to doubt the idea of judgment after death.

Shortly afterward, I was reading Ssu-ma Kuang's *General History* and came upon a passage in its one hundred and thirty-sixth chapter which made me an atheist. The passage in question tells of a philosopher of the fifth century A.D. named Fan Chen who championed the theory of the destructibility of the spirit or soul against the whole Imperial Court, which was then patronizing Mahāyāna Buddhism. Fan Chen's view was summed up by Ssu-ma Kuang in these words: "The body is the material basis of the spirit, and the spirit is only the functioning of the body. The spirit is to the body what sharpness is to a sharp knife. We have never known the existence of sharpness after the destruction of the knife. How can we admit the survival of the spirit when the body is gone?"

This was more thorough reasoning than Ssu-ma Kuang's view that the spirit fades away when the body has decayed—a theory which still admits the spirit as something. Fan Chen fundamentally denies the spirit as an entity: it is only a functioning of the body. This simplification pleased my boyish mind and it gladdened my heart to read that "Although the whole Court and country were against him, no one succeeded in refuting him."

In the same passage, Fan Chen was quoted as being opposed to the Buddhist doctrine of Karma, or the causal chain throughout the various existences. He was talking to the Prince of Ching-ling, who said to him: "If you do not believe in Karma, how can you explain the different states of wealth and poverty, of honor and lowliness?" Fan Chen replied: "Human life may be likened to the flowers on yonder tree. The wind blows down the flowers, of which some are caught by the screens and scattered on the beautifully decorated mats and cushions, while others are blown over the fence and dropped on the dung-heap. Your Lordship is one of those flowers on the cushions, and I, your humble servant, chance to be on the dung-hill. There is the difference in position, but where is the causal chain?"

The doctrine of Karma is one of the few most influential ideas from India that have become an integral part of Chinese thought and life. The ancient Chinese moralists had taught that goodness was always rewarded and evil punished. But in real life, this is not always true. The Buddhist doctrine of Karma has the advantage over the Chinese idea of retribution in that it can always evade the issue by referring to the absolute continuity of the causal chain throughout past and future existences.

Hu Shih

But Fan Chen's figure of speech appealed to my youthful fancy and shook me out of the nightmare absolutism of Karma. It was Chance versus Determinism. And, as a boy of eleven, I took the chances and revolted against Fate. There was no sophisticated reasoning on my part in those days of my boyhood. It was mere temperamental attraction and repulsion. I was my father's son, and Ssu-ma Kuang and Fan Chen attracted me. That was all.

But this mental crisis was not without its comic consequences in my early life. During the New Year Festival of 1903, I paid a visit to my eldest sister, who lived 20 *li* away. After spending a few days at her home I returned with her son, who was coming to pay his New Year visit to my mother. A servant of his was carrying the New Year presents for him. On our way home we passed a shrine with ugly and fierce-looking gods. I stopped and said to my nephew: "Nobody is watching. Let's throw these images into the mud pool." My childish iconoclasm greatly horrified my companions, who persuaded me to move on without troubling the already tottering deities.

It was the day of the Lantern Festival (the fifteenth of the first month). When we arrived, there were many visitors at my house. I was hungry and, when supper was served, my nephew made me drink a cup of strong rice wine which played havoc with my empty stomach. I was soon running about the courtyard and shouting to the moon to come down to see the Lantern Festival. My mother was displeased and sent men to fetch me. I ran before them and the effect of wine worked more rapidly with my running. I was finally caught, but I struggled to get away. My mother held me tight on her lap and many people soon gathered around us.

In my fright, I began to talk nonsense. Then my nephew's

servant stepped forward and whispered to my mother: "Madame, I believe that the little uncle is beside himself. Very likely some god or spirit is troubling him. This afternoon when we passed the Shrine of Three Gates, he proposed to throw the gods into the muddy pool. That must have caused the trouble." I overheard the whisper and a bright idea came to me. I shouted all the more wildly, as if I were actually one of the gods of the Shrine of Three Gates. My mother then ordered incense to be burned in the open and, pleading my youthful ignorance and irresponsibility, made a vow to offer sacrifices at the shrine should my innocent offense be forgiven by the gods.

At that moment report came that the Lantern Procession was approaching, and the people in our house rushed out to see it. My mother and I were left alone. I soon fell asleep. The vow had apparently worked. One month later, when my mother and I visited my grandparents, she made me offer, in all solemnity, our promised sacrifices at the Shrine of Three Gates.

Early in my thirteenth year (1904), I left home on a seven-day journey to seek a "new education" in Shanghai. After that separation I visited my mother only three times and stayed with her altogether about seven months in fourteen years. Out of her great love for me she sent me away without apparently shedding a tear, and allowed me to seek my own education and development in the great world all alone, armed only with a mother's love, a habit of study, and a little tendency to doubt.

I spent six years in Shanghai (1904-1910) and seven years in America (1910-1917). During my stay in Shanghai I went through three schools (none of which was a missionary school) without graduating from any. I studied the rudiments of what was then known as "the new education," consisting chiefly of history, geography, English, mathematics, and some gleanings of natural science. Through the free translations by the late Mr. Lin Shu and others, I made my first acquaintance with a number of English and European novels, including those of Scott, Dickens, Dumas *père* and *fils,* Hugo, and Tolstoy. I read the works of a few of the non-Confucian and Neo-Confucian philosophers of ancient and medieval China and was delighted in the altruism of Mo Ti and the naturalistic philosophy of Lao-tze and Chuang-tze.

Through the popular writings of the late Mr. Liang Chi-chao, the most powerful writer of the age, I came to know a little of such Western thinkers as Hobbes, Descartes, Rousseau, Bentham, Kant, and Darwin. Mr. Liang was a great admirer of modern Western civilization and published a series of essays in which he frankly admitted that the Chinese as a race had suffered from the deplorable lack of many fine traits possessed by the European people, notably emphasis on public morality, nationalism, love of adventure, the conception of personal rights and the eagerness to defend them against encroachment, love of freedom, ability for self-control, belief in the infinite possibility of progress, capacity for corporate and organized effort, and attention to bodily culture and health. It was these essays which first violently shocked me out of the comfortable dream that our ancient civilization was self-sufficient and had nothing to learn from the militant and materialistic West except in the weapons of war and vehicles of commerce. They opened to me, as to hundreds of others, an entirely new vision of the world.

I also read Mr. Yen Fu's translation of John Stuart Mill's *On Liberty* and Huxley's *Evolution and Ethics.* Mr. Yen's translation of Huxley's essay had been published in 1898 and had been immediately accepted by the Chinese intelligentsia with acclamation. Rich men gave money to have new editions made for wider distribution (there being no copyright law then), because it was thought that the Darwinian hypothesis, especially in its social and political application, was a welcome stimulus to a nation suffering from age-long inertia and stagnation.

In the course of a few years many of the evolutionary terms and phrases became proverbial expressions in the journalistic writings of the time. Numerous persons adopted them in naming themselves and their children, thereby reminding themselves of the perils of elimination in the struggle for existence, national as well as individual. The once famous General Chen Chiung-ming called himself "Ching-tsun" or "Struggling for Existence." Two of my schoolmates bore the names "Natural Selection Yang" and "Struggle for Existence Sun."

Even my own name bears witness to the great vogue of evolutionism in China. I remember distinctly the morning when I asked my second brother to suggest a literary name for me. After only a moment's reflection, he said, "How about the word *shih* [fitness] in the phrase 'Survival of the Fittest'?" I agreed and, first using it as a *nom de plume*, finally adopted it in 1910 as my name.

My slight knowledge of the evolutionary hypothesis of Darwin and Spencer was easily linked up with the naturalism of some of the ancient Chinese thinkers. For example, it delighted my boyish heart to find an equally youthful cobeliever of over two thousand years ago in the following story told in the *Lieh-tze,* a spurious work of the Taoist school:

"The House of Tien held a great post-sacrificial feast at which over a thousand guests were present. When fish and wild duck were offered, the host said with a sigh: 'Great is Nature's kindness to man! She has produced grain and fish and birds for the use of man.' The speech was applauded by all the guests present. Thereupon, the son of the House of Pao, who was only twelve years old, stepped forward and said: 'It is not so, my lord. All the beings in the universe coexist with men on a basis of equality. There is no natural order of superiority and inferiority. They conquer and prey on one another only by virtue of their superior strength and intelligence. No species is purposely produced for the sake of another. Men, too, prey on those things which they are able to conquer. How can we say that Nature has produced them for our benefit? Do not mosquitoes suck our blood and tigers and wolves eat our flesh? Shall we say that Nature has produced men for the benefit of mosquitoes and tigers and wolves?' "

In 1906 a few of my schoolmates in the China National Institute founded a periodical called *The Struggle*—another instance of the popularity of the Darwinian theory—which, being primarily interested in instilling new ideas into the uneducated masses, was to be published in the *pei-hua* or spoken language. I was invited to contribute to its first issue, and a year later I became its sole editor. My editorial work on this magazine helped me not only to develop an ability in the use of the living tongue as a literary medium, but also to think out, in clear language and logical order, the ideas and thoughts which had been taking shape since my childhood days. In many of my articles written for this magazine I strongly attacked the superstitions of the people and was frankly iconoclastic and atheistic.

In 1908 my family was in great financial difficulty because of business failures. At the age of seventeen I found myself facing the necessity of supporting myself at school and my mother at home. I gave up my studies and taught elementary English for over a year, teaching five hours a day and receiving a monthly pay of eighty silver dollars. In 1910 I taught Chinese for a few months.

Those years (1909-10) were dark years in the history of China as well as in my personal history. Revolutions broke out in several provinces and failed each time. Quite a number of my former schoolmates at the China National Institute, which was a center of revolutionary activities, were involved in these plots and not a few lost their lives. Several of these political fugitives came to Shanghai and stayed with me. We were all despondent and pessimistic. We drank, wrote pessimistic poetry, talked day and night, and often gambled for no stakes. We even engaged an old actor to teach us singing. One cold morning I wrote a poem which contained this line: "How proudly does the wintry frost scorn the powerless rays of the sun!"

Despondency and drudgery drove us to all kinds of dissipation. One rainy night I got deadly drunk, fought with a policeman in the street, and landed myself in prison for the night. When I went home the next morning and saw in the mirror the bruises on my face, this line in Li Po's *Drinking Song* came to my mind: "Some use might yet be made of this material born in me." I decided to quit teaching and my friends. After a month of hard work, I went to Peking to take the examination for the scholarship founded on the returned American portion of the Boxer Indemnity. I passed the examination and in July sailed for America.

I arrived in America full of pessimism, but I soon made friends and came to be very fond of the country and its people. The naïve optimism and cheerfulness of the Americans impressed me most favorably. In this land there seemed nothing which could not be achieved by human intelligence and effort. I could not escape the contagion of this cheerful outlook on life, which, in the course of a few years, gradually cured my premature senility.

When I went to see a football game for the first time, I sat there philosophically amused by the roughness of the game and by the wild yells and cheers which seemed to me quite beneath the dignity of the university student. But, as the struggle became more and more exciting, I began to catch the enthusiasm. Then, accidentally turning my head, I saw the white-haired professor of botany, Mr. W. W. Rowlee, cheering and yelling in all heartiness, and I felt so ashamed of myself that I was soon cheering enthusiastically with the crowd.

Even during the darkest days in the first years of the Chinese Republic, I managed to keep up my good cheer. In a letter written to a Chinese friend, I said: "Nothing is hopeless except when you and I give it up as hopeless." In my diaries, I wrote down such quotations as this from Clough: "If hopes are dupes, fears are liars." Or this, in my own Chinese translation, from Browning:

> One who never turned his back, but marched breast forward,
> Never doubted clouds would break,
> Never dreamed, though right were worsted, wrong would triumph,
> Held we fall to rise, are baffled to fight better, sleep to wake.

In January, 1914, I wrote this entry in my diary: "I believe that the greatest thing I have learned since leaving China is this optimistic philosophy of life." In 1915 I was awarded the Hiram Corson Prize for the best essay on Robert Browning. The subject of my essay was "In Defense of Browning's Optimism." I think it was largely my gradually changed outlook on life that made me speak with a sense of conviction in taking up his defense.

I began my university career as a student in the New York State College of Agriculture at Cornell University. My choice was based on the belief then current in China that a Chinese student must learn some useful art, and literature and philosophy were not considered of any practical use. But there was also an economic motive: the College of Agriculture then charged no tuition fee and I thought I might be able to save a part of my monthly allowance to send to my mother.

I had had no experience on a farm and my heart was not in agriculture. The freshman courses in English Literature and German interested me far more than Farm Practice and Pomology. After hesitating for a year and a half, I finally transferred to the College of Arts and Sciences at the penalty of paying four semesters' tuition fee at once, which cost me eight months' privation. But I felt more at home in my new studies and have never regretted the change.

A course in the history of European philosophy—under that inspiring teacher, the late Professor J. E. Creighton—led me to major in philosophy. I also took a keen interest in English literature and political science. The Sage School of Philosophy at Cornell was a stronghold of Idealism. Under its guidance I read the more important works of the classical philosophers of ancient and modern times. I also read the works of such later Idealists as Bradley and Bosanquet, but their problems never interested me.

In 1915 I went to Columbia University and studied under Professor John Dewey until the summer of 1917, when I returned to China. Under Dewey's inspiration, I wrote my dissertation on "The Development of Logical Method in Ancient China," which made me reread the philosophical writings of ancient China and laid the foundation for all my later researches in the history of Chinese thought.

During my seven years in America, I had many extra-curricular activities which probably had as much influence on my life and thought as my university work. In days of despondency I took much interest in the Christian religion and read the Bible almost through. In the summer of 1911, when I was a guest at a conference of the Chinese Christian Students' Association held at Pocono Pines, Pennsylvania, I almost decided to become a Christian.

But I gradually drifted away from Christianity, although I did much reading in the history of its development. For a long time, however, I was a believer in the doctrine of non-resistance. Five centuries before Jesus, the Chinese philosopher Lao-tze had taught that the highest virtue resisted nothing and that water, which resists nothing, is always irresistible. My early acceptance of this teaching of Lao-tze led me to take a great liking to the Sermon on the Mount.

When the Great War broke out in 1914, I was deeply moved by the fate of Belgium and became a confirmed non-resister. I lived three years at the Cornell Cosmopolitan Club and made many warm friends of all nationalities. Under the influence of such idealistic pacifists as George Nasmyth and John Mez, I became a zealous pacifist myself. I was one of the founders of the Collegiate League to Abolish Militarism which was formed in 1915 at the suggestion of Oswald Garrison Villard.

When later the International Polity Clubs were founded, under the leadership of Nasmyth and Norman Angell, I was one of the most active members and participated in their first two annual conferences. In 1916 I was awarded the International Polity Club Prize for my essay on "Is There a Substitute for Force in International Relations?" in which I expounded the philosophy of a league of nations on the idea of law as organized force.

My pacifism and internationalism often brought me into serious trouble. When Japan entered the World War by attacking the German possessions in Shantung, she declared to the world that these were to be "eventually restored to China." I was the only Chinese in America who believed in this declaration, and argued in writing that Japan probably meant what she said. For this I was ridiculed by many of my fellow students. When in 1915 Japan presented the famous Twenty-one Demands on China, every Chinese in the United States was for immediate declaration of war with Japan. I wrote an open letter to *The Chinese Students' Monthly*, counseling calmness and cool thinking, for which I was severely attacked from all sides and often denounced as a traitor. War was avoided by China's partial acceptance of the Demands, but the German possessions in China were not restored to China until seven years later.

My reading of Ibsen, John Morley, and Huxley taught me the importance of honest thinking and honest speaking. I read all of Ibsen's plays and was particularly pleased by *An Enemy of the People*. Morley's essay, "On Compromise," first recommended to me by my good friend Miss Edith Clifford Williams, has remained one of the most important spiritual influences on my life. Morley has taught me that "a principle, if it be sound, represents one of the larger expediencies. To abandon that for the sake of some seeming expediency of the hour, is to sacrifice the greater good for the less. Nothing is so sure to impoverish an epoch, to deprive conduct of nobleness, and character of elevation."

Huxley goes still further and teaches a method of intellectual honesty. He merely says: "Give me such evidence as would justify me in believing anything else, and I will believe that [the immortality of man]. It is no use to talk to me of analogies and probabilities. I know what I mean when I say I believe in the law of the inversed square, and I will not rest my life and my hopes upon weaker convictions." Huxley has also said, "The most sacred act of a man's life is to say and to feel 'I believe such and such to be true.' All the greatest rewards, and all the heaviest penalties of existence, cling upon that act."

It is from Professor Dewey that I have learned that the most sacred responsibility of a man's life is to endeavor to *think well*. To think sluggishly, to think without strict regard to the antecedents and consequences of thought, to accept ready-made and unanalyzed concepts as premises of thinking, to allow personal factors unconsciously to influence one's thinking, or to fail to test one's ideas by working out their results is to be intellectually irresponsible. All the greatest discoveries of truth, and all the greatest calamities in history, depend upon this.

Dewey has given us a philosophy of thinking which treats thinking as an art, as a technique. And in *How We Think* and *Essays in Experimental Logic* he has worked out this technique which I have found to be true not only of the discoveries in the experimental sciences, but also of the best researches in the historical sciences, such as textual criticism, philological reconstruction, and higher criticism. In all these fields, the best results have been achieved by the same technique, which in its essence consists of a boldness in suggesting hypotheses coupled with a most solicitous regard for control and verification. This laboratory technique of thinking deserves the name of Creative Intelligence because it is truly creative in the exercise of imagination and ingenuity in seeking evidence and devising experiment and in the satisfactory results that flow from the successful fruition of thinking.

Curiously enough, this instrumental logic has turned me into a historical research worker. I have learned to think genetically, and this genetic habit of thinking has been the key to success in all my subsequent work in the history of thought and literature. More curious still, this historical way of thinking has not made me a conservative but always a progressive. For instance, my arguments for the literary revolution in China have been entirely based upon the undeniable facts of historical evolution and they have been so far unanswerable by my opponents.

The death of my mother in November, 1918, was the occasion which led to the first formulation of the credo for which I had been groping in the vast world for over fourteen years. It was published in February, 1919, in an essay entitled "Immortality, My Religion."

Because of my early boyhood readings I had long since rejected the idea of personal survival after death. For many years I had contented myself with an ancient doctrine of "Three Immortalities" which I found in the Tso Commentary on the *Chun Chiu,* where it was recorded that the wise statesman Shu-sin Pao declared in the year 548 B.C. (when Confucius was only three years old) that there were three kinds of immortality: the immortality of Virtue, of Service, and of Wise Speech. "These are not forgotten with length of time, and that is what is meant by immortality after death." This doctrine attracted me so much that I often spoke of it to my foreign friends and gave to it the name "the doctrine of the immortality of the three W's (Worth, Work, and Words)."

My mother's death set me thinking afresh on this problem, and I began to feel that the doctrine of the Three Immortalities was in need of revision. It is defective, in the first place, in being too exclusive. How many people are there in this world whose achievements in virtue, in service, and in literary and philosophical wisdom cannot be forgotten with length of time? Christopher Columbus, for example, may be immortal, but how about the other members of his crew? How about the men who built his ships or furnished his tools, or the many pioneers who had paved the way for him either by courageous thinking or by successful or unsuccessful explorations of the seas? How much, in short, must one achieve in order to attain immortality?

In the second place, this doctrine fails to furnish any negative check on human conduct. Virtue is immortal, but how about vice? Shall we again resort to the belief in Judgment Day and Hell Fire?

As I reviewed the life of my dead mother, whose activities had never gone beyond the trivial details of the home but whose influence could be clearly seen on the faces of those men and women who came to mourn her death, and as I recalled the personal influence of my father on her whole life and its lasting effect on myself, I came to the conviction that *everything* is immortal. Everything that we are, everything that we do, and everything that we say is immortal in the sense that it has its effect somewhere in this world, and that effect in turn will have its results somewhere else, and the thing goes on in infinite time and space.

As Leibnitz once said, "Each body feels all that passes in the universe, so that he who sees all may read in each that which passes everywhere else, and even that which has been and shall be, discerning in the present that which is removed in time as well as in space." We do not see all, but everything is there, reaching into the infinite. A man is what he eats, and the work of the Dakota farmer, the California fruit grower, and a million other food providers lives in him. A man is what he thinks, and everyone who has influenced him—from Socrates, Plato, and Confucius down to his parish preacher and his nursery governess—lives in him. A man is also what he enjoys, and the work of numberless artists and entertainers, living or long dead, renowned or nameless, sublime or vulgar, lives in him. And so on *ad infinitum*.

Fourteen centuries ago a man wrote an essay on "The Destructibility of the Soul" which was considered so sacrilegious that his Emperor ordered seventy great scholars to refute it, and it was refuted. But five hundred years later a historian recorded a summary of this sacrilegious essay in his great history. And another nine hundred years passed. Then a little boy of eleven chanced upon this brief summary of thirty-five words, and these thirty-five words, after being buried for fourteen hundred years, suddenly became alive and are living in him and through him in the lives of thousands of men and women.

In 1912 there came to my Alma Mater an English lecturer who gave an address on the impossibility of founding a republic in China. His lecture struck me then as quite absurd, but I was amused by his peculiar pronunciation of the vowel *o*, and I sat there imitating it for my own entertainment. His speech has long been forgotten, but somehow his pronunciation of the vowel *o* has stuck by me all these years and is probably now on the tongue of hundreds of my students without anyone's ever being aware that it came through my mischievous mimicking of Mr. J. O. P. Bland. And Mr. Bland never knew it.

Twenty-five centuries ago there died a beggar in a valley of the Himalaya Mountains. His body was decomposing by the roadside. There came a young prince who saw the horrifying scene and was set to thinking. He thought over the impermanence of life and of everything else, and decided to leave his family and go to the wilderness to think out a way for his own salvation and that of mankind. Years later he emerged from the wilderness as Buddha the Enlightened One and proclaimed to the world the way he had found for its salvation. Thus even the decomposition of the dead body of a beggar has unwittingly contributed its part to the founding of one of the greatest religions of the world.

This line of reasoning led me to what may be called the religion of Social Immortality, because it is essentially based on the idea that the individual self, which is the product of the accumulated effect of the social self, leaves an indelible mark of everything it is and everything it does upon that larger self which may be termed Society, or Humanity, or the Great Being. The individual may die, but he lives on in this Great Self which is immortal. All his virtue and vice, merit and sin, all his action and thought and speech, significant or trivial, right or wrong, for good or for evil—everything lives in the effect it produces on the Great Self. This Great Self lives forever as the everlasting monumental testimony of the triumphs and failures of the numberless individual selves.

This conception of Social Immortality is more satisfactory than the ancient Chinese doctrine of the Three Immortalities in that it includes the lowly and the insignificant as well as the heroes and sages, vice as well as virtue, crime as well as meritorious service. And it is this recognition of the immortality of evil as well as of good that constitutes the moral sanction of the doctrine. The decay of a dead body may found a religion, but it may also plague a whole continent. A chance remark of a barmaid may lead to the sudden enlightenment of a Zen monk, but a wrong theory of political or social reconstruction may cause centuries of bloodshed. The discovery of a microscopic bacillus may benefit millions of people, but a tiny sputum from a consumptive may kill multitudes and generations.

Truly the evil that men do lives after them! It is the clear recognition of the consequences of conduct that constitutes our sense of moral responsibility. The individual self owes a tremendous debt to the greater Social Self, and it is his duty to hold himself responsible to it for everything he does or thinks or is. Humanity is what it is by the wisdom and folly of our fathers, but we shall be judged by what humanity will be when we shall have played our part. Shall we say, "After us, the deluge"? Or shall we say, "After us, the millennium"?

In 1923 I had another occasion to formulate my credo in a more general way. An article on "Science and Our Philosophy of Life" by the geologist Mr. V. K. Ting, published in a weekly paper edited by myself, had started a long controversy which lasted almost a whole year. Practically every thinker of any standing in China had taken part in it. When the controversial literature was collected by some enterprising publisher at the end of 1923, it amounted to over two hundred and fifty thousand words. I was asked to write an introduction to this collection. My introductory essay added another ten thousand words to this already voluminous collection and concluded with what I proposed as "a framework for a new philosophy of the universe and life," to which, however, some of the hostile Christian missionaries have mischievously given the name of "Hu Shih's New Decalogue." I now translate it for what it is worth:

1. On the basis of our knowledge of astronomy and physics, we should recognize that the world of space is infinitely large.

2. On the basis of our geological and paleontological knowledge, we should recognize that the universe extends over infinite time.

3. On the basis of all our verifiable scientific knowledge, we should recognize that the universe and everything in it follow natural laws of movement and change—"natural" in the

Chinese sense of "being so of themselves"—and that there is no need for the concept of a supernatural Ruler or Creator.

4. On the basis of the biological sciences, we should recognize the terrific wastefulness and brutality in the struggle for existence in the biological world, and consequently the untenability of the hypothesis of a benevolent Ruler.

5. On the basis of the biological, physiological, and psychological sciences, we should recognize that man is only one species in the animal kingdom and differs from the other species only in degree, but not in kind.

6. On the basis of the knowledge derived from anthropology, sociology, and the biological sciences, we should understand the history and causes of the evolution of living organisms and of human society.

7. On the basis of the biological and psychological sciences, we should recognize that all psychological phenomena are explainable through the law of causality.

8. On the basis of biological and historical knowledge, we should recognize that morality and religion are subject to change, and that the causes of such change can be scientifically studied.

9. On the basis of our newer knowledge of physics and chemistry, we should recognize that matter is full of motion and not static.

10. On the basis of biological, sociological, and historical knowledge, we should recognize that the individual self is subject to death and decay, but the sum total of individual achievement, for better or for worse, lives on in the immortality of the Larger Self; that to live for the sake of the species and posterity is religion of the highest kind; and that those religions which seek a future life either in Heaven or in the Pure Land, are selfish religions.

"This new credo," I concluded, "is a hypothesis founded

on the generally accepted scientific knowledge of the last two or three hundred years. To avoid unnecessary controversy, I propose to call it, not 'a scientific credo,' but merely 'the Naturalistic Conception of Life and the Universe.'

"In this naturalistic universe, in this universe of infinite space and time, man, the two-handed animal whose average height is about five feet and a half and whose age rarely exceeds a hundred years, is indeed a mere infinitesimal microbe. In this naturalistic universe, where every motion in the heavens has its regular course and every change follows laws of nature, where causality governs man's life and the struggle for existence spurs his activities—in such a universe man has very little freedom indeed.

"Yet this tiny animal of two hands has his proper place and worth in that world of infinite magnitude. Making good use of his hands and a large brain, he has actually succeeded in making a number of tools, thinking out ways and means, and creating his own civilization. He has not only domesticated the wild animals, but he has also studied and discovered a considerable number of the secrets and laws of nature by means of which he has become a master of the natural forces and is now ordering electricity to drive his carriage and ether to deliver his message.

"The increase of his knowledge has extended his power, but it has also widened his vision and elevated his imagination. There were times when he worshiped stones and animals and was afraid of the gods and ghosts. But he is now moving away from these childish habits, and is slowly coming to a realization that the infinity of space only enhances his æsthetic appreciation of the universe, the infinite length of geological and archæological time only makes him better understand the terrific hardship his forefathers had to encounter in building up this human inheritance, and the regularity of the movements and changes in the heavens and on earth only furnishes him the key to his dominion over nature.

"Even the absolute universality of the law of causality does not necessarily limit his freedom, because the law of causality not only enables him to explain the past and predict the future, but also encourages him to use his intelligence to create new causes and attain new results. Even the apparent cruelty in the struggle for existence does not necessarily make him a hardened brute; on the contrary, it may intensify his sympathy for his fellow men, make him believe more firmly in the necessity of coöperation, and convince him of the importance of conscious human endeavor as the only means of reducing the brutality and wastefulness of the natural struggles. In short, this naturalistic conception of the universe and life is not necessarily devoid of beauty, of poetry, of moral responsibility, and of the fullest opportunity for the exercise of the creative intelligence of man."

Joseph Wood Krutch

XVII.

JOSEPH WOOD KRUTCH

DURING the course of the Middle Ages it was, I believe, commonly assumed that man is an animal plus. No Darwinian researches were necessary to indicate the obvious fact that his body is constructed along the same general lines as the body of a cow or a pig, and that a very considerable number of his instincts and his desires are related in similar fashion to those of the humbler creatures. But something left out of the lower animals had, it was assumed, been put into man. A soul—something not only immortal but capable of desires and motives quite unknown to beasts—had been mechanically added. This soul came into frequent conflict with the animal part to which it was temporarily linked, but it should and it could (with the aid of God) triumph over it—indecisively in life, but definitively in some future when the troublesome body should have been completely cast off.

Now there are various reasons why it is difficult to accept this theory to-day. Indeed, very grave objections have been raised to even that modern variant called vitalism which assumes that life is something which has, in much the same way, been added to matter. But the theory itself is more than merely delightfully simple, for it serves to symbolize a problem quite as real just now as it ever was. We know even better than they knew in the Middle Ages how much of man is simple animal. We know that his body is, organ for organ and nerve for nerve, almost identical with that of the ape. And we know how much of his conduct can be explained in terms of animal behavior.

Yet try as hard as we may, we cannot quite succeed in bridging the gulf which still lies between us and the creatures whom, all too distressingly it sometimes seems, we so closely resemble. Even the most materialistic among us must distinguish, if only for the sake of convenience, between the human mind and the mind of the beast. We still desire passionately things which no animal could understand. We are still capable of motives unparalleled in animal psychology. And we still need very urgently to know what this difference means.

What of the values which we assign to love, to art, and to knowledge? What of the scruples which afflict us concerning duty, and right, and purity? It is true that the materialistic student of manners and customs may reply that morality cannot possibly exist, because every conceivable action has been at some two times and places considered both obligatory and forbidden. But the fact remains that man has the power and the need to conceive of those abstractions to which he has given the names of right and wrong, and it is that power and that need with which we must deal. Even if it be granted that there is nothing outside of man which corresponds to these conceptions, at least the conceptions are there. They are capable of modifying his conduct very profoundly indeed, and they are a part of the data which any adequate view of man must consider.

You may phrase as you like the question which results. Posing it as one of practical morality, you may ask whether the wise man will cultivate all the quixotic scruples of which his imagination is capable, or whether, brushing them aside, he will strive to attain to a Machiavellian ruthlessness. Putting it in a form more general and abstract, you may inquire whether instinct is, as the naturalists maintain, his only safe guide, or whether, as the dualists insist, man is man only in so far as he denies these natural instincts in the interests of something which he calls the human. But at bottom all of these questions are the same: how great is the difference between man and nature, and what does this difference mean?

If we do not set up as either metaphysicians or scientists, we may neglect if we like the metaphysical and the scientific aspects of the question. Granted that man can conceive a standard of values apparently different from any which is recognized by nature, we may leave to others the attempt to decide whether or not this fact necessarily implies that there must, after all, be something outside of him which corresponds to this standard. And to science, anxious to establish the continuity of phenomena, we may delegate the further problem of determining how the mind—which thinks and wills and judges—has been constructed out of the atoms of matter.

Some scientists, clinging still (and a little desperately) to purely mechanistic theories, may maintain that the most delicate spirit is only the most complicated of the machines which, somehow or other, have gradually got themselves built up out of the dead particles which constitute the ultimate stuff of the universe as it is conceived of in classical physics. Others, hardly less desperate, may lose themselves in the maze of more modern theories and, by speaking of the "free will of the atoms," attribute to even what seems the deadest of dead matter the attributes of mind.

But whatever our theories may be or however great our

willingness to leave theories to others, we are faced by the fact that, for all practical purposes, there still lies a gulf between the two worlds which we as human beings must simultaneously inhabit—between, on the one hand, the world of matter and of animal instinct which we call nature, and, on the other hand, that world of human motives and values which, for convenience' sake, we distinguish as the world of exclusively human things.

Nothing is clearer than the fact that we must deal very often and very intimately with nature. In the first place, we must handle matter both as it exists in the form of that dead material out of which we construct our houses and in the form of those living organisms, plant or animal, which we kill in order that we may eat. Even the most fanatical ascetic must either surrender life itself or acquiesce to some extent in this necessary traffic going on between the human being and that which, living or dead, is at least not human.

But this is not all. For nature is within as well as without that thing which we call ourselves. We have the instincts, the needs, and the desires of the animal. We can no more deny them completely, we can no more refuse to accept that part of nature which is woven into the body with which we act and the mind with which we think, than we can deny that part of her which our hands touch and our eyes see. At every moment of our lives we must be animal in part at least.

And yet the latitude which is nevertheless permitted to us remains enormous. We can be, on the one hand, so nearly a creature of instinct and appetite that we deviate hardly once in a fortnight from the pattern of animal behavior. But we can be, on the other hand, a being so wrapped up in contemplation, so obsessed by scruples, so devoted to quixotic principles, and so hemmed in by the No's which come to us from God knows where, that the average human being can hardly recognize in our emaciated bodies and tortured minds a creature like himself.

Nor is there in the specious doctrine of the golden mean any more than a definition which does not define. For where, between extremes which are separated by a distance at once so great and so difficult to measure by any yardstick yet invented, does any actually determinable mean lie? Indeed, the very fact that the adjective "golden" is traditionally added to this mathematical term should in itself constitute a sufficient warning of the subjective nature of the conception. It is not difficult to observe that in actual practice those who sing its praises agree better among themselves concerning its aureate nature than they do in determining just which human creature—a St. Augustine or an Alcibiades—has most nearly attained it.

By comparison, the doctrine of extremes is logical at least, for though we may not wish to emulate the conduct of St. Simeon on his pillar, we do know what is meant when we are told to mortify as completely as possible the instincts within. But no man, I think, can be very much aided by instructions which consist of no more than the advice to give to the natural and to the human each its "proper" place.

Man has, to be sure, no monopoly on the virtues. The lower animals can be brave just as they can be—toward their offspring at any rate—self-sacrificingly loyal. Indeed, even the insects are said to exhibit a disinterested concern for the welfare of their community and to be capable of something to which the pragmatist at least can hardly refuse to give the name of patriotism.

But in the realm of the lower animals no conflict arises. The virtues appropriate to each creature's way of life are as truly instinctive as the impulses which lead him to defend his individual existence or to gratify the most elementary of his appetites. *His* golden mean—that balance of tendencies which serves to make him just what a tiger or a rabbit or an ant ought to be in order to lead exactly the life characteristic of his kind—is established for him. But though the problem is at least as old as Plato, no one has yet been able to define a good man in the sense in which it is possible to define a good horse, or a good pig, or a good bee.

Nor does there ever arise in the animal realm one of those other conflicts which result from the fact that, with us, all too many of the possible excellences are mutually exclusive. The glorious self-assertiveness of a Cellini is not compatible with the admirable self-negation of a St. Francis; and if the majority of us are hardly capable of becoming either the one or the other, yet we are faced with a thousand choices, similar except for their reduced scale.

Granted that we are not likely either to cultivate a Nietzschean lust for power and glory or to retire to St. Simeon's pillar, granted that (to be still more specific) we are not willing either to renounce the pleasures of the flesh or to devote ourselves whole-heartedly to the career of a Don Juan, then what portion of ourselves are we going to allot to the cultivation of the ego and the pleasures of sense, what part to the denial of instinct in the interest of benevolence and "purity"?

Considered merely as a problem in the calculus of pleasures, the question is unsolvable; no man can really know whether it is more pleasurable to worship an idealized Beatrice from afar or to take one's more substantial pleasures as one finds them. If a worldling cannot imagine the recompenses of the saint, it is no more to be denied that the withered ascetic is no judge of the pleasure enjoyed by the man who is also a vigorous animal, little troubled by those scruples which, so candor compels one to admit, can multiply quite as rapidly as the seeds of what the moralist calls self-indulgence or sin. And if to this mere calculus of pleasures be added the consideration of some "ought," then the already insolvable problem is still further complicated by the addition of another unknown.

Yet all the problems of which this one may be taken as the type reduce themselves ultimately to that same problem of the relationship between man and nature. All these choices are in some sense choices between impulses which are clearly recognized as the common property of all living things and those which exist—at least in other than rudimentary forms—in man alone. He only can be "too virtuous." He only can deny nature to an extent which is ruinous to the good animal within.

In all other creatures some sort of stable equilibrium or harmony is established, automatically and unchangeably, but the power of choice which in him has been so often and so highly lauded is in reality only the sign of an unstable equilibrium—of impulses not completely reconcilable, of potentialities not to be developed together, and of diversely possible excellences all of which can be conceived but of which, in a given man or a given society, only one may be realized.

If ever that missing link hypothesized by the evolutionists should be actually discovered, and if ever we should be called upon to decide whether some creature apparently midway between the ape and the man should be classified as beast or as human being, then we have in this fact a delicate but decisive test. A creature in which harmony is not only possible but instinctive is a beast. One which is aware of a divided allegiance, one which is capable of feeling, however dimly it may be, standards of value different from any plainly perceptible in the world around him and yet conflicting with others no less categorically insistent, is human.

He may imagine, as have the members of most human societies, some invisible world presided over by a spirit which understands the unnatural part of himself. Or he may, like the sophisticated people who have grown weary of many faiths each equally improbable, choose rather to confess himself probably alone in a universe which shares neither his consciousness nor the processes of his mind. But if he is part of nature and yet not really at one with it, then he is surely a human being, for it is the lines which the perception of such a dilemma have worn into the soul which constitute the mark—not of the beast, but of the man.

Doubtless it would simplify things much if there were some guide to which we could submit ourselves as the animal submits himself to his instincts. Doubtless it would be pleasant if there were something which would lead us on to be good men as the tiger is led on to be a good tiger and the ant to be all that an ant should be. And indeed the skeptic can hardly be denied the right to remark that most moral philosophies consist in the philosopher's proclamation that he has discovered just that.

All the naturalistic religions from Rousseau on are founded upon the assumption that nature—which "never did betray the heart that loved her"—is discoverable and ready to serve as an infallible guide. On the other hand, all religions essentially anti-naturalistic in their tendency proclaim that something outside of nature—some revealed code, some theology arrived at by reason, or some inner voice having its origin in the supernatural realm—is equally infallible.

But these faiths unfortunately cancel one another. Nature cannot lead us to anything except herself; and the categorical imperative which seemed to Kant so dependable turns out to be no more than the civilized version of one of those systems of taboos which instruct the savage in an equally categorical fashion that a tattooed face is "right" or that, under certain circumstances, it is immoral to allow oneself to be seen in the act of eating.

All moral codes are true in the sense that each is capable of forming one kind of individual or one kind of culture. As one or the other of them achieves an ascendancy over any united group, it forms a corresponding civilization—a Puritan New England, a Renaissance Italy, or that association of monks which made the Thebaid famous. But the very fact that no one of these civilizations endures, the very fact that humanity ultimately becomes dissatisfied with the limitations of each, is in itself a sufficient proof that no one of them can be described as affording the pattern of *the* Good Life.

Each represents, in other words, an unstable equilibrium. Each is a temporary compromise effected between the natural and the human, but a compromise destined—like all compromises between things essentially irreconcilable—to be no more than temporary. The civilization of the Renaissance comes to an end because human nature finally revolts against the increasing dominance of the animal. The civilization of the Thebaid comes no less surely to an end because nature revolts against the tendency to deny more completely than she will permit the claims which she makes.

Obviously the variety of compromises temporarily possible is great. Obviously a great distance lies between the monk on the one hand and the man of Machiavellian *vertu* on the other. But neither can break the chain which binds him. Neither can cease to be, in some measure, both animal and human. Nor is there any mid-point, permanently fixable by reason, to be determined; for that mean which seems golden is merely the point which we have taken up on the road which is leading to either indulgence or denial.

And thus though all moral codes are, in the sense just defined, equally true, all are nevertheless, and in a more fundamental sense, equally untrue, because none is alone in its power to form a civilization and because no one of these possible civilizations is demonstrably the best or the proper one. Hence it is that when a radical skepticism like that which I here profess comes to deal with the problem of ethics, it expresses a doubt which is more than merely a doubt concerning this system or that. As a matter of course it doubts the all-sufficiency of natural instinct just as it doubts also whether either the Quakers with their inner light or the Roman Catholics with their logically self-consistent corpus of theology have succeeded in getting in touch with anything outside of themselves which may be depended upon to guide them aright.

But these doubts are only corollaries, for the cardinal point of this skepticism is the doubt whether or not there exists anything to get in touch with—whether or not there exists any Idea of Man which actual mankind tends to approach, any "ought" which obligates him to go in any direction, or even any practically applicable epicurean test which will establish any particular sort of life as indisputably the most pleasurable.

The skeptic moreover—and this is fortunate for him—is not obliged to explain how the human dilemma arose. It is indeed one of the advantages of his position that it enables him to shirk that obligation which others seem to feel—that of accounting for all phenomena by some explanation, however improbable.

But he is, nevertheless, permitted to speculate; and if he happens to be (as I confess myself) temperamentally inclined to rationalistic theories, he may find in biology a suggestive clue. It may be that the tiger is not aware of any conflict between things which he would call nature and tigerishness, that the ant is not aware of any conflict between nature and true anthood, simply because no animal is capable of very many or very great deviations from a set type of conduct. But some animals are more variable than others. Man is the most variable of all; and the thing which we call intelligence is, biologically, only the means of utilizing this variability for the purpose of making biologically useful adjustments.

Is it, then, just possible that the sense of conflict of which man is aware is merely the by-product of this variability and that his persistent hypothesization of "oughts" outside himself is merely the effect of a puzzled realization that he can be, not merely one kind of animal, but any one of several? Is it possible that there is, therefore, no more reason in the question whether it is better to be a St. Francis or a Cellini than there is in the question whether or not a tiger is better than an ant? Both exist and both are interesting.

And yet the individual human being is left with the necessity of making choices and with a need of having them made for him so great that he persists in adopting one or another of the faiths which are, quite obviously, contradictory enough. Not even the skeptic is relieved from the necessity of making them, although he may be aware that he chooses in more or less haphazard fashion and without that illusion of knowing what he "ought" to choose which is so comforting to others.

Nor is it likely that any ultimate scientific discovery will solve the dilemma. Man may be part of a purely mechanical nature, or the stuff of matter itself may possess those rudiments of volition which some physicists seem ready to attribute to it. But neither fact would alter the practical aspects of the dilemma. Even the demonstrated existence of a not quite mechanical atom would hardly serve to define an "ought" or prevent individuals and cultures from achieving, for a short while, their own individual but unstable equilibriums.

IRWIN EDMAN

XVIII.

IRWIN EDMAN

THERE are two reasons why it is difficult for a contemporary to be at all certain that he knows what he believes or that he can express it candidly. Modern philosophy has taught us for three centuries to be self-conscious about the veil of consciousness that lies between us and things, the dye of subjectivity that colors and poisons our awareness of the world about us. Modern psychology, especially psychoanalysis, has made us suspicious of the validity of those tenets about which we think we are most in earnest. It has made suspect the deeper motives that lie behind our verbal ones—the instincts that masquerade as faiths and the lusts that parade as ideals. We are deeply dubious that we can know or say what we want, what we are, what we think, what we see.

There is indeed an additional reason why a contemporary hesitates, even upon invitation, to set down his credo about the universe. When there was comparatively little known, it was relatively easy to know or to pretend to know all. Nearly three thousand years ago a Greek philosopher could look about the universe and say "The All Is One," or sum up the universe as fire or water or earth or air, or the sum and combination of them. In the life of the leisure class of the Greek city-state he could prescribe the Middle Way, and specify it as wisdom of life, and know what he meant by it; in the Middle Ages, however much the theme might be modulated, the philosopher could indicate the one thing needful, the salvation of the soul, and prescribe the way toward that salvation.

Every man now knows too little and too much to set down any easy ultimate. The world of knowledge has become too complex and organized; the world of belief has become too distracted and incoherent. No one can speak with authority save on the smallest field of inquiry; there are no sacred sanctions or established civic presumptions from which faith or hope may take a point of departure. It requires audacity unaccompanied by a sense of humor to essay these days to know what is what; it requires a romanticism no modern will permit himself to say what he thinks may come of it, or what may be done about it.

Yet the present writer, for one, believes this self-consciousness to be unwholesome and unwarranted. One does not need the patter of the new physics to recognize the sky above one's head or the earth beneath one's feet, nor will all the newest doctrines of the relativists be able to abolish their omnipresence. In these matters I think it is important to be simple, almost simple-minded. For all the complexity of modern scientific formulas, it is the same old sky with the same things beneath it. Those things include my body and the bodies of other people, the plants and animals, the rocks and stars.

The knife of the skeptic may persuade me to doubt their ultimacy and teach me to seek elsewhere or to find nowhere things-in-themselves. But my hungers and passions, my pains, my raptures, and my expectations compel me to believe in or to act very much as if I believed in the common-sense world of the common man. That world is like Jehovah in the Old

Testament; it is what it is, the source of all that I know and hope and suffer and enjoy. It is that very realm in which even the skeptic is born and in which, however much he doubts it, he is resolved again into dust. A pang of hunger or of love, a loaf of bread, a beautiful face, a stumbling in the dark or a burst of music are all the testimony and all the science I need to give me a sense of the hang of things, and to make me realize that those folds as they hang are the folds of matter.

Nor am I made very much more diffident about my beliefs or aspirations because the psychoanalysts assure me that I cannot, save after long and expensive disillusionment by them, really know what I hope or fear or believe. All belief is periphrasis, the remote subterranean psyche indulging in elocution. I offer the elocution simply for what it is worth. I leave it to the analysts to tinker with the carburetor when the car gets back to the garage. I am not out to soil my hands with the engine. I am out for the ride.

I believe then in the common world of things as they are about us, the things I touch, see, taste, smell, hear, the world that earthy poets celebrate and that worldlings feast and wanton in (the same world which sustains and generates those raptures whose earthiness is so exquisite that one is tempted to call them ethereal). I believe also, though more superstitiously and not on such good evidence, that there is a kind of order in things that for short may be called mechanism, and a fundamental substance, whatever other fancy or pretentious names it be called, that is matter. In this order at a certain remote epoch there was generated life and, at a certain epoch in the history of life, that nervous speck of star dust we call man.

But it neither dismays nor distresses, indeed it scarcely impresses me, that in comparison with the whole nature of things, man is so late, so tiny, and so unregarded an accident. It seems to me not arrogance but honesty to admit, nay to insist, that that last, late incidental fleck of sport of matter called humanity, and the human viewpoint, interest me most. From nature's point of view (if she had any, which she has not), I may be quite unimportant. From my point of view, nature is at once the spectacle I behold, the theater I act in, and the materials and possibilities I can use. And whatever else anybody else may say, he acts—and is compelled to act—as if he believed precisely that.

That the spectacle is interesting it requires nothing more than good health, sensibility, intelligence, wit, and sympathy to discern. I note as part of the spectacle that these requisites are not universally distributed. I believe that with the spread and improvement of education and the possible—though improbable—more equitable distribution of wealth, they may be. There are certain parts of the spectacle that I prefer to others. It is on these grounds that I turn to the arts, to imagination, to friendship, and to philosophy for amusement, sustenance, and consolation.

There are phases of the spectacle that are boring or painful or distressing. Despite all the enormous promise of science and machinery in the way of lives cleaner, easier, swifter, and sweeter, despite all the glamour of suspicious change, I am not altogether at home in my own country and my own century, or yet fool enough to think I could even in fantasy be permanently at home anywhere else. I have no Whitmanesque enthusiasm for everything under the sun. Preference and discrimination are of the very essence of intelligence as I conceive it. I therefore prefer certain friends, places, books, and modes of life to others. Nor by the same token am I content to gloss over certain deplorable phases of the world of nature and of human nature, and of the specifically contemporary and

American world, which honesty and common sense compel me to realize.

I share quite as much as the next man, even if that man happens to be John Dewey or H. G. Wells, the faith that intelligence and contrivance may make this anarchic chaos of industry, mechanism, and capital a little more, nay a great deal more, of a universally shared garden than it is at present. The hope of the world certainly lies in intelligence. Certainly there is no hope anywhere else. I cannot look to anything so remotely definable as God for aid, nor do I ever regret not being able to do so.

But I am convinced that intelligence, though the only hope, is a support both limited and questionable. Some of the noblest and most enlightened minds of the nineteenth century believed ardently, some believe to-day, that the method of physical science applied to human concerns may make human life a brief tenancy of this worldly paradise. Certainly squalor and disease have been greatly eliminated, life has been and may be further lengthened by science, even stupidity may be reduced. Conflicts may be removed between individuals and classes and nations through methods analogous to those of the physical laboratory. But I have an obdurate conviction that human nature is surd, unpredictable, and ultimately unintelligible, that it will not be bound or expressed by formulas or saved by them. It seems to me that human nature and human life will always provide irreducible difficulties and unhappinesses that no House of Solomon, no world-wide scientific foundation can ever cure. Unrequited—and unrequitable—love, loneliness, frustration, and disappointment may be reduced by sociologists and in their extremer consequences eliminated by psychiatrists. But I am certain there would be wistful and regretful citizens in even the most splendidly organized scientific Utopia.

I do not believe that life in general or the world in general has any meaning. I do not think there is any meaning in saying that they could have. But many things, all things in nature, may have meaning; and any life may generate its own purposes or ends. Life itself is what St. Augustine would have called grace, what—in language that, however different, means the same thing—I should call "so much velvet." Not what life means, but what meanings it may have, is what counts. It is possible that, short and doomed though it be, it may be brilliant and varied as well as smooth. It is not the prelude to glory, but the occasional vehicle and revealer of it.

I know I cannot live forever, but I know also that I can know and have experienced immortal things. It is quite clear to me what sort of activities render life to me (and I suspect to a good many others) meaningful and rich, and in which direction they lie. The direction is that of abundance, vitality, and clarity. The activities range from the immediate pleasures of the senses to the wide sweep and contemplations of the mind. There are periods of creation, or enjoyment, and not least of shared enjoyment, when I find that I do not question whether life is good or worth living. For at such times, and for the time being, such questions are affirmatively answered without being asked. But the Good Life to my mind does not consist in scattered moments of felt delight, but in such a general pattern of living as would tend to fill life with richness and significance.

I am well aware that the Good Life cannot be discussed in and certainly not lived in an abstraction Arcadian and aloof. It is dependent on a thousand factors of economic and social well-being which are not yet operative in the world. But I do believe that good will and intelligence (and the spread of the latter might make the former more universal) would make the Good Life more generally available and more generally desired than it is at present.

All this is not by way of saying that I shut my eyes or my heart to the fatality, the frustration, and the tragedy that haunt the life of the most fortunate human creature. Within the possible brilliant brief episode between two oblivions, no observer at once attentive and feeling can fail at times to be discouraged and always chastened. Here again the modern, it seems to me, must come to conclusions as old at least as those of Ecclesiastes and not much more encouraging. For just as I am profoundly convinced that this earth is essentially the same as that trod by Plato two thousand years ago, and by the Bushmen much earlier, so am I impressed by the same facts, poignant and ineluctable, that they must also have observed.

No romantic doctrine of perfectibility and engineered happiness can blind me—I don't think it really blinds anyone—to death and to change. It is the fashion now to exalt novelty—and it goes without saying that only in an unfinished and changing world could anything ever change for the better. But the white peace of eternity (in which I completely disbelieve) I still profoundly care for. The mutations of youth, of friendships, of hopes, of love, may be facts to be reckoned with. I do not see how they are goods to be applauded.

I realize that on this point I differ from most of my alert compatriots and contemporaries. Newness, changes, movement, these have themselves come to be regarded as goods. But I cannot become reconciled to the fact that we live almost completely in the illusions—retrospective and always, even at their best, tinged with melancholy—of memory, and sometimes in the even more painfully illusory fantasies of anticipation.

Nor does it seem to me that crying "Life, life, faster, swifter!" can drown out the insistent fact of death which, in one way or another, the modern seeks to forget or to circumvent or avoid. Death is our name for nature's final and implacable defeat; just as birth is our name for nature's special reiterated triumph. But except that some day I expect to be sick and old and tired, I do not see on what grounds I could welcome death, or on what grounds modern formulas can ease the pang of its imminence or its absoluteness. On this point Ecclesiastes is right, and everything for everyone is ultimately vanity under the sun.

It may be protested that death is too morbid a preoccupation, though obviously it is as patent a fact as life and one that no adult philosophy can fail to reckon with. If it is said that the healthy animal does not brood upon death, it may also be added that he does not reflect on life either. I do not see how anything but weariness can pretend that death is good or anything but cowardice neglect to make peace with it. For my own part, both reflection and instinct have so far persuaded me of the ultimacy of death as a final quietus that no question bores me more than a canvassing of the possibilities of a future life. I cannot, however, hail extinction romantically as once Browning did, as one fight more, the best and the last. It is one of the things hateful to me, as are all the irremediable enemies of life, or even the remediable ones, disease and fatigue and hypocrisy and stupidity. And death is one of those enemies against whom all one can do is hate.

The older religions have tried to do more than hate extinction. They have tried mythologically to wish it away. So far as their literal promise of immortality goes, I am a complete disbeliever. As for the traditional God whose justice, mercy, and benevolence guaranteed an after life, I likewise, of course, disbelieve in Him too. What is more, or worse, or better, I do not even miss Him in the sense in which I miss, at this moment of writing, four thousand miles from home, some of my friends. I believe in nothing that can be called religion by a traditionalist, though I not only respect but find illumination in the insights, at once moral and poetic, of the Jewish prophets, of the Buddhistic way of life, and of the Christian mythology. Literally taken, they are ridiculous and misleading; morally taken, they are metaphors and music on important human themes. They are the most serious art that we have inherited.

Besides God and immortality, traditional religion has promised us, or presumes we have, freedom. In a certain rough sense I suppose I believe in determinism. That is, I believe that every fact has a consequence. But practically and morally I believe in freedom. That is, within the limits of natural conditions, I believe genuine choice is possible, and that that choice is immensely enlarged by education and the habit and technique of understanding.

With respect to the contemporary world to which, after all, these considerations alone have any future or any bearing, I happen, by temperament, to be at once immensely interested and about much of it a little dubious. Unlike some æsthetes I have known, I see no reason, and certainly no use, in trying to flee America. For increasingly America—simply another name for modernity—is becoming the character and quality of that ancient Europe to which the American flees for quietude and refuge.

That we are witnessing the decline of Western culture, of all those habits, things, and values which Athens, Chartres, and Dante enshrine, may well be the case. There is even a chance—to my mind, not a small one—that Western civilization as we know it may be destroyed in a more anarchic and rapid universal war than the last. Intelligence may save us from ruin, and I am on the side of every movement that promises decency and order in a maelstrom of a world. I am ready to believe that science and the machine may save us, if they do not kill or stifle us first. I am ready to believe and work in whatever measure I can toward the realization of an American culture that shall be something more like Greece than like Carthage.

There seems to be little to weep for, naught to bewail. There seem to me objects of enjoyment as intense as those ever given to any race or to any individual possible in our world. There seem to me, without benefit of religion or of clergy, to be the possibilities of worship and of adoration. There are altitudes of the spirit revealed to us in the traditions of philosophy, literature, music, and art that remind me still that divinity was not a human invention but a human discovery. I believe those heights in art or in life may be reached again, and I know the works of contemporaries and the lives of contemporaries that seem to me to bring a renewed faith in the possibilities of life even to a disillusioned and weary generation.

Meanwhile life seems to me, for all its eternal and contemporary limitations, good fun—and possibly much more. At the very least it provokes merriment and, at fortunate moments, in happy instances, it may still be the incitement to beauty and wisdom as well.

XIX.
HILAIRE BELLOC

WE FIND ourselves in a world where we know our own existence and where something which Aristotle called "Common Sense" makes us recognise the reality of existences outside our own. Further, we find in ourselves senses of right and wrong, pleasure and pain. When we set out to interpret ourselves and the universe about us—to find out the meaning of the affair—our own origins and nature and destiny—whether there be a conscious will behind the universe—whether that will is indifferent to us or not, and so on: when we begin *that* supreme inquiry, we are brought to a halt. The great questions, the only questions the answers to which really matter, remain unanswered. It is doctrine indeed that the human mind can, unaided by revelation, discover that God is, that He is omnipotent, one and personal. But it is not doctrine (and still less is it experience) that every human mind can of its unaided power achieve this feat; and it is quite certain that not one in a thousand attempts it. As for the nature and destiny of man, his possible immortality, his responsibility, his free-will, we are left without a clue.

Faced with the great unanswered questions, the tendency of

men, after a first examination, is to proclaim them unanswerable. Of course, where men do not trouble to think, merely accepting what they have been told, they may answer conventionally one or another of these great questions; but the moment they begin to reason, their first, most natural attitude is scepticism. They conclude thus:

"We know nothing of these things. Nothing can be proved upon them, and therefore it is futile to continue the search, and puerile and ignoble to pretend to have discovered an answer. The man who does so is either abandoning the use of his reason and blindly accepting that to which he has been accustomed by long repetition since childhood, or he is a hypocrite and liar, and perhaps the worst sort of hypocrite and liar—the man who lies to himself in order to feel at ease."

Now it so happens that there is a third point of view or attitude of the mind neither sceptical nor the mere product of habit and repetition, but working upon the following lines:

"I have discovered an absolute Authority upon earth; I have heard a Voice which speaks on these affairs in the unmistakable tone of combined integrity and knowledge. I have come upon a Personality whose commands are at once justified, salutary and (as it were) a part of my own being, because they proceed from that which was the Author of my being, to whom I tend and with whom I, like all creation, am in organic connection. The answers given by this Authority to the great unanswered questions, I accept as final and true."

This third attitude, which is neither the high sceptical attitude nor the confused "circular" attitude of mere habit, is called Catholic. It is the attitude which I who am writing these lines adopt in common with a good many other people. I adopt it with all its consequences in political and social action, in the general frame of the mind, in the texture of character which it produces, and in the duties which it imposes apart from, and sometimes in contradiction to, all lesser authorities whatsoever.

This third type of philosophy is unique. One hears men talk, of "warring creeds," "conflicting systems" and "various religions," and including the Catholic Church in that general description as though it were of the same stuff as the rest. Such a confusion argues an ignorance of the matter discussed. Catholicism is not one opinion amongst many, nor one set of doctrines and customs amongst many others. It is of an essence different from all else. It is the only institution on earth which ever has, and still does, proclaim itself infallible and absolutely authoritative. No one of those other institutions which seem to be of its own kind and nature (because they make many statements in common with Catholic statements or because they have a traditional ritual and body of doctrine largely in common with Catholicism—for instance, the Eastern Church) is really of the same stuff at all. For *they* say that there is no visible, localised, concrete, definite, citable authority of the kind. They admit no living and teaching authority among men to be continuously infallible and active to-day and for the future.

At the best they say there *has* been one in the past and *may* be one in the future. But the attitude of those who say that there *is* one, fully alive, and that it always has been and always will be such an authority, is peculiar to Catholics: that is (since one has to define accurately in these days of loose phraseology), peculiar to those who are in communion with the Papacy, accept the infallibility of its decisions and of the General Councils, not only in the past but as they are continued under authority to our own day.

There are certain strange marks to be observed attaching to this institution called "The Catholic Church." In the first place, while making this awful and unique and (in the eyes of most people) incredible claim to certitude based on reason (while no one else has certitude other than blind), it answers some questions only, others not at all. One might imagine that a system of the kind would pretend to universal knowledge; it professes none save in its own field. For instance, it affirms a creation. Our lesser, very interesting, questions upon the *mode* of creation it leaves unanswered. Next, note that it is and has been throughout the ages intensely loved, and even more intensely hated. The violence of that hatred is inconceivable to those who have not felt it. It arises only on contact. It is hardly felt in the absence of the irritant. But in the presence of that irritant hate blazes out like a fire.

Lastly, though hated, it is quite astonishingly unknown. It almost looks as though hardly any man not within this institution could possess the faculties whereby its character may be appreciated.

I have known one or two exceptions (perhaps half a dozen in my whole life) of men born and brought up outside the Catholic Church, never dreaming of accepting it as other than an illusion and man-made, yet really knowing what it was all about and of what stuff it was. These men were men of very wide reading in many languages and of wide travel and experience. But to one such there are a hundred equally well-read and equally widely travelled who are as much in error upon the savour and character of the Catholic Church as, say, the average French journalist is in error upon the nature of an English public school.

For instance, you will find men highly educated, and with a good knowledge of other things, who imagine that Catholicism in some way restricts intellectual exercise. They say this to *us*, to *us* who feel that our intelligence cannot act freely in any other atmosphere, who enjoy the whole range of scholastic inquiry and of those great minds which established the casuistry of Moral Theology! They tell us we are restricted from doing that which the Catholic alone has fully done for two thousand years, that is, looking into everything to find its cause, and searching continually for further and further detail in the general body of truth. Or again, they will regard Catholicism as a bundle of disconnected affirmations, some picturesque, some absurd, some obvious. They may live all their lives reading the history of a Catholic country, or period, and yet remain completely ignorant of the simple fact that the Faith is not only one vast coherent system, explanatory of the universe and of man therein, but a system which is so alive that it ramifies perpetually into a wider and wider exercise of faculty and meets and deals with every new situation with which it is confronted.

Again, you will find many people of fair instruction and fairly wide reading, who imagine that Catholicism refuses to face reality, and organises this illusion, whereas the whole point of Catholicism is the facing of reality and the refusal to be drugged by mere repeated affirmation, or to do anything but laugh at the silly modern systems of self-deception which have arisen from a desire to avoid the ordeal of human life.

It is this character in the Faith—that it is universal, that it has the very ring of reality, that its authoritative voice is recognised at once if it be heard—it is this character, I say, which brought into its orbit, as by an irresistible pressure, the best brains of our time. Among all other kinds of men it has been particularly those men who had the keener senses combined with the highest intelligence who have harked back to the religion of Europe. What that appeal of Catholicism to the intelligence may be I can perhaps best illustrate by a metaphor which I have always found singularly applicable.

The old painters often amused themselves by drawing a picture which at first sight was unintelligible. Put your eye in a particular position, and the picture falls at once into perspective and corresponds with that which it was meant to portray. There is such a detail in the National Gallery; among the objects appearing in a particular picture is one object which at first sight looks like nothing on earth: a long drawn, oval, yellowish thing with meaningless lights and darks upon it. Look at it from a particular point to the side of the picture and you will see it to be a skull; change your position slightly, and it resolves itself into chaos again. Now the Catholic attitude is like that. From the vantage-point of the Catholic attitude the meaningless pattern of the world falls into perspective. Catholic philosophy and action is found consonant with the life of man and with man's normal relation to the world about him. The Faith explains; it explains fully; and it is the only thing that does explain.

Nevertheless, as I have said, it is hated and suffers from a really astonishing ignorance of its character and habits in the minds of onlookers. On this account I suggest that conflict between the Catholic Church and the other forces of the modern world is imminent. Whether we have yet heard the first clash or not is debatable. Whether a recognised and violent open battle will be waged a short time hence or not till after a lifetime or more, no one can tell. But it is coming.

That which is not Catholic in the modern world is not only tending towards, it is racing towards, a new set of laws, a new condition of the civic mind which is incompatible with Catholicism. There cannot but be an atmosphere created in which, in the long run, either Catholicism will not be able to live, or its opponents will not be able to live.

There are many avenues by which we may see that state of things approaching. Perhaps the most important is that of

HILAIRE BELLOC

the debate on Free Will (remember that all political questions are ultimately theological).

The Catholic Church may be called an Exercise of the Will. But as the modern world loses its remnants of Christian doctrine, the function of the Will not only declines, but is in prospect of being denied. The substitution of physical science for philosophy; of the quantitative for the qualitative; of unimportant things, directly demonstrable to the poorest mind, for important things which the greater minds grasp by appreciation—all this process is making for a clash between those who retain the doctrine of Free Will and those who have sunk unintelligently into the drift of materialism and fatalism; a conception that all the process of the world and of ourselves is inevitable. To take but one instance of an issue on which the clash might soon come; this new paganism tends to regard evil as due to impersonal causes. It tends to eliminate moral indignation and to deprive of its meaning the distinction between right and wrong.

Again, the denial of Free Will ultimately tends to restrict more and more the liberty of the individual. It tends indirectly, but with its whole power, to the sacrifice of human dignity for the purposes of a supposed collective temporal and merely material good. Here again the new paganism cannot but clash with the Catholic Church. We may be upon the edge of new laws which will enforce a declaration from parents to promote the sterilisation of the unfit. We may live to see new laws enforcing one system of general education to the exclusion of dogmatic teaching in schools under public authority, to which the mass of people are forced to send their children.

But particular instances give no idea of the magnitude of the quarrel. A whole social tissue is being built up as an organism about us, and the more coherent it becomes, the more its new personality is emphasised, the more violent and emphatic is its necessary quarrel with that opposing institution whereby alone, as I conceive, can man fulfil his being, or even achieve such poor happiness as freedom and responsibility breed in this brief preparatory life between birth and death.

BEATRICE WEBB

XX.

BEATRICE WEBB

OUT of the social environment and mental climate in which I was born and bred, there seemed to arise two outstanding questions, questions perpetually recurring in my own consciousness from girlhood to old age: Can there be a science of social organization, in the sense in which we have a science of mechanics or a science of chemistry, enabling us to forecast what will happen, and perhaps to alter the event by taking appropriate action or persuading others to take it? Secondly, assuming that there can be, or will be, such a science of society, is man's capacity for scientific discovery the only faculty required for the reorganization of society according to an ideal? Or do we need religion as well as science, emotional faith as well as intellectual curiosity? In the following pages will be found my tentative answer to these two questions—that is, my philosophy of work or life.

The first of these questions, Can there be an applied science of society? led me early in life to choose a particular vocation—the study of social institutions by the methods of personal observation, actual participation in the organization concerned, the taking of evidence, statistical inquiry, and the examination of historical records. My reaction from this long-continued practice of the art of the social investigator has been an ever-deepening conviction of the supreme value in all social activity of the scientific method.

Let me give one or two examples of an applied science of society taken from the public administration of Great Britain during the past hundred years. In the early part of the nineteenth century the business of government, whether national or local government, was honeycombed with favoritism, corruption, and barefaced peculation. This wholesale dishonesty on the part of representatives and officials has been largely swept away by the adoption of a social invention of definitely scientific character, namely, the audit—a device which is scarcely a century old. The systematic checking of the cash transactions of all public officials by a special class of independent experts has been found to have an amazing influence not only upon their accuracy but also upon their honesty. Thus, the world can, by taking thought, so far predict and alter the future as positively to grow the habit of honesty on a large scale. Another instance is the discovery, during the past three-quarters of a century, of better methods of selecting persons for responsible or specialized work. During the eighteenth century, alike in central and in local government, nearly all positions of trust and authority were jobbed; that is to say, they were given by those in authority to their own relatives, political supporters, or social hangers-on, however incapable or badly conducted these persons might be. To-day this jobbery has been very nearly eliminated in the British civil service by two or three simple devices. One of these devices, applicable to nearly all first appointments of young persons, is selection by competitive examination, through a non-political board, wholly unconnected with the public authorities which are engaging new employees. Another expedient, more suited to persons of mature age where specific attainments are indispensable, is the device of a prescribed qualification—a qualification tested by the appropriate professional organization—again an organization wholly unconnected with the public authorities concerned. This we have for our official doctors and nurses, civil engineers, accountants, and architects.

Let me give one more instance of the advantage of the scientific study of facts in the way that I have described. A hundred years ago the accepted way of dealing with extreme poverty—what was called destitution—was poor-law relief. This relief took one of two forms—maintenance in the general mixed workhouse or a niggardly dole of unconditional outdoor relief. A century of experience has discredited both. As a result of long-continued observation and experiment by all sorts of persons, officials and philanthropists, recorded in innumerable bluebooks and scientific treatises, there has been gradually created a whole series of new social institutions vitally affecting human behavior—a veritable framework of prevention. Instead of threatening the sick person with the workhouse if he applied for relief, the public-health authority has come more and more to seek him out, in order to cure him and to prevent any spread of disease. The local education authority now welcomes every child to school, insists that the parents send the child to school reasonably clean, even feeds the child if it is found to require it, and prosecutes the parents who are guilty of wilful neglect. The infant-welfare center endeavors to look after every birth, instructs the mother how to rear the baby, and offers periodically to examine and weigh the growing infant, so that the mother may know how it is progressing. This may seem a small matter. But the statistician proves to us that during the past thirty years, since these things have been done, only half as many babies die as in the previous generation. What is even more striking is the vast alteration for the better that has been effected by these preventive services in the behavior of the parents and the children in the way of healthy living, in cleanliness, and even in manners.

There are some of us who believe that it will yet be found practicable, through observation and experiment, to invent an analogous framework of prevention applicable to that terrible disease of modern industry, mass unemployment.

Have I succeeded by these few illustrations in making the reader realize why I believe that we have already a science of society—a young and very incomplete science, but one that is steadily growing and that is capable of indefinite extension? But it is a science with limitations. Unlike iron and stone and machinery, human beings and social institutions are always changing. They even alter while you are studying them. This is a difficulty which the science of society shares with the science of biology or with that of medicine. But the changes in social institutions are sometimes so catastrophic and far-reaching as completely to baffle our generalizations and nullify our predictions. No student of social facts, however competent, could have forecast the Russian Revolution or the nature of the Soviet Government. No one could have foreseen the sudden development of the Fascist state in Italy. No one could have predicted the rapid rise to prosperity and power of the Czecho-Slovakian republic, the very name of which we can barely pronounce and the exact position of which is unknown to most of us. Here and there, from time to time, there emerges from the mass a man or a group of men whose uncommon qualities are exceptionally influential with the particular race of human beings with whom they come in contact. It may be a captivating personality, it may be religious exaltation, it may be superlative efficiency in the organization of war or in the administration of the state. William James called such great men "ferments," influences which change the course of life of a whole nation. We may recognize such a ferment in the great leader of the Czecho-Slovakian race, Masaryk. Sometimes these potent individuals appear more like volcanic eruptions—as with Lenin in Russia and Mussolini in Italy and Gandhi in India. These are as unpredictable by science as an earthquake. But woe betide the great man, be he prophet or warrior or statesman, who forgets not only that the common man exists, but also that it is with the common man that he has to deal. If a Lenin, a Mussolini, or a Gandhi wants to reduce the infant death-rate or to adopt summer time, to create a universal system of public education or to build up a stable democratic state out of millions of men of different races and antagonistic creeds, in Russia, Italy, or India, he must, for all his volcanic power, learn from the knowledge of past and present social institutions the particular devices by which one or other of these things can be created. Before he died Lenin had to admit that in ignoring one common characteristic of the tens of millions of the Russian peasant-cultivators—the desire to better his own circumstances—he had made a big mistake. He had, indeed, to reverse his policy of complete communism, and to permit, at least temporarily, a measure of individual accumulation and private trade. Mussolini may yet find that in suppressing all independence of speech and freedom of the press he has alienated an indispensable factor in a stable and progressive state.

To sum up: The generalization and predictions of the science of society relate to that strange abstraction, the average human being. Here we recognize what might be termed the mystical element in the work of the statistician. What he tells us is the truth, even truth of a high order. But he does not deal with our individual peculiarities. He predicts what will be found true of what is common to all the individuals who make up the group or race of men with which he is dealing. The uncommon, the exceptional, the peculiar characteristics of the individual man, and the manner of his influence, are at present and possibly always will be outside the scope of a science of society.

I pass to the second question which has continuously confronted me in my passage through life. Is man's capacity for scientific discovery the only faculty required for the reorganization of society according to an ideal? Or do we need religion as well as science, emotional faith as well as intellectual curiosity?

Very early in my career as a social investigator I realized that science deals only with the processes of life; it has little to say of the purpose of life. We can learn through science how best to kill a man or slaughter a multitude of men; we can discover how to cure a human being of specific diseases and thus raise indefinitely the standard of health. But no amount of personal observation or statistical inquiry will tell us whether we *ought* to kill or to cure. Our behavior, as parent or child, as colleague or rival, as employer or employed, as private citizen or public official, is largely dictated to us by law or public opinion. But whenever we settle it for ourselves, it seems to depend on intuition or impulse, on likes or dislikes, or to put it in another way, on our emotional outlook on life. Historically, codes of conduct, scales of value, patterns of behavior—to use the term of my friend, Graham Wallas—are intimately related to contemporary conceptions of man's relation to the universe, whether these notions are woven into magic rites, wrought into religious creeds, or expressed in systems of philosophy incapable of objective verification. My own experience is that in the nobler type of men these guides to conduct appear to rise out of emotive thought, connecting the purpose of individual man with the purpose of the universe, the visible with the invisible world. "Man lives in two worlds," Professor Haldane tells us in his brilliant exposition of What I Believe, "the visible world which changes with time, and an invisible world whose constituents do not change." "I have not very much use for people who are not in touch with the invisible world," he adds somewhat scornfully. The trouble is that when we ask to be put in touch with this invisible world we are given, by this eminent scientist, not the bread of spiritual guidance but the hard stone of pure intellect and a short measure of that! "Among the components of the invisible world are the realities corresponding to mathematical statements like $16 + 9 = 25$." This, literally, is all that he vouchsafes us! Memory recalls my friend Bertrand Russell arguing that the arithmetical proposition that two and two makes four cannot be proved by pure logic, and is merely an empirical truth derived from experience, thus belonging to the visible and not to the invisible world. However that may be, to an undeveloped mind like mine Professor Haldane's exposition of the invisible world is meaningless. It arouses no response either from my intellect or from my emotions.

But why should we expect to describe the invisible world? All we can do is to explain our own state of mind, so that we may enter into communion with those of like temperament, and thus encourage and strengthen each other in our common pilgrimage through life. For my own part, I believe that the mind of man, as distinguished from the appetites and instincts which he shares with other animals, is divided into two parts —the intellectual and the emotional, each having its own methods and sanctions. What is called the scientific method is the highest expression of the intellect; by observation, verification, and reasoning, we can discover how things happen and predict how they will happen under like circumstances, and, in many instances, by applying this knowledge, we can alter this happening in the direction we desire.

The highest expression of the emotional side of human nature is the attainment of the beautiful and the good; the one represented by art in all its manifestations, the other by varieties of religious experience, leading to what is felt to be the right conduct of life. I have not the artistic temperament and I know not in what state of consciousness this may be embodied; what may be its discipline and its sanctions. But like the majority of the human race I have an incipient religious temperament—a yearning for the mental security of a spiritual home. "Religion," we are told by Professor Whitehead (*Science and the Modern World*, p. 238), "is the vision of something which stands beyond, behind, and within, the passing flux of immediate things; something which is real, and yet waiting to be realized; something which is a remote possibility, and yet the greatest of present facts; something that gives meaning to all that passes, and yet eludes apprehension; something whose possession is the final good, and yet is beyond all reach; something which is the ultimate ideal, and the hopeless quest."

This vision of something which is real and yet waiting to be realized is associated in my experience with an intuitive use of prayer. A secularist friend once cross-examined me as to what exactly I meant by prayer; he challenged me to define the process of prayer; to describe its happening. I answered I would gladly do so if I could find the words. The trouble is, as Tagore observes about poetry, that words have meanings, or, as I prefer to say, predominantly intellectual meanings; and in prayer it is emotion, not reason, that seeks an outlet. It is by prayer, by communion with an all-pervading spiritual force, that the soul of man discovers the purpose or goal of human endeavor. That is why down all the ages of human development prayer has been intimately associated, whether as cause or effect, with the nobler and more enduring forms of architecture and music; associated, too, with poetry and painting, with the awe-inspiring aspects of nature, with the great emotional mysteries of maternity, mating, and death.

To Professor Haldane my longer string of words may seem as meaningless as his curt arithmetical formula does to me. Perhaps we can find common ground in *The Will to Believe,* eloquently expounded by William James, or in *The Philosophy of "As If,"* logically developed by Vaihinger. So far as I understand the conclusion of these eminent metaphysicians —a conclusion which I understand is also held by Einstein— it can be summed up in the proposition that wherever no hypothesis can be scientifically proved or disproved, and yet some hypothesis must be accepted as a starting-point for thought or as a basis for conduct, the individual is justified in selecting the hypothesis which yields the richest results in the discovery of truth or in the leading of a good life. Such a justifiable hypothesis seems to me the faith I hold: that man is related to the universe by an emotional as well as by a rational tie, that there is a spirit of love at work in the universe, and that the emotion of prayer or aspiration reveals to man the ends he should pursue if he desires to harmonize his own purpose with that of the universe; exactly as the working of his intellect discovers the means by which these ends may be best achieved. "Did I ever tell you," writes one of the greatest of British scientific thinkers, Francis Galton, "that I have always made it a habit to *pray* before writing anything for publication, that there may be no self-seeking in it, and perfect candor, together with respect for the feelings of others" (*Life of Francis Galton,* by Karl Pearson, III A, 272).

But I realize that in the world of to-day science is in the ascendant, while the religious impulse is in eclipse. This decay of religious faith is, I think, a reaction from what is false within the current religious creeds. Throughout the ages, prophets and priests, saints and Sadducees, have dictated to the faithful mythical accounts of how things happen, how they have happened, and how they will happen—whether concerning the beginnings of life on this earth, or the course of the stars, or the diagnosis and cure of disease, or the better organization of society. This unwarranted intrusion of religion into the realm of science, this illegitimate attempt to supersede reason by emotion in respect to the processes of nature has always led and will always lead, at best, to failure to attain the desired ends, at worst, to superstitious practices and degrading magic. Few believers in the scientific method accept as evidence of fact the Biblical narrative of the creation of the world in six days or that of the miracles of the Immaculate Conception and the resurrection from the dead of the physical body of Jesus of Nazareth. I am aware that these "dogmas" are deemed by some practicing Christians to be not statements of fact at all, but merely symbols of some invisible truth—appeals to the emotion and not to the intellect. This gloss on the creed of Christendom seems to me lacking in candor.

Thus, like many of my contemporaries, I am a religious outcast; I cannot enjoy, without sacrificing intellectual integrity, the immeasurable benefit of spiritual comradeship, the inner peace arising out of traditional forms of worship, the inspiration of noble motive—all of which I recognize as embodied in the discipline of the great religions of the world, such as Christianity and Buddhism. And while I rejoice in the advance of science, I deplore the desuetude of regular religious services with their encouragement of worship and prayer for the good reason that personal experience and the study of history convince me that this absence of the religious habit leads to an ugly chaos in private and public morals and to a subtle lowering of the sense of beauty—witness the idol of the subhuman, the prevalence of crude animalism, in much of the music, art, and literature of the twentieth century.

But to my mind there is one hopeful portent. Men of science endowed with the religious temperament are to-day reinterpreting the mystical meaning of the universe; and it is they who may bring about a new synthesis between our discovery of the true and our self-dedication to the beautiful and the good.

XXI.

WILLIAM RALPH INGE

Not long ago Mr. Lowes Dickinson wrote, if my memory serves me, "For myself, I am no democrat." Still more recently he confessed to being one. It all depends on what you mean by democracy. In America it means anything you like, but when the word is mentioned you are expected to salute the star-spangled banner. For instance, an American divine exclaimed, "You cannot separate God and democracy. For if we believe in God, we believe in God's purposes, God's ideal, and that is believing in God." The logic seems to halt. Or I may cull this gem from the *New York Medical Journal,* in an article on gout: "Uric acid is tottering upon its throne. Democracy is advancing in medical theory as well as in political practice."

Well, it is bad manners to smile at our friends when they are at their devotions. But, as a matter of fact, democracy is neither an attribute of the Deity nor a method of therapeutics. It is the name of an experiment in government. During the war we said we were fighting to make the world safe for democracy. That was a lump of sugar for the American eagle, and, fortunately for us, he swallowed it. At present, most of the world seems to have made up its mind that democracy is not safe for itself.

We must, however, distinguish between democracy as a form of government, in which all the citizens legislate without representation; democracy as a form of State, which means that the electors, under universal suffrage, have the last word; and democracy as a form of society, which means equal consideration for all. The first is possible only in a small city State, like ancient Athens or a Swiss canton. The second is what we have got. The third is a Christian principle, and as a Christian I believe in it. Number two I do not much believe in, and I fancy very few people believe in it any longer. Mr. Shaw has said that the great political problem is to find a good anthropometric method, and that we have not found it. The silliest of all methods is to break heads; the next silliest is to count them. Practically, universal suffrage means that the worldly goods of the minority are put up to auction at each election, and there is no limit to the absurdity of the promises made by candidates except the fear that they may be called upon to redeem them. It is a ridiculous arrangement; but I frankly admit that I do not know what we could put in its place.

As for the notion of abolishing private gain, I will only make one obvious remark. If you destroy the chief motives which induce people to work hard, namely, the desire to improve their own position, and still more to give their children a good start in the world, a few people will work as well as they do now (I hope I should, but I doubt it), the majority will work badly, and a considerable number will refuse to work at all unless someone stands over them with a whip. The output of commodities would beyond question be enormously reduced; and the country would be very poor. At last in desperation we should adopt the whip, or some equivalent.

WILLLIAM RALPH INGE

As Herbert Spencer said, "Socialism would mean slavery, and the slavery would not be mild."

I do not want to give all my space to politics, but one thing I must say before I leave the subject. Those who go about abusing our social system, calling it a hell upon earth and so forth, are doing about the worst disservice to their country that any man could do. For, in spite of all the faults that may justly be found with it, it is a simple fact that there has never been a time in the history of the world when the average citizen, the working man and woman, could command anything like the comforts and amusements and opportunities for education and intellectual pleasure that he and she have now. With all its faults, the civilisation of the twentieth century is the happiest and best for the average man and woman that the world has seen. And then these gentry go about poisoning people's minds, and stirring up discontent everywhere, till the temper of society becomes sour, embittered, despondent, and quarrelsome. Our social arrangements are better for the poorer citizens than they have ever been before, and they are in the way to become better still. America leads the way. By mass production on a large scale, by standardisation, and by improved machinery, rough manual toil is being eliminated, and comforts hitherto undreamed of are being put within the reach of almost all, without lengthening the day's work or diminishing wages. This is the American alternative to Socialism; it *works,* whereas Socialism has always been a dead failure.

There is, of course, a very awkward snag in our way—unemployment, due partly to the dole and partly to over-population. Our social problems can be solved if our numbers are properly regulated; if they are not, they are hopeless. But my studies in this subject lead me to think that in this country we shall adjust our population to something like the optimum number, though we may go through a bad time first. My calculation is that between 1940 and 1945 the population will become stationary. If it is too large now, and I think it is, the best remedy is State-aided colonisation. The dole is utterly demoralising; its chief effect is to turn the unemployed into the unemployable.

I am more anxious about quality than quantity. The young science of eugenics is going to be extremely important some day; but I am not in favour of very drastic measures to stop the procreation of the unfit, till we know rather more than we do now. But let us all agree that the test of the welfare of a country is the kind of men and women that it produces; and that nature is more important than nurture. There are two great factors in our modern civilisation. One is industrialism and the growth of applied science; the other is the scientific faith.

I am not a man of science, as Mr. Haldane will perhaps remind you; but I read scientific books, and I think I understand the scientific spirit. On the whole, I think the moral influence of the new knowledge has been beneficial. The air that blows round science is like the air of mountain tops, cold and thin, but pure and bracing. I will mention some of the gains which the scientific temper has brought us.

Even in politics and religion, where passion and prejudice are most potent to obscure the intellect and distort the judgment, there is a higher standard of veracity and more respect for evidence. Rhetoric and advocacy are distrusted. The scientific spirit has transformed history, and has imposed rather more conscientiousness even upon controversial literature and public speaking.

Curiosity, which was condemned by monkish morality, is now praised, as it was by the Greeks. To seek for the truth, for the sake of knowing the truth, is one of the noblest objects that a man can live for. Huxley thus states the aims of his own career: "To promote the increase of natural knowledge, and to forward the application of scientific methods of investigation to all the problems of life, in the conviction that there is no alleviation of the sufferings of mankind, except veracity of thought and action, and the resolute facing of the world as it is, when the garment of make-believe is stripped off."

The centre of gravity in morals, as in theology, is changing from authority to rational motive and the conscience of the individual. New moral demands arise from new knowledge and new circumstances, and these new demands are easily stifled by authoritative tradition. Among the big questions which the new morality will have to tackle are our duty to posterity, our duty to the so-called lower animals, and our duty to our habitation, the earth, the beauty of which we are spoiling as fast as we can. We shall have to fight the politician, who remembers only that the unborn have no votes and that since posterity has done nothing for us we need do nothing for posterity; the traditionalist theologian, who tells us that the animals have no souls, and therefore no rights; and the Philistine who cannot see a waterfall without wishing to turn it into a power station.

Again, although science is for the most part agnostic about the existence of a personal God, it is positive in rejecting much that has been falsely taught and believed about God. God is, at any rate, not a capricious and cruel Oriental sultan, nor a magnified schoolmaster, nor the head of the clerical profession. This purification of the idea of God is a great gain. Such as men themselves are, such will God appear to them to be; and such as God appears to them to be, such will they show themselves in their dealings with their fellow men.

The abandonment of miracle, as a fact of present-day experience, is a clear gain. Though we are still plagued with priestly frauds and bogus cures, ghostly apparitions, and superstitions of every kind, science has laid the axe to the root of the tree, and we may hope that by degrees such beliefs and half-beliefs will either be discredited or placed on a scientific basis.

Lastly, the greatly extended horizon which science has opened for the human race gives us "the rapture of the forward view" which we never enjoyed before. The secular faith of to-day is the belief in rational self-determination, the hope that humanity has its future in its own hands.

So much in praise of science. It does not follow that we must adopt the very poor philosophies which scientific men have constructed. In philosophy they have much more to learn than to teach. The notion that the real is what can be weighed and measured, and that all our higher interests are a kind of luminous haze floating above the real world and unable to affect it at all is very bad philosophy, and theology is quite right to protest against it. It would leave us with no art, no religion, and no science either. The eternal and absolute values are at least as much parts of reality as atoms and electrons.

Nor need we accept the very unscientific superstition of the nineteenth century, the belief in an automatic law of progress. It was held by most of the scientists, but it is quite unscientific. Progress is a rather rare phenomenon in nature and it cannot go on for ever. When we look at the moon, airless, waterless, cold, and dead, we know what the ultimate fate of our planet must be. "But we have a very long lease, almost as good as a freehold." Yes, we have; but there is no law of progress. When we think of the insect civilisations, which advanced to a more complete socialism than even Mr. Shaw has pictured, we may infer that at least a possible fate for us is to reach a condition of stable equilibrium, when the faculty of thought, which will be no longer useful, will be withdrawn, and instinct will take its place. We shall be in purgatory, but we shall not know it. We shall then have a Socialist and Suffragette millennium, governed by our maiden aunts, who will be armed with stilettos to extinguish the men when they have performed the only function which will be left to them. This may be the end of nature's queerest experiment, the evolution of our noble selves. However, since the human race does not possess the virtues of the little busy bee, and of the ant who is an example to the sluggard, and since all our progress has been the result of our fixed propensity to live beyond our incomes and save ourselves trouble, it is more probable that we shall go on indefinitely as we are, trying new experiments, all of which will be interesting, and some of them successful.

You will expect me to say something about religion in an age of science. Christianity, after breaking the first moulds into which the precious metal, still hot and liquid, was poured, congealed and petrified—you may spell petrified with a capital P if you like—at a rather unhappy period of the history of Europe. The Greeks and Romans knew that their civilisation was on the wane, and they had no hopes for the future.

The Jews had hopes for the future, but what they hoped for was a supernatural deliverance, which would enable them to bruise their oppressors with a rod of iron. The consequence was that neither from Palestine nor from Greece could the early Christians get any evolutionary doctrine of history. The framework of Christianity was catastrophic. There was no significance in history apart from a few tremendous events in the past and future—the creation of the world a few thousand years ago, the fall of man, his redemption in the first century A.D., and the end of the world, which was thought to be very near. We now live in an age when all educated people believe in a very different world order. We are now told that the sun has been in existence about eight billion years, the earth about two thousand million, the human race about one million; and that there is no reason, so far as we know, why there should not be men and women on this planet a million years hence. Further, we believe that the changes in the world are slow and gradual, and in accordance with natural laws. The supreme question for Christians is whether the catastrophic scheme which we have inherited by tradition can be fitted into the evolutionary scheme in which we have come to believe. Personally I think it can, but only at the cost of greater changes than most churchmen are willing to face.

As Protestant Christians, we are bound to the New Testament, and the New Testament only. We are not bound to accept the extreme asceticism which captured the Church—it was not originally a Christian movement—nor the theocratic monarchy which established itself on the ruins of the West Roman empire. I can accept the dictum of Rudolf Eucken, a great German thinker: "We not only can be, but we must be Christians; only, however, if we recognise that Christianity is a progressive historical development still in the making."

There is only one omission in the moral teaching of the New Testament, and I have already indicated what it is. There is no vision of an earthly future either for State or Church, no glimmering that there might be a very long time before the predicted end of the age, no help towards constructing a better social order. When Christ was asked to arbitrate in a case of disputed property, He replied that it was no business of His, and added, "Beware of covetousness."

I have explained this omission; but it is really a good thing. If Christ had laid down laws for the better government of society, He would not only have done no good in the state of society then existing, but His rules would have been a positive hindrance to later societies, whose conditions are totally unlike those of Palestine in the first century. He gives us broad principles, and has a good deal to say about selfish and wasteful consumption; as for problems of distribution, He leaves them for Christian governments to settle in their own way. It is really a great gain.

Christianity, however, is a religion of spiritual redemption, not of social reform. Christ cared very little for the paraphernalia of life. He lived on a higher plane, in the conscious presence of His Father in Heaven. And the religion which He meant to found was a religion of the Spirit, a life of purity and holiness, of faith and love, a Church from which no one is excommunicated except by himself, a brotherhood of men and women who find nothing hateful except hypocrisy, hard-heartedness, and calculating worldliness. Some people have called it a feeble religion, which glorifies weakness and littleness as such. There could not be a greater mistake. It is a heroic religion; but it has its own standard of values; it has broken down all man-made barriers by ignoring them; and, by making the perfection of the divine life the standard of measurement, has made all differences except moral ones sink into insignificance.

This religion is a permanent acquisition of the human race; it is a treasure which we can never surrender. If anyone thinks that the man of the future will want no religion, he must be a very foolish person. The grandest spirit of Western Christianity, St. Augustine, did not even claim that Christianity was new. He wrote, "What is now called the Christian religion was in existence among the men of old time, and has never been lacking since the beginning of the human race, till Christ Himself appeared in the flesh. Since that time the true religion already in existence began to be called the Christian religion." What happened at the Incarnation was that the eternal Christianity appeared for the first time upon the plane of history, and became a power in the world. To suppose that we shall need no religion is nonsense. And as for starting a new religion, as some suggest, you might as well try to build a tree.

Do you object, as evolutionists, to the perfect character being supposed to have appeared nineteen hundred years ago? Then listen to Rodin, the great French sculptor: "In art there is no law of progress. Beyond Pheidias sculpture will never advance." So in the sphere of character we may say, "Beyond Jesus of Nazareth man will never advance."

I base my faith in Christianity mainly on two things. First, the testimony of my heart and conscience (and, may I not say, of the heart and conscience of all right-minded people?), that in the New Testament are to be found "the words of eternal life"; for, as one of the Cambridge Platonists said, "Christianity is a divine life, not a divine science." And my second ground is what is called mysticism or personal religious experience. St. Paul's faith was based on communion with the Spirit-Christ, an experience which was to him absolutely certain. I cannot have his tremendous conviction, for I have not deserved it. Spiritual things are spiritually discerned. But I think I am sure that when I pray in the name of Christ I am not merely talking to myself, or practising moral dumbbell exercises.

So much, then, for my views about religion. I think we shall have to let some traditional dogmas go, but I do not think that will matter. The worst enemies of Christianity are bad Christians; and if I had to find a name for that view of life which is incompatible with Christianity, I should call it *secularity*, that which the New Testament calls "the world," human society as it organises itself without thought of God and the spiritual life.

Some of you may have expected that I should dwell more on the dangers that lie ahead of us. Ten years ago I did think that civilisation was in great danger, and I still think that it was. Now I am inclined to think that we have turned the corner, but we are not out of the wood yet. Another war, or a revolution, might yet plunge us into another dark age.

But I do not want you to confound reasoned hopefulness with optimism. An optimist is a barometer stuck at Set Fair, whatever the weather may be. The man who says, "I am always an optimist," is a very irritating kind of fool. He is the kind of man who would buy from a Jew and sell to a Scot and expect to make a profit.

I repeat that there is no law of progress. Our future is in our own hands, to make or to mar. It will be an uphill fight to the end, and would we have it otherwise? Let no one suppose that evolution will ever exempt us from the struggles. "You forget," said the Devil, with a chuckle, "that I have been evolving, too."

XXII.

J. B. S. HALDANE

I DIFFER in several respects from many of the other contributors to this book. To begin with, I am much younger than many of them. And my intellectual background is perhaps very different. As a child I was not brought up in the tenets of any religion, but in a household where science and philosophy took the place of faith. As a boy I had very free access to contemporary thought, so that I do not to-day find Einstein unintelligible, or Freud shocking. As a youth I fought through the war, and learned to appreciate sides of human character with which the ordinary intellectual is not brought into contact. As a man I am a biologist, and see the world from an angle which gives me an unaccustomed perspective, but not, I think, a wholly misleading one.

In describing the world as I see it in so short a time, I cannot avoid being dogmatic. I do not doubt that some of the statements which I am going to make are false. A survey of the beliefs which intelligent men in the past have held as certainties makes that sufficiently clear. One cannot order one's life without a set of beliefs of some kind. But the intellectually honest man must recognise the utterly provisional nature of his beliefs. So when I make an apparently definite statement, I must ask you to put before it some such words as "It seems to me very probable that . . ." I will now try to state my point of view.

Man lives in two worlds, the visible world which changes with time, and an invisible world whose constituents do not change. But both worlds can only be described as they appear to us, that is, from a human and imperfect standpoint. Among the components of the invisible world are the realities corresponding to mathematical statements like $16 + 9 = 25$. This is a statement of a fact as real as the Albert Memorial, which any sane person must recognise when it is pointed out to him. But unlike the Albert Memorial, it was a reality 10,000 years ago, and will be 10,000 years hence. There are also invisible realities corresponding to scientific laws, and I think also to some of our general notions of what is beautiful and good. These latter realities are harder to apprehend because we approach them through a mist of emotion. We know very little about what may be called the geography of the invisible world. The religions, if I may continue the metaphor, have covered the vacant spaces of its map with imaginary monsters, the philosophies have ruled them with equally imaginary parallels of latitude. But both have affirmed, in opposition to the so-called practical man, that the meaning of the visible world is to be found in the invisible. That has been the secret of their success. They have failed when they tried either to describe the details of the visible world or to dictate the details of conduct in it. The churches are half empty to-day because their creeds are full of obsolete science, and their ethical codes are suited to a social organisation far simpler than that of to-day. But they still command the allegiance of a number of intelligent people because, amid a world of transitory interests, they support in some measure the claims of the ideal. I am not a member of any religious body, because I find those claims upheld elsewhere. If I thought that the aims of science and art were merely material I should belong to some church. But I believe that the scientist is trying to express absolute truth and the artist absolute beauty, so that I find in science and art, and in an attempt to lead a good life, all the religion that I want.

I have not very much use for people who are not in touch with the invisible world. At best they are good animals, and too often not even that. The men and women who have done best, both for themselves and their fellows, are those who have brought these two worlds into relation. For example, you can listen to your radio to-night because James Clerk Maxwell fifty-six years ago embodied an extremely important set of properties of electro-magnetic waves in a set of equations. Those equations represent an eternal truth—something in the invisible world. Their discovery rendered wireless communication possible. If you do not make any contact with this timeless world (in other words, have no inner life) you have at best a very precarious hold on happiness. Given that contact, you enjoy a very considerable security from the results of misfortune in the visible world, and a complete immunity from boredom. Dean Inge, H. G. Wells, and I, agree to a considerable extent about the nature of the invisible world, because we are all, in some degree, disciples of Plato.

One does not come naturally to the realisation of eternal truths and values. One is brought there by education in the widest sense. It is one of my principal functions to teach certain scientific truths to students at Cambridge University. Many of them are both able and eager to learn. But others are neither able nor eager. Under our present economic system they are enabled to come to Cambridge because their parents are wealthy. By so doing they keep out others who are better qualified intellectually to learn, and more willing to do so. As a teacher I cannot support a social system which is responsible for this injustice. We have got rid of physical starvation. We still have intellectual, æsthetic, and spiritual starvation, which to my mind are greater evils than any mere economic inequality. Until our educational system is so altered as to give a fair deal to every boy and girl who desires a first-rate education and is capable of benefiting by it, my political views are likely to remain, as they are now, on the left.

There is a worse evil than intellectual starvation, and that is the deliberate suppression of free thought and free speech. I rejoice to live in a country where this evil, though it exists, is less serious than in most other countries. But I believe that even in England freedom of publication is unduly restricted in the names of decency, morality, and so on. There is much more liberty in this respect across the Channel, and no one who has worked beside the French in peace and fought beside them in war can accuse them of degeneracy. So many new ideas are at first strange and horrible though ultimately valuable that a very heavy responsibility rests upon those who would prevent their dissemination.

Moreover, the censorship to which I refer is applied in a very partial way. A book glorifying war may be quite as antisocial, and to my mind quite as obscene, as one glorifying illicit love, but it is never suppressed, and seldom publicly denounced.

I now turn from the world of ideas to the visible world. I am a biologist, that is to say, I study the nature of living creatures, and I naturally look at things from a biological point of view. I feel at home in the world because I know that the other animals, and the plants, too, are my blood relations. Even the inert matter has mostly been alive in the past. When I look at a limestone mountain I realise that, grim and lifeless as it appears, it was made by countless billions of my microscopic fellow creatures. What is more surprising, I think that I can even have some very dim inkling of what it feels like to be limestone. We know material objects in general from the outside. We know our own bodies from the inside. Just as everyone knows what it feels like to be hot, so I know from my own personal experience what it feels like to consist of an abnormally large or small amount of calcium carbonate, of which the limestone mountain is built. In this concrete and detailed way I feel my relationship to the world around me.

I am a part of nature, and, like other natural objects, from a lightning flash to a mountain range, I shall last out my time and then finish. This prospect does not worry me, because some of my work will not die when I do so.

As a biologist I am interested in my body. Most people are only interested in anything below their skins when they are ill. I like to study the performance of mine as my friends do that of their motor-cycles or receiving sets. It amuses me to know what my heart does when I run upstairs, or how quickly my finger nails grow. To a biologist even a toothache can be interesting. Naturally I regard health as extremely important, far more so than wealth, and I shall regard my life as well spent if I can do a little, by research and education, to make my fellow creatures healthier. There is still an immense amount to be learnt about health, but if what is at present known to a few were part of the general knowledge, the average expectation of life in this country could probably be increased by about ten years. Two difficulties lie in the way: ignorance and the dissemination of falsehoods. To take a simple example of the latter. Enormous sums are spent in disseminating lies about health in order to advertise medicines and "health foods" which are generally useless and often dangerous. A widely advertised vitamin preparation contains, besides vitamins, a substance definitely poisonous to children. Under the law of the land I might have to pay thousands of pounds in damages if

I mentioned the preparation in question, even if my statement could be proved to be true. On the other hand, I am at liberty to say publicly that diphtheria antitoxin is useless, which is a plain lie.

Now for an example of the prevailing ignorance. When a father advises his son on a choice of occupation, he is generally guided mainly by economic, and partly by ethical considerations. He wants his son to avoid bad wages and bad company. He does not think about bad health, though he may be impressed by the risk of violent death. Yet the health of different occupations differs to an extraordinary extent, and the average man knows very little about the risks of even his own job, let alone his neighbour's. Otherwise no sane man would take up such an occupation as that of metal grinder or barman, with a mortality double that of the average man, when he might become a carpenter or a railwayman, and thus enjoy an expectation of life above the average. Our rulers are equally ignorant of these matters. Protective duties and subsidies are granted quite impartially to healthy occupations like agriculture, and unhealthy ones such as the cutlery trade. When this policy is opposed it is opposed on economic grounds, and never because, by encouraging an unhealthy trade, you are condemning some of your fellow countrymen to death. All parties agree in putting economic considerations before biological; wealth before health. I could give you plenty more examples of this ignorance if space permitted.

Even a healthy man or woman is incomplete. For a large number of men the main interest in life, the main object of their desires, the main source of their satisfaction, is Woman. For me the fascination of woman is only second to that of science. In most cases man's interest in woman culminates in marriage. Provided it does not then cease, the marriage is generally a success. Successful marriage requires a certain effort by both hus-

J. B. S. HALDANE

band and wife. But, speaking as a happily married man, I can assure you that no other effort is so amply rewarded. Marriage has a biological basis, and would be far more often a success if its biology were generally understood and the knowledge acted on. But you can only study the physiology of marriage against a background of general human physiology. If you do so the facts fit into their proper places. If not, you get a distorted and unhealthy view of them.

The psychological, even the intellectual, benefits of marriage, seem to me to be enormous. If a man has lived for some years in the closest intimacy with a woman, he learns to look at life from her point of view as well as his own. A man who cannot do this is like a man blind in one eye. He does not appreciate the solidity and depth of the world before him. The ideas I am putting before you here are largely my wife's, or at any rate, family ideas, rather than my own private productions. The unmarried woman is perhaps even worse off than the unmarried man; and few women seem to me to be psychologically complete till they have become mothers. During the Middle Ages Europe was far too much influenced by celibate men. To-day much too big a part in public life is played by the celibate woman, and too little by mothers. I find few ideas more genuinely disgusting than that held by many education authorities that a woman ceases to be suitable as a teacher when she becomes a mother. Because I have so high an opinion of marriage at its best, I think that it should be possible to end it if it fails for any of a number of reasons, instead of, as now, for one only. This is called "undermining the sanctity of marriage."

Marriage generally brings children. Everyone will agree that it would be an evil if the birth-rate of this country were halved, in which case the population would rapidly fall; or doubled, in which case it would increase too quickly. But they will disagree whether too many or too few children are born at present. I do not know myself, though I am clear that too many children are born in the slums, too few in the well-to-do suburbs. But we shall not arrive at a sensible solution of the population problem till we realise that it is a question of numbers, like the design of a motor-car or the framing of a budget, and cannot be settled by an appeal to abstract principles alone.

Our present educational system is unjust to children because the majority of them do not get a fair chance, and practically none are taught the truths of science from a human point of view. Science teaching should begin, not with a mythical body in rest or uniform motion, but with the human body. Mine did so begin at the age of three.

Between different men and women there are immense inborn differences which no amount of education can overcome. I do not believe that any training could have made Ramsay MacDonald into Jack Hobbs, or *vice versa*. The ideal society would enable every man and woman to make the best of their inborn possibilities. Hence it must have two characteristics. First, liberty, which would allow people to develop along their individual lines, and not attempt to force all into one mould, however admirable. Second, equality of opportunity, which would mean that, as far as is humanly possible, every man and woman would be able to obtain the position in society for which they were best suited by nature. The waste of human beings under our present system is a far worse evil than any merely economic waste. I believe in democracy because equality of opportunity is impossible where inherited rank or wealth is important, but for no other reason. I do not know what would be the ideal form of government in a community where that equality had been achieved. Democracy appeals to me, not as an end in itself, but as the most hopeful route, at least for England, to a classless society. In a classless society far-reaching eugenic measures could be enforced by the State with little injustice. To-day this would not be possible. We do not know, in most cases, how far social failure and success are due to heredity, and how far to environment. And environment is the easier of the two to improve.

I am a citizen of the British Empire, which includes the great Dominions. My high-brow friends complain that the Dominions have produced little great art or literature. I answer that at least they have done something unique. Before the war the average expectation of life of a baby born in New Zealand was sixty years, in Australia fifty-seven years, in Denmark, the next healthiest country, fifty-six years. England also ran. Since then other countries have caught up to a large extent, but New Zealand and Australia still seem to be leading. I am proud to belong to a Commonwealth which has won the first and second places in the great race against death.

I am also an European, and proud of it. Europe is sick to-day, but it is at least making some attempt to cure that sickness by a federal union of its states. And it still leads the world in science, literature, art, and music. In methods of production the United States are ahead of us, and many Europeans think that we should copy them. Dean Inge believes that the working class in the United States is better off than our own. His opinion is shared in unexpected quarters. When my wife and I were in Moscow last year at a great scientific congress we only saw two propaganda films. One was against alcohol; the other showed the manufacture of Ford cars as an argument for American industrial methods. I take a different view for the following reasons. Though they are still reducing their infantile mortality, since 1921 the death-rate of Americans at every age from thirty upwards has been increasing steadily. Whether as the result of hustle, prohibition, or the spread of medical cults, such as "Christian Science" and osteopathy, which reject the results of science, America is at present heading for death, and not life. Europe has much to learn from America, a little even from Asia, but I do not think that we should imitate either of these continents.

Some of you probably think I have laid too much emphasis on death-rates; I have talked about them for two reasons. Firstly, they are the only means we have of comparing the health of two trades or two nations; and I think that there is a very close connection between health and happiness. Secondly, otherwise well-informed people are ignorant of the facts concerning them.

For example Mr. Bernard Shaw, in a recent book, stated that while the lungs of Sheffield cutlery grinders used to be unhealthy, they were now as healthy as those of other people, thanks to Government Inspectors. Unfortunately the latest available statistics show that the death-rates of cutlery grinders, both from consumption and bronchitis, are between seven and eight times those of the general population.

I am an Englishman, and, what is more remarkable, though of Scottish origin, I believe in England. At the present moment our country counts for less in international politics than during last century. Nevertheless some of our ideas and practices are at present conquering the world. In Moscow, which has rejected the great British invention of Parliament, there was a word which I constantly noticed on posters. It was not "soviet," nor "red," nor yet "revolution," but "phutbol." The same is happening all over the world. Spanish bull-fighters are becoming centre-forwards. German students are taking to football instead of slashing one another's faces. And with British sport goes the ethical code called Sportsmanship, which future historians may perhaps consider a British invention as important as Parliament and Railways. I hope to see British sport conquer most of the world. But I am no narrow patriot, and would welcome a French invasion of the British kitchen.

England is only likely to regain her former pre-eminence if we can be ten years ahead of the rest of the world in industry, as we were a century ago. We should, of course, reorganise our industries, but other countries have already done so. We shall not regain our place by doing that. We have probably no great undeveloped mineral resources. But we have undeveloped human resources, especially among the children of the skilled artisan class. Our best hope for the future lies in giving them a chance to become Watts and Stephensons.

Finally, I am a human being, a citizen of the world which applied science is daily unifying. My own profession of scientific research knows no frontiers and no colour bars. Japanese, Indians, and Chinese, as well as Europeans and Americans, are, or have been, among my colleagues. I am naturally in favour of any measures tending to unify humanity and prevent war. But my views as to the best methods of achieving these aims are not informed by sufficient knowledge to be worth stating. For the same reason I am saying nothing about economics.

I am glad that I live to-day and not at any time in the past. In the 4,000 years before about A.D. 1800 civilisation had spread over a gradually widening area, but its quality had not greatly improved. A century ago in England children were hanged for theft, and a married woman could own no property. Neither of these evils existed in Ur of the Chaldees 4,200 years earlier. In the nineteenth century we doubled our average expectation of life, quadrupled our average real wage, and vastly improved our education and morals. This was made possible, in the main, by the application of science. To-day the whole form of civilisation is changing. We are trying unheard-of experiments. The great experiment of Socialism is being tried in Russia and will doubtless be tried elsewhere. We meet with huge and unexpected accidents like the Great War. We shall go on having such accidents so long as our rulers are not merely ignorant of science, but think on pre-scientific lines. (You will remember how the Kaiser talked of the war in terms of "shining armour," and Mr. Asquith of "unsheathed swords.") We have got to learn to think scientifically, not only about inanimate things, but about ourselves and one another. It is possible to do this. A single mind can acquire a fair knowledge of the whole field of science, and find plenty of time to spare for ordinary human affairs. Not many people take the trouble to do so. But without a knowledge of science one cannot understand current events. That is why modern literature and art are mostly so unreal.

We live in a dangerous age, but an extraordinarily interesting one. History is being made on a vaster and quicker scale than ever before. For humanity as a whole I am hopeful. For England I am only moderately hopeful, though I believe that if we are willing to adapt ourselves to the new conditions of life, we may yet be as great a nation as ever. But even if I am blown to pieces in the destruction of London during the next war, or starved to death during the next British revolution, I hope that I shall find time to think as I die, "I am glad that I lived when and where I did. It was a good show."

BIOGRAPHICAL NOTES

ALBERT EINSTEIN, winner of the Nobel Prize and author of the Theory of Relativity, is generally regarded as the world's most distinguished living scientist.

BERTRAND RUSSELL is known on two continents as mathematician, educator and philosopher. Some of his better-known books are *Education and the Good Life, Marriage and Morals,* and *Philosophy.*

JOHN DEWEY, Professor of Philosophy in Columbia University, is America's most influential philosophic force. His radical empirical thinking in a dozen fields is summed up in numerous books, among which may be named *How We Think, Human Nature and Conduct, Democracy and Education, Nature and Reality* and *Individualism, Old and New.*

ROBERT ANDREWS MILLIKAN was in 1923 awarded the Nobel Prize for isolating and measuring the electron.

THEODORE DREISER'S best-known novels include *An American Tragedy, Sister Carrie, The Titan, The Financier,* and *The "Genius."*

H. G. WELLS has recently crowned a lengthy career as novelist, social prophet and humanizer of knowledge with his *Science of Life,* a monumental work written in conjunction with his son, G. P. Wells, and the English biologist, Julian Huxley.

FRIDTJOF NANSEN died in 1930. Known widely as Norwegian explorer, scholar and diplomat, he was awarded the Nobel Peace Prize in 1922.

SIR JAMES JEANS is the Astronomer Royal and the author of many widely known books including *The Universe Around Us, Astronomy and Cosmology, The Mysterious Universe,* and *The Stars in Their Courses.*

IRVING BABBITT, Professor of French Literature at Harvard University, is America's chief exponent of the Humanist doctrine. His best known book is *Rousseau and Romanticism.*

SIR ARTHUR KEITH, famous for his researches in the antiquity of man, was in 1927 President of the British Association for the Advancement of Science. He is Hunterian Professor in the Royal College of Surgeons, London.

JAMES TRUSLOW ADAMS is one of the most notable of American historians and social critics. Among his books are *The Adams Family, Our Business Civilization* and *The Founding of New England.*

H. L. MENCKEN is perhaps America's most generally influential critic. His most recent work is *Treatise on the Gods.*

JULIA PETERKIN won the Pulitzer Prize for 1929 with her novel *Scarlet Sister Mary*.

LEWIS MUMFORD, one of the keenest of the younger American critics, is equally well-known as essayist, social historian and architectural authority. Among his books are *Sticks and Stones*, *The Golden Day* and *Herman Melville*.

GEORGE JEAN NATHAN is the author of a long series of critical works, most of them dealing with the drama. His most recent volume is entitled *Testament of a Critic*.

HU SHIH is known as the "Father of the Chinese Renaissance" and is largely responsible for the new sense of cultural responsibility alive in China to-day. His most monumental work is a History of Chinese Philosophy.

JOSEPH WOOD KRUTCH is the dramatic editor of the New York *Nation*. Among his books are *Edgar Allan Poe: A Psychological Study*, *The Modern Temper* and *Five Masters*.

IRWIN EDMAN is Associate Professor of Philosophy at Columbia University and has established his reputation as teacher, essayist and poet.

HILAIRE BELLOC is internationally known as poet, historian, essayist, novelist and Catholic apologist.

In conjunction with her husband (Lord Passfield) BEATRICE WEBB has written several standard books on sociological problems.

WILLIAM RALPH INGE is the Dean of St. Paul's, London, and the author of numerous works in the fields of religion and philosophy.

J. B. S. HALDANE is Sir William Dunn Reader in Bio-chemistry at Cambridge University. Among his books are *Possible Worlds, The Last Judgment, Dædalus*.

THIS BOOK

is published by the publishers of

JEAN RICHARD BLOCH
And Company · *A Night in Kurdistan*

WILLIAM BOLITHO
Twelve Against the Gods · *Camera Obscura* · *Overture-1920*

ERNEST DIMNET
The Art of Thinking

WILL DURANT
The Story of Philosophy · *The Mansions of Philosophy*
Transition · *The Case for India* · *Studies in Genius*

ALFREDO ALOYSIUS HORN
Trader Horn

JOHN COWPER POWYS
Wolf Solent · *In Defence of Sensuality*

FELIX SALTEN
Fifteen Rabbits · *Bambi* · *The Hound of Florence*

ARTHUR SCHNITZLER
Casanova's Homecoming · *Rhapsody*
Beatrice · *None But The Brave* · *Theresa*
Daybreak · *Dr. Graesler* · *Little Novels*

FRANZ WERFEL
Class Reunion · *Verdi* · *The Man Who Conquered Death*

and Others

from The Inner Sanctum *of*
SIMON and SCHUSTER
Publishers · 386 Fourth Avenue · New York

THIS BOOK
is published by the publishers of

JEAN RICHARD BLOCH
—*And Company* · *A Night in Kurdistan*

WILLIAM BOLITHO
Twelve Against the Gods · *Camera Obscura* · *Overture-1920*

ERNEST DIMNET
The Art of Thinking

WILL DURANT
The Story of Philosophy · *The Mansions of Philosophy*
Transition · *The Case for India* · *Studies in Genius*

ALFRED ALOYSIUS HORN
Trader Horn

JOHN COWPER POWYS
Wolf Solent · *In Defence of Sensuality*

FELIX SALTEN
Fifteen Rabbits · *Bambi* · *The Hound of Florence*

ARTHUR SCHNITZLER
Fräulein Else · *Casanova's Homecoming* · *Rhapsody*
Beatrice · *None But The Brave* · *Theresa*
Daybreak · *Dr. Graesler* · *Little Novels*

FRANZ WERFEL
Class Reunion · *Verdi* · *The Man Who Conquered Death*

And Others

from The Inner Sanctum *of*
SIMON *and* SCHUSTER
Publishers · 386 Fourth Avenue · New York